Greenhill Books

At Her Majesty's Secret Service

Also by Nigel West

Spy!: Six Stories of Modern Espionage (with Richard Deacon)
MI5: British Security Service Operations 1909–45
MI6: British Secret Intelligence Service Operations 1909–45
A Matter of Trust: MI5 1945–72
Unreliable Witness: Espionage Myths of World War II
The Branch: A History of the Metropolitan Police Special Branch
GARBO: The Personal Story of the Most Successful Double Agent Ever (with Juan Pujol)
GCHQ: The Secret Wireless War
The Friends: Britain's Postwar Secret Intelligence Operations
Molehunt: Searching for Soviet Spies in British Intelligence
Games of Intelligence: The Classified Conflict of International Espionage
Seven Spies Who Changed the World
Secret War: The Story of SOE
The Faber Book of Espionage
The Illegals: Double Lives of the Cold War's Most Secret Agents
The Faber Book of Treachery
The Secret War for the Falklands: SAS, MI6 and the War Whitehall Nearly Lost
Counterfeit Spies: The British Secrets at the Heart of the KGB's Archives
Crown Jewels (with Oleg Tsarev)
VENONA: The Greatest Secret of the Cold War
The Third Secret: The CIA, Solidarity and the KGB Plot to Kill the Pope
Mortal Crimes: The Greatest Theft in History – Soviet Penetration of the Manhattan Project
The Guy Liddell Diaries (ed.)
MASK: MI5's Penetration of the Communist Party of Great Britain
The Historical Dictionary of British Intelligence

Fiction

Blue List
Cuban Bluff
Murder in the Commons
Murder in the Lords

At Her Majesty's Secret Service

The Chiefs of Britain's Intelligence Agency, MI6

Nigel West

Greenhill Books, London
Naval Institute Press, Annapolis, Maryland

At Her Majesty's Secret Service
The Chiefs of Britain's Intelligence Agency, MI6

First published in 2006 by Greenhill Books, Lionel Leventhal Limited,
Park House, 1 Russell Gardens, London NW11 9NN, England
www.greenhillbooks.com
and
Published and distributed in the United States of America and Canada by the
Naval Institute Press, 291 Wood Road, Annapolis, Maryland 21402-5034
www.navalinstitute.org

British Library Cataloguing-in Publication Data
West, Nigel
At Her Majesty's secret service: the chiefs of Britain's intelligence agency, MI6
1. Great Britain. MI6 – Officials and employees – Biography 2. Great Britain.
MI6 – History 3. Intelligence officers – Great Britain – Biography
4. Intelligence service – Great
Britain – History
I.Title
327.1'2'0922'41

Greenhill edition

ISBN-13: 978-1-85367-702-1
ISBN-10: 1-85367-702-7

NIP edition
ISBN-10 1-59114-009-9

Library of Congress Catalog Card No. 2006932046

For more information on our books, please visit www.greenhillbooks.com,
email sales@greenhillbooks.com, or telephone us within the UK on 020 8458 6314.
You can also write to us at the above London address.

Edited and typeset by Donald Sommerville
Map drawn by John Richards

Printed and bound in Great Britain by
Creative Print and Design (Wales), Ebbw Vale

Contents

Acknowledgments

My thanks are due to the many intelligence professionals who made this book possible. I owe particular gratitude to those that assisted my research, among them Sir Colin McColl, Anthony Cavendish, Brian Crozier, Jeff Morley, and the late Christopher Phillpotts, Charles Seymour, Harford Hyde, Cleveland Cram, Arthur Martin, Nicholas Elliott, Andrew King, Fergie Dempster and others who cannot be named.

Illustrations

Glossary and Abbreviations

Abwehr	Military intelligence service, Nazi-era Germany
AIOC	Anglo-Iranian Oil Company
ANA	Arab News Agency
BND	Federal German Intelligence Service
BOSS	South African Bureau of State Security
CIA	Central Intelligence Agency
CIFE	Combined Intelligence Far East
CIO	(Rhodesian) Central Intelligence Organisation
CPGB	Communist Party of Great Britain
CX	Secret intelligence
DCI	(American) Director of Central Intelligence
Dezinformatsia	(Soviet) disinformation scheme
DGSE	French intelligence service
DIE	Romanian Intelligence Service
DMI	Director of Military Intelligence
DNI	Director of Naval Intelligence
DST	French security service
FBI	(American) Federal Bureau of Investigation
FCD	KGB First Chief Directorate
FCO	Foreign and Colonial Office
FO	Foreign Office
FOA	Foreign Office Adviser
GC&CS	Government Code and Cypher School
GCHQ	Government Communications Headquarters
GRU	Soviet Military Intelligence Service

Haganah	Intelligence branch of the Jewish agency
IAEA	International Atomic Energy Authority
IONEC	Intelligence Officers' New Entry Course
IRA	Irish Republican Army
ISC	Parliamentary Intelligence and Security Committee
ISG	Iraq Survey group
ISLD	Inter-Services Liaison Department
JIC	Joint Intelligence Committee
KPD	German Communist Party
KGB	Soviet Intelligence Service
MECAS	Middle East Centre for Arabic Studies
MI5	British Security Service
MI6	British Secret Intelligence Service
NID	Naval Intelligence Division
NKVD	Soviet Intelligence Service
NSA	(United States) National Security Agency
OGPU	Soviet Intelligence Service
PA/CSS	Personal Assistant to the Chief of the Secret Service
PCO	Passport Control Officer
PET	Danish security police
PIIC	Public Interest Immunity Certificate
PIRA	Provisional Irish Republican Army
PNG	*Persona non grata*
PUS	Permanent Under-Secretary
RCMP	Royal Canadian Mounted Police
Referentura	KGB office
Rezident	Senior KGB officer
Rezidentura	KGB organisation
SCD	Second Chief Directorate
SDECE	French Intelligence Service
Sicherheitsdienst	Security Service, Nazi-era Germany
Sigint	Signals intelligence
SIME	Security Intelligence Middle East
SIS	Secret Intelligence Service
SISMI	Italian Intelligence Service

StB	Czech intelligence service
SVR	Russian Federation intelligence service
UB	Polish intelligence service
WMD	Weapons of Mass Destruction

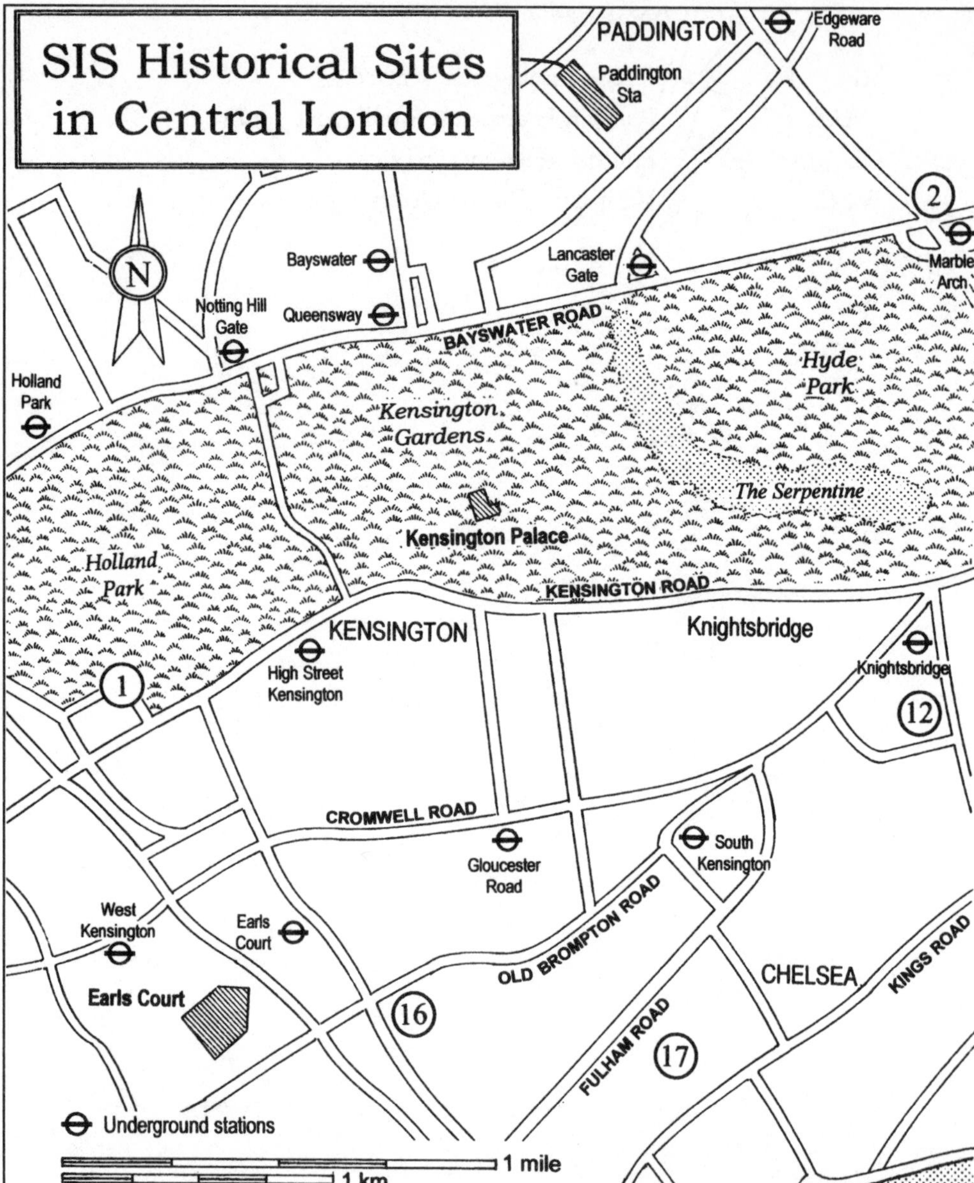

KEY

1 **1 Melbury Road** Home of Sir Mansfield Smith-Cumming
2 **Mount Royal Hotel** Marble Arch. Location of Penkovsky debriefing in April 1961
3 **White's Club** 37 St James's Street. Stewart Menzies and David Boyle were members
4 **14 Ryder Street** Wartime headquarters of Section V
5 **3 Carlton Gardens** Headquarters of SIS's Y Section
6 **21 Queen Anne's Gate** C's apartment
7 **54 Broadway** SIS headquarters from 1924 to 1966
8 **2 Whitehall Court** SIS headquarters in World War I until 1924

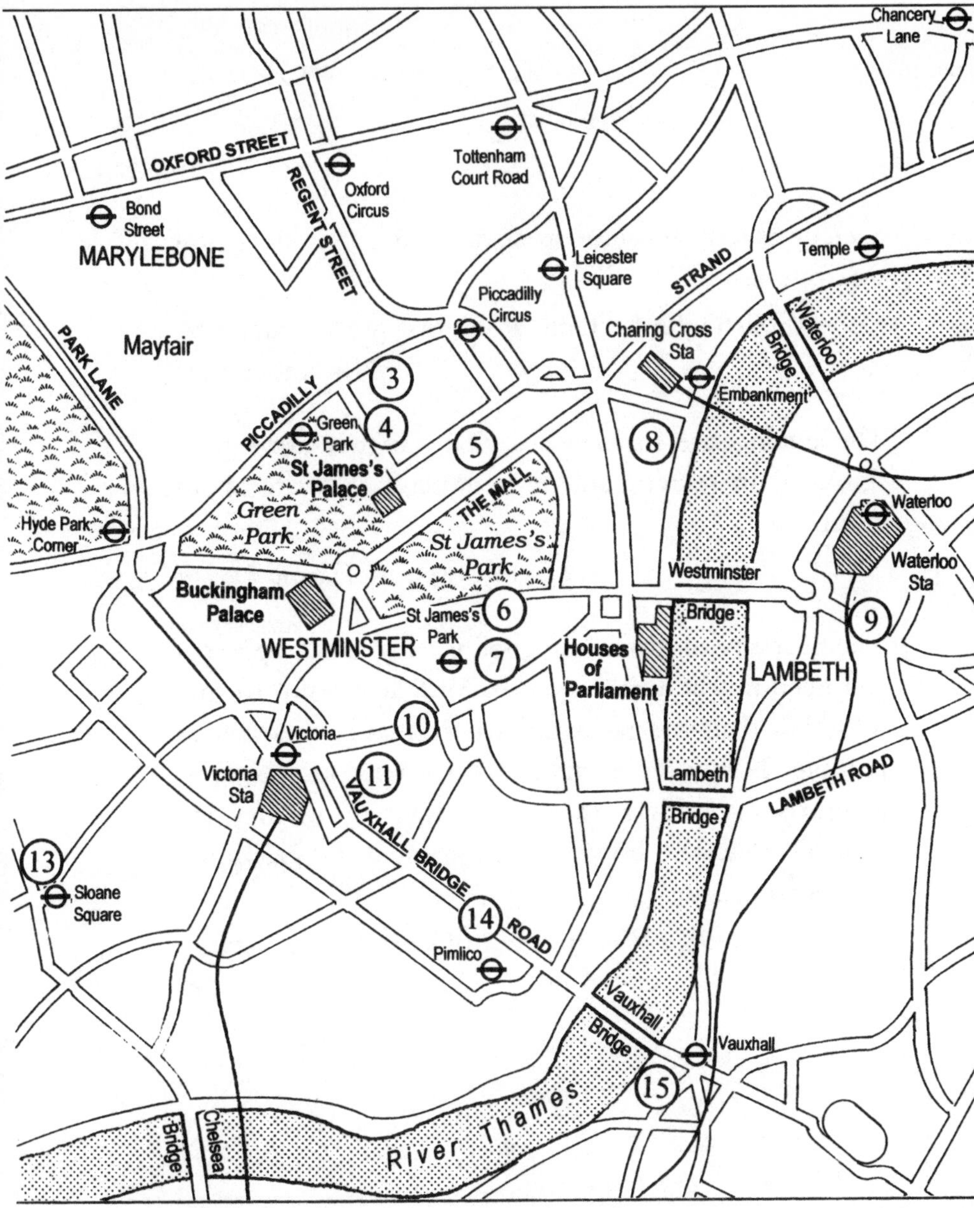

9 **Century House** SIS headquarters from 1966 to 1996 at 100 Westminster Bridge Road
10 **Artillery Mansions** Postwar headquarters of SIS's Production Research Department
11 **Ashley Gardens** SIS's first office in C's flat
12 **23 Hans Place** SIS training section for officers
13 **Sloane Square** Safehouse where Kim Philby was interrogated in 1955
14 **60 Vauxhall Bridge Road** SIS's London Station
15 **Vauxhall Cross** SIS's headquarters from 1995
16 **Coleherne Court** Safehouse where Oleg Penkovsky was debriefed in July 1961
17 **111 Old Church Street** SIS training section for agents

'Secrecy is our absolute stock in trade, it is our most precious asset.'

Sir Colin McColl, at C's first press conference,
November 1993

'The intelligence services are vital but they are rightly shrouded in secrecy and it is difficult to write about them.'

David Owen in *Time to Declare*

'The necessity of procuring good intelligence is apparent and need not be further urged. All that remains for me to add is that you keep the whole matter as secret as possible. For upon Secrecy, success depends on most enterprises of this kind and for want of it, they are generally defeated, however well planned and promising a favourable issue.'

George Washington to General Elias Dayton,
26 July 1777

Introduction

> 'Through many books on secret service published in England since the War a shadowy figure goes gliding. A man of power and mystery looms up, the guiding hand behind our Secret Service. His appearance is described, his remarks are quoted, but his name is mentioned never. He is always spoken of, tout court as "C".'
>
> Valentine Williams in *The World of Action*

THE Chief of the Secret Intelligence Service (SIS) was, from the foundation of the organisation in August 1909, one of the most influential figures in Whitehall, yet, from the outset, the position was always a constitutional anomaly, one of those ambiguities which thrive in Whitehall, because as a department of state SIS simply did not exist.

The idea that a modern liberal democracy with an effective parliament should tolerate or even endorse a clandestine body that is not accountable to the electorate is an aberration yet, until the enactment of the Intelligence Services Bill in 1994, that was precisely the position held by SIS and its successive Chiefs. Their organisation was only officially acknowledged as having existed as a wartime unit within the orthodox military intelligence structure and the convenient fig-leaf of 'MI6', which is often used to this day, allowed successive prime ministers and foreign secretaries to avoid awkward questions in the House of Commons. As David Owen recalled, 'As Foreign Secretary I never publicly mentioned MI6 until years later in Opposition, after James Callaghan had decided not to comply any longer with the pretence that it does not exist.'[1] Whilst this expedient might have had the advantage of allowing the Chief to operate independently of his political masters, the reality is that successive Chiefs rarely exercised this option and instead ensured that the Service remained an instrument of the government, in the postwar years fulfilling requirements set by the Joint Intelligence Committee. As Sir Dick White observed, the practice of obtaining a ministerial sanction for most operations, and certainly the risky ones, negated the need for the Service to endure bureaucratic and potentially leaky oversight procedures. Unlike the American system, where presidents hid behind the White House's executive privilege of disowning unsuccessful operations, thereby leaving a hapless Central Intelligence Agency to the tender mercies of Congress, SIS rarely embarked on a project without the fullest ministerial approval. On only one occasion was SIS caught over-stepping the mark, and the then Chief, Sir John Sinclair, paid a heavy price for what turned out to be a failure of communications in the Buster Crabb affair, rather than a manifestation of wilful disobedience or misconduct. SIS was never to be accused of behaving like 'a rogue elephant' the (subsequently withdrawn) allegation notoriously made by Frank Church during his Congressional committee's investigation of the CIA's misdeeds in 1974.

For the first eighty-five years of its existence, the Secret Intelligence Service, known variously as 'the firm', 'the funnies' and within the Foreign Office as 'the friends', was supposed to be secret, with the identities of successive Chiefs undisclosed. No Chief went into the public print, nor published his memoirs, although Smith-Cumming bequeathed his meagre diaries to his successors and, according to Valentine Williams, once boasted to his astonished staff, 'When I retire I intend to publish my memoirs. I shall call them "The Indiscretions of a Secret Service Chief". It will be a splendid-looking publication bound in red with the title and my name embossed in gold and consisting of 400 pages – every one of which will be blank!'[2]

The paradox at the heart of the British system is that, thanks to a succession of novelists, many of whom like Valentine Williams served in SIS, the ubiquitous British Secret Service is the best known intelligence agency in the world, with half the globe's population having watched a

James Bond movie. Although Ian Fleming himself never served in SIS, he certainly drew on many authentic details for his books and was probably inspired to publish his first thriller, *Casino Royale*, by another novelist, Phyllis Bottome, who wrote about a dashing, womanising British Secret Service officer, Mark Chalmers, in 1946, six years before James Bond emerged. Like Bond, the equally fictional Chalmers was also fluent in German, had been educated in Switzerland and 'climbed like a mountain goat'. As Bottome was married to the SIS officer who had been tutor to the Fleming brothers, the link is hard to avoid, arguably making SIS the most publicised, but unavowed organisation on the planet.

The real SIS was not headed by 'M', but by 'C', and its personnel were identified by five-figure code-numbers, whereas Bond was simply '007'. SIS did operate stations overseas, and although 'Universal Import-Export' was not its London cover, the SIS headquarters at 54 Broadway for many years bore only one brass plate, that of the Minimax Fire Extinguisher Company. The parallels were all too obvious to the *cognoscenti* who easily spotted the verisimilitude, and one Chief, Colin McColl, for one gratefully accepted the Bond genre as 'our best recruiting sergeant. Everyone, everywhere, knows the British Secret Service.'[3]

Not all Chiefs were so pleased to see their work trivialised and fictionalised. Dick White upbraided Graham Greene over a convivial lunch after the release of *The Human Factor*, complaining to the author (who himself had been a wartime SIS officer) that SIS did not kill people. It was precisely because SIS had not indulged in such excesses, he claimed, that the organisation had avoided the kind of inhibiting Congressional oversight that had hamstrung the CIA. Equally Maurice Oldfield, on the other hand, strongly disapproved of the handiwork of David Cornwell/John Le Carré, another former SIS officer who, so the Chief claimed, had amassed a fortune from his experiences under consular cover in Germany during the Cold War but never made a contribution to the SIS Widows' and Orphans' Fund. Although Oldfield, who had expressed his irritation at Cornwell's tour of SIS's Far Eastern stations while researching *The Honourable Schoolboy*, knew he had not been the model for Le Carré's enigmatic spy-master George Smiley, he nevertheless asked to meet the actor Alec Guinness who played the role on television and in fact bore a strong physical resemblance to him. The honour of being the original of Smiley had fallen to Jack Bingham (Lord Clanmorris) for whom Cornwell had worked when he had joined MI5, prior to his career in SIS. Oldfield, wearing his characteristic light-coloured suede shoes, large spectacles and flamboyant gold cuff-links, met Guinness for lunch at La Poule au Pot at the end of August 1978 and afterwards the actor followed C down Ebury Street in an effort to imitate his distinctive walk, which was more like a waddle.

SIS delights in such yarns, and is full of traditions. The Chief's vast, carved mahogany desk supposedly comes from Admiral Lord Nelson's *Victory*, and the grandfather clock that continues to grace his current office in Vauxhall Cross was actually constructed in its entirety by the first Chief, Captain Sir Mansfield Smith-Cumming. SIS's intelligence product, circulated to its eager customers in Whitehall and beyond, has always known by the prefixed reference 'CX', which originally was an abbreviation of 'Cumming Exclusively.'

SIS's origins, and the appointment of Smith-Cumming, can be traced back to the decision of the Committee of Imperial Defence, following the intelligence failures of the Boer War, to create a Secret Service Bureau, divided into home and foreign sections. As we shall see, Smith-Cumming proved to be an inspiring and charismatic spy-master whose personality and unusual physical attributes gave him a near mythological status for those who wrote about him. Among those who have described encounters with C were Sam Hoare, Somerset Maugham, Edward Knoblock and A. E. W. Mason. Most famously, when in October 1932 Compton Mackenzie was prosecuted and fined for revealing in *Greek Memories* that his 'supporter and friend', Captain Mansfield Cumming RN, was the Chief of the British Secret Intelligence Service, was known as 'C', and often used the alias 'Captain Spencer', the author took his revenge by publishing *Water on the Brain*, a cruel satire of bungling incompetence in the world of secret intelligence. At one point in the trial the Attorney-General, Sir Thomas Inskip KC, MP, complained that the defendant had 'revealed the mysterious consonant by which the Chief of the Secret Service was known', prompting the judge to ask 'If C is such a dangerous consonant, why is it still being used fifteen years after the war?'[4]

C himself was a kindly, stout, balding, Punch-like figure with a cordless, gold-rimmed monocle whose study was packed with books, models of aircraft and submarines, a high-powered telescope, a compass and a collection of chemicals in test-tubes. Beside his desk was a bank of telephones and dominating the room was a large portrait of a group of French villagers facing a Prussian firing-squad during the war of 1870. He delighted in gadgets, loved secret inks, commanded great loyalty and affection from his staff, and drove at high speed in a Rolls-Royce bearing a Chief Constable's distinctive number-plate, allowing him to ignore the traffic regulations. Compton Mackenzie recalled that in October 1916 Smith-Cumming had commented that he had 'intended to make myself extremely unpleasant to you; but I said that when I saw you I should probably find you a man after my own heart and fall on your neck. We'll have dinner at the Savoy one night soon.'[5]

Smith-Cumming was evidently fond of Mackenzie, whom he introduced to his wife, as they dined together in Whitehall Court, below a portrait of his beloved son Alastair in his Seaforths' uniform, describing Mackenzie as 'the man who had given him more trouble than anyone else in his service',[6] although it was long after his death that people would write openly about him. In 1930, when Sam Hoare referred to him in *The Fourth Seal*, he observed of 'this remarkable personage' that:

> If I describe him in detail, I may be charged, even though the circumstances of the work have completely changed, with disclosing secrets about the holiest of Intelligence holies. If I pass him by without a word, it may be thought that he is not worthy of being placed as a peer in the company of General Macdonogh and Admiral Hall.[7]

Indeed, in March 1938 when Sir Paul Dukes gave a detailed description of his recruitment and first interview with Smith-Cumming, and dedicated *The Story of 'ST-25': Adventure and Romance with the Secret Intelligence Service in Red Russia* 'To the memory of The Chief', he even then declined to name him.[8]

Today the role of Chief, now fulfilled by John Scarlett, Smith-Cumming's thirteenth successor, is much changed, but is still recognisable.

His objectives are set at the weekly meetings of the Joint Intelligence Committee, which he attends in person, and much of his predecessors' independence is curtailed by continuous contact with two individuals whose posts did not exist until the latter half of the twentieth century, that of the Intelligence Coordinator to the Cabinet, and the Prime Minister's Foreign Policy Adviser. The Chief remains answerable to the Secretary of State for Foreign Affairs, and retains the right of direct access to the Prime Minister, but is now accountable to the Intelligence and Security Committee, the Parliamentary oversight committee created by the 1994 Intelligence Services Act. Nevertheless, the role of Chief is quite unique, given the post's triple responsibilities for collecting intelligence, managing a network of overseas stations and maintaining a relationship with Whitehall. By the nature of the work, SIS attracts some unusual personalities, and it is C's task to direct and protect the careers of some 2,000 men and women who have joined arguably the world's most prestigious intelligence agency.

Chapter I

Mansfield Smith-Cumming 1909–1924

'I have no use for the usual channels except in the early morning.'

Mansfield Smith-Cumming[1]

The first Chief of the Secret Intelligence Service was appointed in August 1909 as head of the Foreign Section of the Secret Service Bureau, and it is directly to him that much of the Service's mystique and tradition is due. He signed his correspondence with the single letter 'C', in green ink, a tradition that survives to the present day, as does his unique sobriquet of 'Chief'.

When Mansfield Smith-Cumming was summoned to London in August 1909 by the Director of Naval Intelligence, Admiral the Honourable Alexander Bethell, he was fifty years old and had come to the end of a not very distinguished naval career that had been handicapped by chronic sea-sickness. His Royal Navy service record, although believed by many including his biographer to be lost, can in fact be inspected in the National Archives and records that in the opinion of Captain Walter Hunt-Grubbe he was 'a clever officer with great taste for electricity. Has a knowledge of photography' but had been stricken with severe sea-sickness while serving in the Straits of Malacca on operations against Malay pirates. He was obliged to take sick leave, and was invalided off HMS *Magnificent*. In 1883 his ill-health forced him back to England to recover, and when he was appointed Transport Officer on an Indian troopship, the *Pembroke Castle*, he succumbed again. Finally, after he had transferred to another troopship, the *Malabar*, he was declared unfit for further service and in 1886 his name was added to the Retired List with the rank of lieutenant-commander, with an annual pay of £109 10s. His personal file is entirely unremarkable, chronicling his services as ADC to Captain Buller in 1876 during operations of the Naval Brigade against Malay pirates, his knowledge of French, his ability to draw, and the acquisition of a Royal Aero Club flying licence in 1913.[2]

Smith-Cumming had been born on April Fool's Day 1859 as plain Mansfield Smith. His change of surname from Smith to Smith-Cumming occurred in 1889, following his marriage to his second wife, the heiress Leslie Valiant, in order to preserve her maternal grandfather's name. He went on to drop the hyphenated Smith in 1917. His enthusiasm for his adopted name is reflected in the bookplates he had printed for his library, which bear the impressive coat of arms granted to the Cumming family in 1781.

Already a wealthy man, Smith-Cumming received a considerable settlement from his wife who had inherited a substantial property at Logie in Morayshire. Following his official retirement on half pay, to a houseboat at Bursledon on the Hamble, Smith-Cumming attended an Admiralty torpedo course, and later became an expert on boom defences, working at HMS *Australia* and HMS *Venus*, both shore establishments on Southampton Water. Here his research was greatly valued, but precisely why he was selected by Bethell to join the Secret Service Bureau is unknown, though the choice was inspired. As well as his knowledge of French, his interest in electricity and photography, and his skill as a draughtsman, he kept fast motor boats (among them the *Command*, *Communicator*, *Competitor* and *Comedy*) at a boatshed on Badnam Creek, loved the new sport of motoring, and even learned to fly.

As can be seen from his naval record, he was seriously injured in a car accident in France soon after the outbreak of the First World War, breaking both legs. What the file does not show is the death of the driver, his only son Alastair, who was a 24-year-old subaltern in the Seaforth Highlanders. C had driven his Rolls-Royce Silver Ghost to GHQ, where Alastair had been seconded to the Intelligence Corps, and picked him up for ten days' leave in Paris. At about 9.00 p.m. on 1 October, driving at 60 miles an hour, they had hit an unlit farm cart and then careered into a tree, to lie there undiscovered for the next nine hours. Reportedly Smith-Cumming was trapped under the vehicle and cut off his own crushed left foot with a penknife so as to be able to reach Alastair who was dying. When he was found, C was rushed to Meaux hospital and operated on, before being taken to Neuilly for further surgery. This is the version retailed in part by Somerset Maugham and has been generally accepted, but, whatever the truth of the circumstances of the crash, thereafter Smith-Cumming often disconcerted his visitors by absent-mindedly stabbing his wooden leg with a paper knife. According to one witness, C did this deliberately while interviewing candidates recommended for SIS posts, and rejected those who winced at his performance.

When Smith-Cumming joined the Secret Service Bureau it was accommodated in a small office in Victoria Street opposite the Army & Navy Stores, and shared with Captain Vernon Kell of the South Staffordshire Regiment who was to head the Home Section, the forerunner of the Security Service. While relations between the two men were to remain cordial for many years Smith-Cumming disliked commuting from Bursledon and resented the fact that the only other member of staff, William Melville, a retired Special Branch detective, really worked full-time for Kell. Accordingly he quickly lobbied for, and obtained permission, to rent a flat nearby at his own expense and use part of it as his office. The first flat he found was in Ashley Gardens, where he installed a typewriter and a safe and set about the business of espionage by approaching retired military men living abroad to act as agents. His relative success can be judged by the very first SIS intelligence report, dated 18 January 1910, based on a message from 'WK' who described German naval developments and the construction of submarines. Cumming had taken no time at all to adopt the now standard tradecraft of concealing the names of individuals and places by codenames, holding clandestine meetings with his sources away from his office, and even referring to his Secret Service activities in correspondence as 'C.C. work'.

Cumming did not establish his first overseas station, in the British Consulate-General in Rotterdam under Richard Tinsley, until the autumn of 1913. The early development of his organisation was handicapped by its lack of funds and facilities, to the point that he complained he was unable to take a break away from his work because of the necessity of maintaining contact with his handful of sources, with whom he corresponded by the regular mail. Smith-Cumming's first sponsored mission abroad using British personnel ended in disaster with the arrest of Lieutenant Vivian Brandon RN and Captain Bernard Trench RM by the German police while undertaking a survey of the forts in Heligoland in August 1910. Brandon and Trench had already completed one mission, to Kiel, the previous year, but on this occasion their photography, of the fortifications on the island of Wangerooge, attracted the attention of the sentries and Brandon was taken into custody. The British government immediately denied knowledge of his 'movements, which were entirely unauthorised'[3] but the seizure of pictures of the Kaiser Wilhelm Canal, Borkum and Wilhelmshaven sealed the fate of the two officers at their trial in Leipzig in December 1910, and they were sentenced to four years' imprisonment.

Although they only admitted to having been in contact with a naval intelligence officer named 'Reggie' (actually NID's Captain Cyril Regnart), Brandon and Trench were actually Cumming's agents, code-named respectively BONFIRE and COUNTERSCARP, and their arrest caused 'rather a panic' at the War Office.[4] The DNI, Admiral Bethell, decreed that the Whitehall line would be complete disavowal. 'We had ascertained that the two unfortunately were not military men, not connected in any way with any C.C. work. We knew nothing at all about them',[5] thereby establishing a position intended to protect the government from the embarrassment of association with officially-sponsored espionage, and maybe offer the two defendants an opportunity to portray themselves as hapless, harmless tourists. In the event both men were convicted and served their sentences in the fortresses of Königstein in Saxony and Glatz in Silesia respectively, but were released in an amnesty to celebrate the marriage of Kaiser Wilhelm's daughter to Prince Ernst Augustus, the Duke of Cumberland.

Also freed was another of Smith-Cumming's agents, Bertrand Stewart, an Old Etonian, lawyer and Territorial Army officer who had been arrested in Bremen early in August 1911. Unlike Brandon and Trench, who were C's men but had been run jointly with the NID, Stewart seems to have been an enthusiastic amateur whose services, originally volunteered to the War Office, had been accepted by C with some reluctance. While Brandon and Trench resumed their normal duties upon their return home, apparently accepting that their imprisonment had been an occupational hazard, Stewart demanded huge compensation, complaining that he had been betrayed by a double agent who had planted a codebook on him to incriminate him, and that the avoidable debacle had been everyone else's fault except his own. C insisted that 'He has never done anything for us which merits even the barest thanks'[6] but, undeterred, Stewart visited the new DNI, Captain Jackson, and then tried to see the First Sea Lord, Lord Fisher. Finally he made representations to Colonel George Macdonogh, the Director of Military Intelligence (DMI) at the War Office, and engaged a lawyer to demand £10,000, repayment of his trial costs in Germany and a testimonial letter from C in recognition of his valuable services addressed to the King, the Secretary of State for War and the First Sea Lord. Smith-Cumming not only refused to participate in this, but objected strongly to the criticism directed at him. 'I urged in vain that this man might do me a great deal of harm if allowed to go round to my superiors and tell a one-sided story, and that I should like to be allowed to meet him and answer any charges he had to make.'[7] The dispute was resolved finally when Stewart went to France with his territorial regiment and was killed, whereupon his widow received £10,000 in compensation.

The outbreak of war did not result in any dramatic escalation in the size of C's office, and in December 1914 he noted, for the War Office, that his staff consisted of three other officers, four clerks, two typists, a messenger and two outside men, one of whom, Ernest Bailey, acted as his chauffeur. His monthly expenditure was estimated at £4,310, almost a quarter of which was allocated to his Dutch organisation which ran agents in German-occupied territory. Early in the new year C made a list of his agents, who amounted to twenty-three, run at an annual cost of £6,500, a figure that exceeded the limit set by the Foreign Office by £1,500. Only gradually did C's staff increase, and in 1915 consisted of an actor, Guy Standing, a mining engineer named Cockerell, the office manager T. F. Laycock, a mining engineer from Colombia named Newnun, and Sub-Lieutenant Jolly who had joined from the *Tatler*.

In 1916, with the reorganisation of the War Office, Kell's Home Section adopted the military intelligence designation MI5 and moved into large premises in Charles Street, Haymarket, while C's office became MI1(c) and operated from a flat on the seventh floor of 2 Whitehall Court, a large Victorian mansion block overlooking the Embankment next to the National Liberal Club and the Authors' Club. Later he was to expand the office space and acquire more accommodation at 4 Whitehall Court, with a separate Air Section at 11 Park Mansions, Vauxhall Bridge Road.

C's office was typically labyrinthine and ramshackle, being a maze of corridors, steps and walkways on the roof of the building, a veritable rabbit warren on two levels which were accessed by a private lift, operated by C's man, and described by various visitors, among them Valentine Williams, Paul Dukes and George Hill. Compton Mackenzie recalls an interview with C in Whitehall Court at which he was presented with a swordstick that Smith-Cumming claimed he had carried 'on spying expeditions in time of peace. "That's when this business was really amusing" he said. "After the war is over we'll do some amusing secret service work together. It's capital sport."'[8]

C's offer to dine his staff at the Savoy was characteristic. His deputy, appointed in 1916 but without the formal title of vice-chief, was Colonel Freddie Browning, an Oxford-educated Grenadier from the War Office's Trade Intelligence Department, who was a director of the hotel and, according to Sam Hoare, 'the friend of more people in the world than anyone I ever knew.'[9] Horrified that the secretaries only had buns for lunch, the ever-hospitable and generous Browning built a canteen on the roof of Whitehall Court for the staff, installed a chef and had him buy the food through the hotel. He was independently wealthy, being chairman of the family firm of Twiss, Browning and Hallowes, and at the outbreak of war had been appointed aide-de-camp to Field Marshal Lord Roberts VC. Exceptionally well-connected, he was an inveterate partygoer and associated with a long list of beauties from the stage, provided by his life-long friend Rupert D'Oyly-Carte. In 1932, when George Hill named Browning as a senior SIS officer in his memoirs *Go Spy the Land*, both Smith-Cumming and Browning were dead, yet he omitted to identify the Chief, saying only that 'I had not the least idea that Colonel Browning, an old acquaintance of mine, was in the secret service, and our meeting was a most happy one.'[10]

In terms of operations. C was fortunate to recruit one source, Dr Otto Kreuger, who was to 'pay the rent' for SIS for more than two decades. Codenamed TR-16, Kreuger was a marine engineer from Godesberg who had made the mistake of striking a brother officer, who happened to be related to the Kaiser. He was court-martialled, and in November 1914, when he offered his services to Tinsley at the British legation in The Hague, was an embittered 39-year-old. Kreuger proved to be an exceptional agent, with access to all the German naval bases, Zeppelin sheds and construction yards, and with the professional skill to know precisely what he was looking at. He possessed a phenomenal memory and made regular trips to Holland to report to Tinsley without the necessity of carrying any notes over the frontier. He was also sufficiently adept to escape any suspicion, even being elected as a director of the Federation of German Industries, until 1939 when he was finally trapped by the Gestapo and beheaded.

Within Whitehall, C's organisation was a strange hybrid, apparently created jointly by the War Office and the Admiralty, but paid for by the Foreign Office. This bureaucratic anomaly left C very exposed, but he evidently used his considerable skills to play each of his masters off against the others, and thereby neatly avoided the oft-threatened perils of amalgamation. While he always maintained cordial relations with Kell, known as 'K', there were several attempts to expand MI5's role beyond the United Kingdom, and eventually a division of responsibilities was agreed that allowed MI5 to play a role within the Empire, with the exception of Malta and Gibraltar, and to share Hong Kong, but to limit its activities to security, and emphatically not the collection of intelligence.

C's role was initially defined by the Permanent Under-Secretary (PUS) at the Foreign Office, Sir Arthur Nicholson, in a memorandum to the War Office in November 1915. This referred to him for the first time in any official document as 'the Chief of the Secret Service', and this arrangement was later confirmed in what amounted to a charter, entitled 'Cabinet Orders with regard to this Special Intelligence Service of the British government'. This guaranteed C a measure of independence, called upon other government departments to cooperate, ensured that SIS personnel were not disadvantaged in their career by service with SIS, and required the Foreign Office to provide 'one nominal acting or supernumerary post' for SIS at each overseas diplomatic mission. In fact, of course, SIS had precious few representatives abroad, as can be seen from this list prepared by C in October 1916, following the recruitment of a baronet, Lieutenant-Colonel Sir William Wiseman, who had been gassed at Hooge and invalided out of the Army, to go to New York for SIS.

Staff and agents: Headquarters 60; Aviation 11; Holland 10; 240; Norway 10; Sweden 10; Denmark 80; Russia 12; Alexandria 300?; Athens 100; Romania 30; Salonika 40; Malta 8; New York 8; South America ?; Switzerland 15; France 20; Italy 8; South Africa 3; Spain about 50; Portugal 2; odds and sods? Total 1,024.[11]

Initially C had structured his organisation into geographical regions, which had a superficial, logical appeal, but thus arrangement caused dissatisfaction, especially with the DNI, Admiral 'Blinker' Hall, who complained about the poor quality of SIS's intelligence product. Initially, according to an early recruit, Commander Frank Stagg RN, C had assigned Newnun to cover Greece and the Mediterranean, Cockerell, to Belgium and Holland, and Guy Standing to all the Americas, leaving Stagg in charge of NID liaison, Scandinavia, the Baltic and Russia. The solution was to separate requirements from production and to bring in officers from the individual services to head sub-divisions, so Claude Dansey was seconded to join Colonel Rhys Sampson (formerly C's man in Athens) to head an Army Section, H. E. Crowther Smith to be in charge of the Air Section, Browning to run Economics, and Captain James Somerville to take charge of the Naval Requirements Section.

This reorganisation may have assuaged the DNI's complaints, but the War Office continued to undermine C's authority overseas, withdraw personnel from his staff as soon as they had been trained, attempt to take over his most successful networks and create friction between his representatives abroad and the War Office's military attachés. Exasperated at yet another bid from the War Office for 'amalgamation' with MI5, which he interpreted as subordination of his service, Smith-Cumming complained to (Sir) Ronald Campbell, the PUS's private secretary that:

> From the day of my appointment I have been disgracefully treated, my authority has been deliberately undermined and my influence even among my own staff damaged by constant fights and humiliations . . . They have made many promises to secure my submission to their scheme of spoilation, but have never kept one of them, and in all my dealings with queer people in my strange and unique service I have met no one who was so thoroughly unscrupulous and untrustworthy as the author of the proposal put forward.[12]

Following the Armistice C fought two lasting battles. One was against the government which sought to impose swingeing cuts on the overseas stations, and the other was against the Bolsheviks. The two were not unconnected because Smith-Cumming argued that the threat from Russia could only be met by a properly-funded SIS. Lord Hardinge of the Foreign Office agreed and urged the Foreign Secretary Lord Curzon that SIS should be 'distinct from any Government Department and free from Parliamentary control'.[13] C's problem was that he only paid the salaries of a small part of his organisation, the lion's share being met by the War Office, which was now effectively discharging men in C's service. In addition, the Foreign Office was pressing to close down a dozen of his key stations, and staff confidence was not enhanced when termination notices were sent out, and then withdrawn a few days later. It was during this chaotic period that C accomplished two important goals. One was that SIS personnel would remain exempt from income tax, argued on the basis of the need for complete confidentiality about SIS's employees, and the more practical expedient that in any event SIS would have to increase its pay to cover any new tax liability that might arise. The other achievement was an acceptance of the ingenious cover of Passport Control Offices for SIS stations overseas. Hitherto SIS had relied upon a variety of unsatisfactory billets, such as Military Control Officers and MI1c officers seconded to military commands, which were heavily dependent upon uncertain War Office cooperation. Numerous incidents had occurred which had demonstrated military hostility to C's men, who had gained a reputation for unorthodoxy, indiscipline and unmilitary behaviour, and in any case there was the need to find a convenient slot within the Foreign Office. The PCOs provided just such a remedy, and one that was to be adopted across the globe. This uniformity undermined the integrity of the cover, but nevertheless offered numerous other advantages.

By the time C received his knighthood, on 25 July 1919, he was firmly in the saddle, preparing the Service to engage a new adversary, this time with the support of a new Cabinet sub-committee, the Secret Service Committee (SSC), which was ready to allow C's organisation to operate into the peace. In reality, as a reflection of SIS's independence, the SSC held only three meetings between 1921 and 1931.

C's trump card remained the Bolshevik menace, and his adventurers actively plotting against Lenin included the Russian-born and educated Stephen Alley, Paul Dukes, who was knighted by the King when he recounted his experiences to him at Buckingham Palace, Augustus Agar who was decorated with the VC and DSO, George Hill, who later described his exploits in *Dreaded Hour* and *Go Spy the Land*, and of course the extraordinary, swashbuckling Sidney Reilly, codenamed ST-1 and later inappropriately dubbed 'the Ace of Spies'. The activities of these larger-than-life characters during the Russian Civil War served to convince Lenin that he would always be the target of assassination plots, and be vulnerable from émigré groups funded by his enemies in the West. In consequence the feared Cheka set about penetrating almost all the leading opposition organisations. The Cheka soon came under the control of the wily Felix Dzerzhinsky, who planted legions of double agents on his adversaries, and succeeded in luring Reilly into Russia and entrapping him. Of C's men in Russia, only Ernest Boyce, his station commander in Petrograd, and Stephen Alley, would continue their SIS careers into peacetime, the former in Helsinki, the latter in the expatriate community that had gravitated to Paris.

In May 1921, having sacked 58 people at headquarters, and reduced the budget by £69,000, C listed his establishment as 65 staff, plus 132 posted abroad, running 484 agents, producing 13,000 intelligence reports a year. These reductions had been accepted by the Chief as part of the price of the SSC's recommendation that he should retain his independence but come under the ministerial control of the Foreign Office.

After the war C developed heart trouble and, anticipating his imminent retirement, took steps to canvass for a successor. His choice, accepted by all, was the head of the Submarine Service, and former DNI, Admiral Hugh Sinclair. C died at his home at 1 Melbury Road, Kensington, on 23 June 1923, at the age of sixty-four, following a meeting with Valentine Williams, who recalled in his autobiography:

> He had lent me a small collection he had made of books about secret service published before the War, including the memoirs of Major Le Caron, the celebrated Fenian spy – C had known Le Caron and called him an unmitigated liar – so, hearing that my old friend was to leave London shortly, I called to return his books and bid him good-bye. I spent the afternoon with him, chatting over old times. I left him about 6 p.m. comfortably installed in the corner of a sofa. When his secretary went in to him soon after she found him dead.[14]

In his will Smith-Cumming left the bulk of his considerable fortune to his widow and made bequests of £100 to his three secretaries, and to his driver, Ernest Bailey.

Chapter II

Hugh Sinclair 1923–1939

'The Secret Service as a definite profession in peacetime – No.'

George Hill in *Dreaded Hour*[1]

THE succession of the DNI, Admiral 'Quex' Sinclair (so called because of 'the wickedest man in London' in Sir Arthur Pinero's play *The Gay Lord Quex*) upon the death of Sir Mansfield Cumming after he had been at SIS's helm for more than thirteen years, was marked by continuing financial pressure from the Treasury, and a crisis inherited from Cumming's anti-Bolshevik adventures.

Despite a difficult private life and a divorce in 1920, Sinclair was exceptionally well-qualified to take over C's mantle, and his Royal Navy service record, which dated back to 1886 when he first went to sea, reads considerably better than his predecessor's:

> Came home in Opal on sick leave granted by Commander-in-Chief [indecipherable] England in Tocca 4 August 1891. Order to [ ] England in *Tocca* cancelled and transferred to *Benbow* before she [ ] was stationed 92 to England in her. October 1892 to be borne in flagship Portsmouth on *Benbow* P.O. 14 December 1892 acting sub-lieutenant by first coming home in *Tyne*. Arrived home 4 January 1893. 11 January 1893 joined College Part I. Arrived 7 April 1895, 14 July 1895 discharged on half pay and granted leave to go abroad till end of first week in July. Arrived home 6 July

1895. May 1896 selected to qualify for torpedo duties. Completed course of introduction at Royal Artillery College, Woolwich for (T) [indecipherable] 11–15 July 1898. NL 7922 Retired Curzon Howe reports satisfactory condition of the *Magnificent* creditable to this officer. To remain in *Magnificent* until ordered to leave owing to the commander being invalided. As of 19 August 1903 G 3437 appointed to War Office committee on Brenan Torpedo. War Office committee abolishes April 1904. NL 12943 / 1905 Satisfaction expressed as a favourable report of [indecipherable] of *Bevallion* – G 5826 / 1906 contributed to good results [indecipherable] G [indecipherable] 1905. NL 11509 / November 1096 Satisfaction of *Leviathan* by Rear Admiral Lambton. NL 128 5 December 1907 [indecipherable] Portsmouth. Showed unremitting zeal and attention in assisting to regenerate [indecipherable] and commitment. Recommended for promotion by Commander-in-Chief Portsmouth. Satisfaction expressed. Recommended by Admiral Fanshawe ADAL November 1908. Inspection of RN Bks, 15 June 1908 much credit due to Commander Sinclair. [indecipherable] P A Fanshawe May 1909 recommended for promotion special by Fanshawe NL 11353/ 04 very creditable inspection of RN Bks Portsmouth by Admiral Fanshawe. TC satisfaction expressed specially recommended for early promotion. Specially recommended for immediate promotion by Admiral Fanshawe November 1909. Reappointed [indecipherable] captain on appointment of Rear Admiral Cradock 29 August 1911. 14 May 1912 assisted commander of *Hibernia* 29 August 1912 ceased command of *Hibernia*. 17 March 1914 appointed member of committee to inquire into the question of employment of Royal Marines at the Divisions on other than military work. M 15579 / 14 appointed [indecipherable] ember of a committee to consider question of the conveyance of men to their home ports for long leave 10 June 1914. 25 May 1916 appointed member of East Coast Bases Committee. [indecipherable] AL.CW 8 September 1916 T.L. appreciation expressed of services rendered by him as Dr of M

> division during the war. Credit for the success of the drafting arrangements being due to him. Granted leave from 15 February 1917 – 23 February 1917 included. Gave up command of *Renown* D.M 16 August 1917. CW 6544 – 20 January 1918 to receive employment as chief of staff. full pay plus 18 shillings per day command money on his appointment as captain 2nd class. CW 40234/18 granted Order of Rising Sun 3rd class) gazetted 29 November 1918. CW 37028/18 granted Legion of Honour (officer) gazetted 12 December 1918.[2]

In 1919 Sinclair, now serving as Admiral Hall's deputy, was appointed to succeed Hall as DNI, and in 1923 he was named Chief of the Submarine Service, a post he held only briefly because of C's death. According to his entry in *Who's Who*, which omits all mention of his family, he went onto the retired list in 1926, whereas in fact he had been appointed C two years earlier.

SIS's battle with the Treasury ended in the closure of the stations in Madrid, Lisbon, Zurich and Luxembourg, and staff reductions at Rome and The Hague, but the Service had at least established the right to an independent existence, albeit under the Foreign Office's Secret Vote, and with an annual budget of £90,000, reduced from £240,000 in 1919. This achieved, Sinclair was unexpectedly engulfed in a major crisis. The document which created the problem had been sent by courier in September 1924 from the SIS station in Riga where Colonel Ronald Meiklejohn had acquired what purported to be a copy of a Comintern directive from a source with access to files in Moscow. The document was originally typed in Russian in Cyrillic script, and dated 15 September 1924. Meiklejohn's secretary had translated it and found what seemed to be a letter signed by Grigori Zinoviev, Lenin's appointee as President of the Third International, and addressed to the Central Committee of the Communist Party of Great Britain (CPGB), advocating sedition on a grand scale and agitation within the armed forces, all eloquent proof that the Soviets had deliberately reneged on the terms of the recent Anglo-Soviet Trade Agreement which had opened diplomatic relations between the two countries, but remained to be ratified by Parliament.

When the document had been received in London by SIS's Chief of Production, Major (Sir) Desmond Morton it had been circulated routinely to the services, MI5 and the Foreign Office, although as was customary there was no indication of how or where SIS had acquired it. Morton was later to claim that he had not appreciated the political potential of the text, just as the country was preparing for a general election, and when asked for verification of its authenticity he confirmed that an SIS source inside the CPGB had reported that the CPGB's Central Committee had met recently to discuss Zinoviev's instructions. While nobody quibbled with the general sentiments expressed in the directive, which were entirely in conformity with the Comintern's policy of exporting Soviet-style Communism, there were immediate demands for assurances of its *provenance* but on 25 October, four days before polling day, the entire content was published in the *Daily Mail*. As a consequence Ramsay MacDonald's first Labour administration, which had already lost a vote of confidence in the Commons, and was losing its Liberal support, was portrayed as having been willing to tolerate the Kremlin's subversion, and Stanley Baldwin was swept to office in a landslide victory. The fact that Zinoviev protested that he had never sent any such letter, and the CPGB denied ever having received it, was dismissed as typically, predictably duplicitous and spurious.

SIS's involvement in the Zinoviev Letter affair, and the Labour Party's preoccupation with the scandal, survived into 1998 when one of the first acts of Tony Blair's new Foreign Secretary, Robin Cook, was to commission an investigation of SIS's files to establish once and for all whether the letter was a forgery, as the left had maintained for the past seven decades, and if so who had been culpable. Cook appointed the Foreign Office's chief historian, Gill Bennett, to undertake the task, and she was able to travel to Moscow to examine the relevant files in the KGB's archives. Her subsequent report,[3] which drew on an earlier investigation conducted by Millicent Bagot of MI5, established the sequence of events which had followed safe receipt of the document from Riga. Recently retired from MI5, Miss Bagot had been commissioned to write a report on the affair following the publication in 1967 of *The Zinoviev Letter* by three *Sunday Times* journalists, a book claiming that the letter had been forged in

Berlin. She took three years to complete her task and her report (which remains closed to the public) was submitted to the Director-General of the Security Service, Sir Martin Furnival Jones.

Bennett established that Desmond Morton had circulated the three-page letter to the usual recipients, any number of whom could have had a motive for leaking it first to Conservative Central Office, and then to the newspapers. Among the suspects, apart from Morton himself, was the former DNI, Admiral Hall, who had been elected to the Commons as a Conservative MP in 1922; Smith-Cumming's former deputy Freddie Browning (who died in 1929, at the age of fifty-six, of cirrhosis of the liver); the head of SIS's Army section, Stewart Menzies, who allegedly later acknowledged to Morton that he had sent a copy to the *Daily Mail*; Donald im Thurn, a well-connected former MI5 officer who had been actively lobbying for the letter's publication, but had not actually seen it for himself; C's aide Bertie Maw, and Colonel W. A. Alexander, an MI5 officer close to Kell. Precisely who actually delivered the document to the *Daily Mail* is unclear, but a strong candidate must be Freddie Browning. His daughter Grace acted as his wartime assistant in SIS and she and her family always believed he had been responsible, which was why he had been given a silver cigarette box by Lord Northcliffe, engraved with the words 'Today A Great Victory Was Won', and dated the day of the General Election.

Despite the strong possibility of Browning's involvement, the common denominator linking most of the principal candidates is Donald im Thurn whose diary reveals that he was in touch with the new DNI, Admiral Sir Alan Hotham, who had put him in touch with SIS's Bertie Maw, and he was anyway talking to MI5's Colonel Alexander, and to Bunty Saunders of Scotland Yard, in what now appears to be a race to see who would publish the Zinoviev letter first. As for the intermediaries at Central Office, there were any number of possibilities, including Joseph Ball, the MI5 officer who in 1929 was to be appointed director of Central Office's Research Department, and the Party's Chairman, Lord Davidson, who later may have paid im Thurn £5,000.

When the document was first circulated the Foreign Office's Northern Department contacted Captain Hugh Miller, Scotland Yard's expert on Communism, and he confirmed that the content was similar in tone to what he read in the Comintern's regular journal, *International Press Correspondence*. The final proof, as presented by SIS, was Morton's assertion that he had met his spy inside the CPGB, Jim Finney, on the evening of 10 October, that Finney had corroborated receipt in London of Zinoviev's directive, and he had written a memorandum recording the fact on 11 October. However, close scrutiny of Morton's minute revealed that Finney had not made any direct reference to a specific letter from Zinoviev, and MI5 and Scotland Yard's Special Branch, both surprised and dismayed to learn that Morton had been running an agent inside the CPGB without sharing that knowledge with them, expressed reservations about the strength of this meeting as corroboration. It also seemed that Finney, who had used the alias Finlay, had previously worked briefly for MI5, but had not proved reliable.

Having accepted Morton's agent report as confirmation of the CPGB's receipt of the Zinoviev letter, Sinclair himself weighed in on 23 October to reveal to the Foreign Office that 'Additional confirmation that such a document was in existence was furnished by an individual in touch with M. Rakovsky and the Arcos Bank.'[4] In fact C's information had come from his friend Donald im Thurn, who had been active from the outset, spurred on by a mysterious informant who wanted to ensure that the British government did not suppress news of the incriminating letter. Im Thurn also suspected a cover-up, and contacted many of his old friends from the intelligence world to get confirmation of the letter's existence, and ensure that, one way or another, its explosive contents were made public. According to im Thurn's source, the Soviet Chargé d'Affaires in London, Christian Rakovsky, definitely knew of the letter and had even discussed it with a left-wing Labour MP, Jimmy Maxton; both men had recognised the implications and allegedly had cursed Zinoviev for his gaffe. Thus, im Thurn reported, when Rakovsky had been told of the existence of the letter, he had believed it, having no reason to doubt its authenticity until later, when the CPGB and Moscow denied all knowledge of it. This was the news conveyed by im Thurn to Sinclair, in a telephone call on 21 October, and then relayed to the Foreign Office two days later by C as yet further proof that the letter was authentic.

Sinclair's link to im Thurn was via Bertie Maw who had lunched with im Thurn on 18 October and written up a report of the meeting, in which he said that im Thurn had identified his original source as a woman, the mistress of a Russian monarchist 'in touch with Rakovsky and Arcos',[5] and had offered to send someone to Moscow to obtain a copy of the letter for £10,000. It would seem that im Thurn's motives for his involvement were not entirely patriotic, and it seems clear that he was later paid a substantial sum by Lord Davidson for his help during the election campaign, and maybe his silence.

At the Foreign Office's request, SIS contacted Meiklejohn at Riga on 27 October to establish that his Russian version appeared to be a copy of the original in the Moscow file, and that the version mailed to London by the Comintern, if it ever came to light, would most likely have been written in English, and therefore would differ slightly from Meiklejohn's translation. In fact the only version that anyone ever examined was Meiklejohn's, and this reached London on 12 December. It was only on 28 October, after this contact with Meiklejohn, that SIS revealed to the Foreign Office that the letter had been acquired in Riga, a disclosure made on the strict condition that it went no further than the PUS. Until that moment there had been considerable speculation about how the incriminating letter had fallen into SIS's hands. Was Arthur McManus of the CPGB, to whom the letter was addressed, the subject of a clandestine letter intercept? Had an informant betrayed it from inside the CPGB? Did SIS have a spy in Moscow?

The problem for Sinclair, which emerged as various investigations were conducted into the origins and authenticity of the Zinoviev letter, was that SIS found it hard to refute Labour accusations of collusion with the Conservative Party and interference and manipulation during the general election campaign. As Gill Bennett eventually concluded, the letter itself was undoubtedly a forgery, although its composition was sufficiently skilful to persuade those who read it of its intrinsic authenticity. No blame could be attached to Ronald Meiklejohn for acquiring this tantalising item and sending it to headquarters, and Desmond Morton acted quite properly by circulating it to SIS's clients. Hugh Miller, who later joined MI5, confirmed that the content coincided with the Comintern's declared policies, and nobody in officialdom, including C, the DNI or Scotland

Yard, ever encouraged im Thurn in his quest for publication. However, Sinclair had two embarrassments. Firstly, he had used Bertie Maw as an intermediary with im Thurn, an intervention that was never disclosed (and even those reading im Thurn's diary years later misinterpreted his various references to 'MAW' as someone's initials) and, secondly, he had depended on Morton's unreliable memorandum of 11 October, and Maw's report of 18 October, to give his personal assurance to Sir Eyre Crowe, the Permanent Under-Secretary at the Foreign Office, that the bogus document was authentic.

Thereafter Sinclair's pivotal role in the Zinoviev letter would remain known to only a very few, for im Thurn himself died in March 1930, taking the secret of Maw's involvement to the grave. As for who actually peddled the original Russian document in Riga, the Soviets, who were as interested as anyone else in who had been counterfeiting Comintern directives, concluded that a notorious White Russian forger, Vladimir Orlov, who had been General Wrangel's chief of intelligence during the Civil War, was responsible. Orlov had made a good living fabricating ostensibly plausible Soviet documents, mainly for propaganda purposes, and when SIS contacted Meiklejohn to conduct investigations into his source, yet more supporting evidence conveniently materialised, including a record of the minutes of an emergency meeting of the Sovnarkom, the Council of People's Commissars, supposedly convened on 25 October 1924 to discuss the crisis in Britain, and chaired by Leo Kamenev. This second document, containing admissions that the Zinoviev directive was genuine, was sent to London on 6 November, and was seized on by Sinclair as empirical proof but, as we now know, this too had been forged by Orlov! Better still, Meiklejohn's agent reported on 1 November that Dzerzhinsky himself had conducted a molehunt to plug the leak in the Comintern and had arrested two suspects and introduced a series of new security procedures to protect the integrity of all future typed documents. Although this did not amount to further evidence of the authenticity of the Zinoviev letter, and merely signalled Dzerzhinsky's predictable interest in what was supposedly a major breach of the Comintern's security, real or imagined, Sinclair listed this material too in support of his case.

Meiklejohn had been educated at Rugby and had joined the Army, becoming an officer in the Royal Warwickshire Regiment, in 1898. He had fought in the Sudan two years later and subsequently won a DSO in the Boer War. He had served in the North Russia campaign in 1919 and in 1920 led the British Military Mission to east Finland. The following year he had been appointed C's man in Riga, a post he was to retain for the next seven years, assisted by two subordinates, L. G. Goodlet and H. T. Hall, until he was replaced by Norman Dewhurst. With the benefit of hindsight, Meiklejohn's behaviour in Riga looks very odd, and it is unclear why this experienced officer should have been duped, if that is indeed what happened. However, his record in Riga as an SIS officer was not entirely unblemished, for his star agent, codenamed BP-11, was a Volga German, supposedly a cipher clerk on the staff of Deputy Foreign Commissar Maxim Litvinov's headquarters in Estonia, who sold him 200 'paraphrases' of what he claimed were Litvinov's secret wireless messages. When eventually this traffic was intercepted and read by the Government Code and Cypher School (GC&CS) the 'paraphrases' were exposed as somewhat inaccurate, and BP-11 had been sacked. In short, Riga was a hotbed of revolutionaries and counter-revolutionaries, all anxious to cash in on SIS's generosity. In the example of BP-11, Meiklejohn's man had failed his first litmus test and on the assumption that either Sinclair or Morton, or both, knew of his record, one might have expected a degree of scepticism in London when the station produced another well-placed agent.

When Rakovsky finally delivered his rebuttal he cited numerous textual problems with the letter, and even named Orlov as a notorious forger in Berlin who was likely to have been responsible for the fabrication, but these objections were brushed aside by Meiklejohn, who claimed he knew about Orlov's group and insisted that his source did not operate in Berlin, where Orlov was known to be based. SIS headquarters then demanded that the station produce a piece of Soviet notepaper headed 'Third Communist International', but none was forthcoming, the somewhat dubious explanation being that the Comintern's new security measures made the removal of such a specimen impossible.

The issue of the letter's authenticity could not be decided by Ramsay MacDonald before he submitted his resignation to the King on 4 November 1924, but the new Conservative administration immediately set up a Cabinet committee, chaired by the Foreign Secretary, Austen Chamberlain, to consider the same matter. Naturally, one of those called to give evidence to the enquiry, which was conducted entirely in secret, and issued no concluding report, was C, who left a five-point memorandum in SIS's files listing the arguments he used to prove the case for authenticity. This document is quite explosive as it can now be seen to provide damning proof that Sinclair actively misled Chamberlain's committee, which consisted of Lord Curzon, Lord Birkenhead and the Viscount Cecil. At the outset C claimed that the source run by the Riga station worked for the Comintern secretariat in Moscow and had access to the Comintern's secret files, whereas Meiklejohn had only ever claimed to have run an agent in Riga who in turn was in touch with such an individual (whose identity was unknown to him). Thus Sinclair concealed one link in the chain, and compounded the offence by stating, falsely, that the source had been of proven reliability over several years, when in fact he had no idea who he (or she) was. Sinclair then went on to quote the Sovnarkom document as supporting evidence, and the testimony of his informant of 18 October (who was, of course, actually Donald im Thurn's mysterious source). Considering that the Sovnarkom minute was also a forgery, and im Thurn's information to Bertie Maw was proof of nothing, C's case looks decidedly flimsy. Then, incredibly, it was to get worse with his assertion that he was well aware of the White Russian forgers in Berlin, 'but in this particular case we are aware of the identity of every person who handled the document on its journey from Zinoviev's files to our hands'.[6] This was, quite obviously, a flat lie.

Sinclair was on safer ground when he made his fourth point, that the letter's content was entirely consistent with what were known to be the Comintern's policies, but his fifth and final argument, that if the document had been a forgery, it would have been uncovered as such, seems bizarre and even desperate. Nevertheless, the committee reported to the full Cabinet on 19 November that they 'were unanimously of the opinion that there was no doubt as to the authenticity of the Letter.'[7] Clearly C's evidence had swayed a committee of Tory politicians who must have been predisposed to accept his assurances, but if there was any weight in Sinclair's belief that a forgery would surely have been discovered, it perhaps follows that he had indeed made just such a determination. After all, there is no other explanation for his most comprehensive deception. The deceit is all the greater, considering the evidence of Assistant Commissioner Sir Wyndham Childs, the head of the Special Branch, who declined repeatedly to offer an opinion on the letter's authenticity, but insisted that 'the document was secured by the Foreign Office organisation and their opinion must outweigh that of any other living person, otherwise the Secret Service would be an impossibility.'[8] Thus Childs, who doubtless must have had his own suspicions, passed the buck to SIS and placed the very existence of the Service in the balance. Equally, Sinclair's blatant lies can only be explained if he knew for certain that he had mistakenly given his imprimatur to a fake. While his original error may have been made in good faith, his subsequent cover-up made him all the more culpable. On the other hand, it is easy to see that, given the option, further lies were more attractive than the grave constitutional crisis into which the country would have fallen, knowing that SIS's intervention during a general election campaign was certainly believed by the Labour Party to have helped change history.

We now know that, contrary to the assertion that the text of the letter conformed to the Comintern's known general policy, a formal decision had been taken *not* to indulge in any inflammatory propaganda in Britain until after the Anglo-Soviet Trade Agreement had been ratified. This is confirmed by recently declassified files in Moscow. The text was unquestionably a forgery, and there was no molehunt organised to trace a leak because Zinoviev and Dzerzhinsky knew the document to be bogus. Furthermore, for Zinoviev to have sent such a letter to the CPGB would have been sheer madness, bearing in mind that only a year earlier the Party headquarters had been raided by the police and the Party's records removed for scrutiny by Scotland Yard. Given the sheer improbability of the version averred by Sinclair, the only reasonable explanation for his deception is that the Riga station accepted a forged document at face value at a moment that was to have the most extraordinary consequences, of constitutional proportions.

It might be asked why Millicent Bagot's report, completed some years after these events had occurred, did not reveal what others in MI5 must have known. The answer may be because MI5 employed Derek, one of Sinclair's two sons, or that MI5's own hands were not entirely clean, considering the role played by Joe Ball and maybe Bunty Saunders, who was soon to join the Security Service from Scotland Yard. The Bagot report focused on the discrepancies surrounding Morton's alleged agent inside the CPGB, whose information was completely at odds with MI5's own sources inside the Party, and cast doubt on the efforts made by SIS's station in Riga to ascertain the truth. In particular, Bagot found that the same source had supplied the station with fourteen 'surprisingly accurate' Soviet documents since 1923, and was still active in 1931, yet there was absolutely no trace of his, or her, true identity, nor the motive for providing them. In the circumstances, the apparent reluctance of the Riga station to cooperate with the original inquiry seems highly suspicious, especially as doubts continued to mount about the source's reliability. Every intelligence source ought to be the subject of rigorous tests of integrity, conducted by somebody other than the agent's own case officer, and when such an exercise was conducted in Riga, with a false rumour spread as bait, Meiklejohn's source picked it up and reported it as a fact. As we have seen, the Cabinet committee had absolutely no knowledge of these concerns, for it had accepted Sinclair's wholly false assurances that the source was indeed known, and was entirely reliable.

Such momentous events might have been expected to dominate Sinclair's nineteen-year tenure as Chief but, although this episode must have coloured his relationship with Menzies and Morton, who must have learned the truth, there were other events, in the Soviet Union and Germany, which would preoccupy him. Certainly his complicity in the Zinoviev affair did little to undermine SIS's status within Whitehall for C even proposed to the SSC, in 1925 and 1927, that his organisation might be the most appropriate to absorb MI5, GC&CS and even the Special Branch. This was a complete reversal of the position in which Smith-Cumming had found himself, fending off 'amalgamation' from the War Office, but Sinclair argued that such a strategy would eliminate wasteful duplication. MI5 fought back, and C retired from the field with control over the codebreakers of GC&CS who were moved from Queensgate and accommodated in SIS's main office block, at 54 Broadway. Simultaneously he moved up from his home in Fishery Road, Maidenhead, and installed himself in a splendid, eighteenth-century town house at 21 Queen Anne's Gate (which conveniently backed onto Broadway Buildings), with his sister Evelyn acting as his housekeeper, although as a bachelor he reportedly spent much of his time at his club, the Naval and Military, in Piccadilly, typically surrounded by a thick cloud of cigar smoke.

Internally, Sinclair's principal challenge came from one of his predecessor's officers, Henry Landau, who became the first SIS officer to write about his work for Smith-Cumming. Born in South Africa of Anglo-Dutch parentage, Landau had graduated from Cambridge shortly before the outbreak of the Great War and had volunteered for military service, to be commissioned in the Royal Field Artillery. In 1916 he had received a summons to Whitehall Court where he was tested in his claimed fluency in German, Dutch and French. Thereafter Landau was instructed to rebuild SIS's train-watching service in Belgium which monitored the enemy's troop movements right across the Western Front. The ring operated behind the German lines and had been codenamed WHITE LADY, which became part of the title of Landau's second book, *Secrets of the White Lady*, published in 1935. SIS's embarrassment at the publication was enhanced considerably by the author's assurance that the documents quoted in the text 'have been taken from secret service records which have hitherto been unavailable for publication'.[9]

After the war, following the success of his train-watching activities, Landau had moved to America where he had been out of reach of the British courts. No action was taken against his first book, *All's Fair*, which was released in 1934, but the government apparently threatened to place a ban on the distribution in Britain of the sequel. In his book the author admitted that he had 'not attempted to disguise the names of Allied agents. My friends in Belgium and France assure me that if damage could be done by divulging them, it was done years ago when a complete list of agents' names was published in the various decoration lists.'[10] His other books were *The Enemy Within* and *Spreading the Spy Net*. Both were published in 1937 and dealt in some detail with his experiences in SIS and can today be recognised as the first in a genre. Landau did take some elementary precautions to avoid identifying, for example, Otto Kreuger, SIS's German marine engineer, whom he mentioned only as being a Dane but, if he had ever returned to Britain, he would certainly have faced arrest and prosecution. However, as he remained abroad outside the jurisdiction of the High Court C was powerless to prevent him haemorrhaging SIS's wartime secrets. Although Kreuger was to be arrested and executed in 1939, he was betrayed not by Landau, but by a former SIS officer in The Hague, a station that was to be beset by scandal.

The problem in the Netherlands developed as a consequence of SIS's reliance on personnel with a private income. SIS pay was poor, and this was long before SIS offered a pension scheme, and the temptations were great, especially when the Passport Control Officers issued visas to Palestine under the terms of the League of Nations mandate. As Fascism took a grip in Germany and Italy thousands of European Jews were anxious to emigrate, and were willing to pay for the opportunity. In The Hague the PCO, Major Hugh Dalton, took advantage of their plight and accepted bribes in return for visas, and one of his subordinates, Jack Hooper, who learned of the lucrative racket, was taken on as his partner. When Dalton's extracurricular activities came to light in September 1936 during an SIS audit, he shot himself, while Hooper confessed his complicity and was sacked. Short of money, Hooper sold the true name of TR-16 to the Germans, who immediately placed Dr Kreuger under surveillance and eventually watched him meeting his SIS contact. SIS parsimony was also to be blamed for the treachery of C. H. ('Dick') Ellis, another career SIS officer, who sold out to the Germans in Paris, but who was to escape undiscovered until long after his retirement.

The system of charging for visas was intended to help bolster SIS's precarious finances but, as the demand for emigration increased, individual PCOs found their intelligence-gathering activities were handicapped by the pressure to handle hundreds, and sometimes thousands of desperate applicants. Frank Foley in Berlin took advantage of the chaotic scenes around his office to recruit two spies, both of whom would 'pay the rent' for some years. Johann deGraff, later to be known as 'Jonny X' was an experienced Comintern agent. He was a German who had run away to sea in 1907 at the age of fourteen and served in the Kaiser's navy during the war. In 1917 he had been one of the leaders of the Communist-inspired mutiny on the battleship *Westfalen* and later attended the Lenin University in Moscow. Having become disenchanted with the Soviets, deGraff simply volunteered his services to Foley who used him as a human encyclopedia on the Comintern's activities in Germany and his Comintern missions across Europe, to Britain and to Shanghai. When deGraff was sent to Brazil to foment revolution there in 1935, SIS played a key role in providing the Brazilian authorities with the detailed information they needed to suppress the rising. When he was arrested in Brazil in 1940 and threatened with deportation back to Germany, and certain death as a by-now notorious member of the KPD, deGraff was rescued by SIS and resettled in Canada.

Foley's other star agent was Paul Rosbaud, the editor of German scientific journals who provided large quantities of technical data which, under the Nazis, was banned from publication abroad. Another walk-in, Rosbaud was an Austrian physicist whose wife was Jewish, and his role as adviser for Springer Verlag gave him access to valuable information about the latest scientific advances, including Hitler's secret weapons and plans for an atomic bomb. Additional scientific material also came from Professor Hans Mayer, the anonymous author of the mysterious Oslo Report which first alerted SIS to Nazi interest in proximity fuzes, and the development of flying bombs and ballistic missiles on the Baltic island of Peenemünde.

Despite the cultivation of such impressive sources, Sinclair remained impotent in dealing with the Treasury, and he often complained that SIS, with its Secret Vote of £180,000 cost the Exchequer less in a year than a single destroyer operating in home waters. SIS's unpopularity in Whitehall was in part because his message, especially on the subject of the scale and speed of German rearmament, was unwelcome. On more than one occasion he clashed with Stanley Baldwin over official estimates of the size of the Luftwaffe, and on one occasion, in May 1935, threatened to resign unless the Prime Minister returned to the Commons to correct a misleading statement about German aircraft production figures. The issue led to a secret Cabinet inquiry chaired by Philip Cunliffe-Lister (then Secretary of State for Air, and later Lord Swinton) in July 1935 to take evidence on the true strength of German front-line aircraft. In his evidence the Chief was supported by Desmond Morton and the head of SIS's air intelligence section, Fred Winterbotham. The reality was that SIS had produced some very precise statistics but Baldwin, claiming that he had been misled, had been reluctant to accept them because he believed, as he later acknowledged, that rearmament was politically unacceptable to the British electorate in May 1935. However, Sinclair and his team persuaded the committee that SIS's estimates were accurate, and the government belatedly recognised the need to strengthen the RAF. Sinclair had warned Winterbotham that their future had lain in the balance, but once the Air Staff's opposition collapsed the Chief triumphed. 'On our way back to the office', recalled Winterbotham, 'the Admiral congratulated Morton and myself on our performance. It was, in a way, a turning-point for my career in MI6. We all had a drink in the Admiral's flat.'[11]

Sinclair, who must have known and probably approved of Morton's copious leaks to Winston Churchill, his near neighbour in Kent, took a close interest in Nazi rearmament and always remained in close contact with his friend the British Ambassador in Berlin, Sir Nevile Bland. It was on a visit to him in 1939 that a young Nicholas Elliott was deputed:

> . . . to look after the great man, drive him around and ensure that he was suitably wined and dined – he was a *bon viveur* and an excellent cook.
>
> We descended together to Nevile's cellar and selected the wines he would wish to drink during his stay. Some weeks previously the Admiral's sister, Evelyn Sinclair, had come out to stay with the Blands and we had to get on well together – so much so that she briefed me on how to behave towards him. She told me that he invariably adopted a disconcerting technique with younger men by maintaining a stony silence and simply not answering any questions they put to him. This, of course, was intended to throw the victim right off balance and cause him, in his shyness, to make a fool of himself. The right technique was, initially, only to speak when spoken to. The first time therefore I found myself alone with the Admiral I followed Evelyn's advice. Why, he inquired after a time, was I so silent? Had I lost the use of my tongue? I then confessed the advice his sister had given to me. Happily he was much amused.[12]

Soon afterwards Elliott, now serving as an honorary attaché at the embassy in The Hague, would be a witness to the Venlo incident (described below), and later joined MI5, only to transfer to SIS's Section V in 1942.

Having survived the debacle over the Zinoviev letter, Sinclair's legacy was a series of rearguard actions against Treasury parsimony which left his stations abroad badly depleted and strapped for cash. In failing health, Sinclair was to succumb to cancer at the London Clinic on 4 November 1939, probably his greatest achievement being his dress-rehearsal for war, conducted during the Munich Crisis of 1938, which had temporarily moved the entire organisation to its secret war station at Bletchley Park, a hideous mansion and estate the Chief had bought with his own funds so as to avoid a further drain on the Secret Vote, which had been increased belatedly to £350,000. Accommodated alongside SIS's various individual sections at Bletchley was GC&CS which, through bureaucratic inertia, had remained under C's umbrella and had mobilised a cadre of academics to exercise their code-breaking skills. This apparently unpromising investment was to prove to be a war-winner, but until the source, initially codenamed BONIFACE and then ULTRA, came on stream, Sinclair would be recalled by Winterbotham principally as a Chief 'whose absolute personal loyalty and fairness to his staff were qualities which were rarely found in his successors'.[13]

Chapter III

Stewart Menzies 1939–1952

'He would not have held the job for more than a year if it had not been for Bletchley.'

Victor Cavendish-Bentinck[1]

MENZIES occasionally reflected to friends that he had spent his entire career either at, or preparing for, war with Germany, and when he stepped into C's shoes, with the blessing of the Prime Minister and the Foreign Secretary Lord Halifax, the country had been at war for almost exactly two months. The succession, as it turned out, was not entirely automatic, for Churchill, as First Lord of the Admiralty, had felt duty-bound to remind the Cabinet that the Chief was, by tradition, a naval man, and he proposed Captain Gerald Muirhead-Gould, commander of HMS *Devonshire* in 1939 but formerly naval attaché in Berlin between 1933 and 1936. Muirhead-Gould's candidacy proved not to be a match for Menzies and a minute from the Secret Service Committee meeting in 1923 was found to note that the appointment of C should be rotated among the services. The issue was decided at Cabinet on 28 November when Sir Alexander Cadogan confided to his diary, Halifax 'played his hand well and won the trick' for Menzies.[2] It was sheer bad luck that one of Sinclair's final orders was to plunge SIS into a major crisis that would handicap his successor for the remainder of the conflict.

Menzies had begun his career as a regular officer in the Grenadiers but had soon transferred to his stepfather's regiment, the Life Guards. His first experience of what had been termed MI1(c) had been in December 1915 when he had been posted to Sir Douglas Haig's headquarters staff at Montreuil. Earlier in the war Menzies had fought at Ypres and had won the DSO and MC, but he was not to return to regimental duties for the remainder of the conflict, during which he was engaged on 'secret service and security' work under Colonel (Sir) Walter Kirke.

Menzies's friends sometimes thought that he promoted the idea that he was the future Edward VII's illegitimate son, a rumour often in circulation in polite society, fuelled by his refusal ever to mention his father, Jack Menzies, in his *Who's Who* entry. Known as 'Hell-fire Jack', Menzies senior was the Master of the Linlithgow and Stirlingshire Hunt, and for much of his lifetime a wealthy director of the Distillers Company, previously run by his father, Stewart's grandfather, Graham. However, by the time of his death in May 1911 at the age of fifty, Jack had stood unsuccessfully for Parliament, lost almost all of his fortune, and seen his wife live with Colonel Sir George Holford, an equerry to the Prince of Wales. Soon after the funeral, Holford married the beautiful Susannah Menzies, but the gossip about her relationship with the late King persisted.

In November 1918 Stewart Menzies married Lady Alice Sackville, the daughter of the 8th Earl de la Warr, but thirteen years later they were divorced so she could wed Colonel Fitzroy Spicer of the 16th Lancers. The following year Menzies married Pamela Beckett, one of the four daughters of the Hon. Rupert Beckett, an immensely wealthy Old Etonian who was chairman of the Westminster Bank and proprietor of the *Yorkshire Post*. Later Menzies was to have a string of mistresses, including Freda Portarlington (wife of the 6th Earl), the wife of a near neighbour at his country home in Wiltshire at Bridges Court, Luckington, and, it was rumoured, his secretary Evelyn Jones.

When Menzies had effectively accepted the mantle from the ailing Sinclair in November 1938 he had been head of Section II, SIS's Army section, although in reality he had always acted as C's deputy. Nobody else inside the organisation could match his experience or the breadth of his contacts, but probably few outsiders realised the true nature of the poisoned chalice he had been handed. SIS was not highly regarded in Whitehall, mainly because of disastrously poor reporting on Italian intentions prior to the invasion of Abyssinia, and the complete lack of firm production figures for German rearmament. Naturally, Sinclair had blamed his lack of financial resources for the paucity of accurate SIS reporting from Germany, but it was Menzies who received the benefit of an increased annual budget for 1940/41, to £5.6m.

Menzies spoke good French and German, was admired as a horse-man, hunting with the Beaufort and Quorn, had an eye for a pretty pair of legs and, aged forty-nine at the time of his appointment, either knew, or had been at Eton with, most of the Cabinet. However, almost as soon as his appointment had been confirmed, SIS was engulfed by a disaster of huge proportions on the Dutch border with Germany near the town of Venlo.

The background to what became known as the Venlo incident can be traced back to Sinclair's decision to allow the PCO in Rome, Claude Dansey, to build a parallel organisation to SIS's well-established networks in Europe which reported through the semi-transparent Passport Control Officers. Dansey, accurately described by R. V. Jones, the wartime head of scientific intelligence, as 'a man who delighted in intrigue',[3] had served with MI5 and MI1(c) during the Great War and, after some unsuccessful adventures in private business in the United States, had been appointed by Sinclair to go to Rome in 1929. There he had remained until 1936 when the Ambassador's wife, Lady Drummond, suffered the theft of her jewels. One of two brothers named Constantini, both employed in the chancery as servants, fell under suspicion, and Francesco was sacked, prompting an investigation of the embassy's security conducted by Valentine Vivian, a senior SIS officer. His report was damning and suggested that the embassy had been haemorrhaging secrets for years, probably since 1924, and identified Secondo, not Francesco, Constantini as the likely suspect. Embarrassed by these developments, Dansey had returned to London under a cloud but had undertaken to recover his standing by creating an independent SIS network, based on his own commercial and journalistic contacts, that would not be dependent on local PCOs. Sinclair, perhaps in recognition of the vulnerability of his PCOs, had accepted the proposal and thus 'Z' had been born, under a variety of business covers, some authentic, others created specially to accommodate Z agents.

The fundamental attraction of the Z network was, of course, its isolation from the PCO organisation which was known to have been compromised. Dr Otto Kreuger had been arrested following problems at the Hague station, and Thomas Kendrick, the PCO in Vienna, had been arrested by the Gestapo during the Anschluss. However, Sinclair had directed that upon the outbreak of war the two separate structures should combine, with the heads of both in each country identifying themselves to their counterparts. In Holland this meant that the local Z representative, Captain Sigismund Payne Best, introducing himself to the PCO, Major Richard Stevens, and working together on a joint project, contact with a senior Luftwaffe officer who had presented himself as an anti-Nazi linked to a group of other dissidents. Unfortunately the entire operation had been an elaborate entrapment scheme masterminded by the Sicherheitsdienst which ended in the abduction of Stevens and Best on 9 November as they approached the frontier to hold a rendezvous with the enemy officer. Their Dutch escort, Lieutenant Dirk Klop, having been shot dead, the two SIS men were dragged into Germany at gunpoint for interrogation and remained in concentration camps for the remainder of the war.

The capture of two such well-informed men so soon after the outbreak of hostilities was a huge loss to SIS, for Best had been one of Smith-Cumming's recruits, and had remained in contact with SIS when he returned to private business in the Netherlands after the war. As for Stevens, he had only recently arrived in The Hague as PCO, and had received a very comprehensive briefing on the latest developments at Broadway before he had left. Accordingly, two potentially key sources had fallen into German hands, and Menzies had no way of knowing the extent to which the networks known to Best and Stevens had been compromised. The whole purpose of running parallel, insulated networks had been subverted, and both structures had been place in jeopardy.

Almost worse, the Nazi Blitzkrieg had already overrun Poland and would shortly sweep across Western Europe and Scandinavia, so that SIS was obliged to evacuate its stations in all these countries, none of them having prepared stay-behind networks which could continue reporting after the PCOs had left. By the late spring of 1941 Menzies was watching the Nazis from Lisbon, Madrid, Cairo, Istanbul, Berne, Helsinki and Stockholm, having been forced to withdraw from Athens, Bucharest, Prague, Sofia, Belgrade, Vienna, Berlin, Oslo, Copenhagen, Paris, The

Hague, Warsaw, Tallinn, Riga and Brussels. The consequence of these evacuations was a concentration in London of experienced officers who had worked abroad for years and knew the leading personalities and security officials of their host countries well. Of course, London was also to play host to remnants of the Czech, French, Polish, Belgian, Latvian, Lithuanian, Estonian, Norwegian and Dutch intelligence services, which were allowed to continue their operations on behalf of their governments-in-exile, on condition SIS handled their communications. Thus SIS station commanders like Biffy Dunderdale (from Paris) and Harold Gibson (from Prague) took on new liaison responsibilities and also found themselves the beneficiaries of information from their former hosts. In Gibson's case, he had accompanied the Czech intelligence chief, Colonel Frantisek Moravec, on a flight to Croydon in March 1939, accompanied by his senior staff and their files, thus allowing Moravec to maintain contact with his star agent, Paul Thümmel. Codenamed A-54, Thümmel was a well-placed Abwehr officer who continued to supply Moravec with top quality intelligence until he was arrested by the Gestapo in March 1942.

Truly, SIS was virtually in a state of collapse yet, thanks to some cryptographic breakthroughs achieved on the Abwehr's hand ciphers, and a few Enigma keys, there was a chance that C would not be entirely blind. By the end of 1940 GC&CS had exploited the early achievements of the codebreakers at Bletchley Park, an organisation that was to expand world-wide to 12,500 personnel. Thereafter SIS very largely became a branch of the signals intelligence (Sigint) organisation with a specialist, global section devoted to analysing the counter-intelligence material, and another branch dedicated to the distribution of the product, initially disguised as having originated from a source codenamed BONIFACE. When that pretence was finally dropped, because of the unwillingness of military commanders to put their faith in SIS reports, a new security classification of 'ULTRA Secret' was introduced in March 1941 to distinguish the Sigint summaries from other SIS product.

While historians generally agree that ULTRA probably shortened the war by two years, it is no exaggeration to say that ULTRA probably also saved SIS, enhanced its reputation and ensured its survival into the peace. Victor Cavendish-Bentinck, then Chairman of the Joint Intelligence

Committee (JIC) who did not think much of the SIS officers he dealt with on an almost daily basis, remarked that Menzies 'was not a very strong man and not a very intelligent one'.[4] Nevertheless, Menzies succeeded in forging a close relationship with the fledgling American intelligence organisation, the Office of Strategic Services (OSS), a complete neophyte in the tawdry world of espionage. C accepted American personnel to work alongside SIS officers, indoctrinated them into the ULTRA secret, ran an office in New York to coordinate activities in the Western Hemisphere, and responded quickly and effectively to the unexpected challenges of the enemy's development of secret weapons, jet fighters, ballistic missiles and in atomic research. However, SIS lost a turf war with Special Operations Executive (SOE) to conduct irregular warfare behind enemy lines, and played only a minor role in fostering resistance in the occupied territories. SIS's real achievement was in the field of counter-intelligence, having dominated the principal adversaries, the Abwehr and the Sicherheitsdienst across Europe without having to descend to the expedient of accepting defectors. The key was the skilful exploitation of the ULTRA source and ensuring its security, not just to defeat the Nazis, but to continue the work of wireless interception and cryptanalysis into the peace.

While it may have been sheer serendipity that enabled Menzies to capitalise on GC&CS, he was certainly shrewd in his management of his scarce resources. He took an active role in the Wireless Board, the inter-agency body created to supervise the radio deception perpetrated by MI5's double agents, a programme that was to encompass an impressive but unpublicised number of double agents run by SIS in Europe, including Iceland where COBWEB and BEETLE made important contributions, and the Middle East. SIS created representative organisations based in Cairo and Delhi to conduct local operations, thereby turning Broadway into the hub of a truly global intelligence undertaking. The need to manage this dramatic expansion brought its own pressures on Menzies, but he proved adept at recruiting, quite often in the bar of White's Club, men of his own social stratum to work for SIS. Among them were his personal assistants, Peter Koch de Gooreynd and David Boyle, who acted as foils for the diplomats, (Sir) Patrick Reilly and Robert Cecil, kindly provided by the Foreign Office to assist with liaison. Both the latter, who were successively placed in Broadway to keep an eye on C, were charmed by him, and the atmosphere. Menzies found former remittance men to go to Portugal and Tangier, country gentlemen to open the diplomatic bags of neutral countries and London playboys to risk their lives on dangerous missions in the Balkans. Among the talent brought into Broadway were Graham Greene, Malcolm Muggeridge, Rex Fletcher, Derek Verschoyle, Hugh Trevor-Roper, Robert Carew-Hunt and a dozen others who were later to write about their adventures. Although not a university man himself, Menzies placed no restrictions on assembling the hired help – they came from academia, Fleet Street and just about anywhere else where suitable skills might be found and harnessed. Christian names were preferred to military rank, and the informality of the prewar era continued during the conflict, even if Menzies himself rarely ventured from his red-carpeted office on the fourth floor, into the maze of frosted-glass cubicles, corridors and flimsy partitions in which his subordinates worked on the fifth and sixth floors above. The club-like atmosphere was enhanced during the war years by the roster, applied to everyone, for fire-watch and night duties, which were performed either on the roof or in the basement bar where some staff preferred to spend the night during the air-raids. Regardless of rank or experience, SIS officers and their pretty secretaries met for pre-dinner or pre-theatre drinks in the bar, in preference to The Feathers across Broadway, and during the Blitz sometimes remained there until dawn.

Deliberately remote from his subordinates, Menzies's management style was one of delegation, leaving Claude Dansey and Valentine Vivian to run their separate branches, Vivian supervising the counter-intelligence effort while Dansey concentrated on the collection programme. Neither personally was easy to deal with but nobody could doubt their experience and professionalism, even if they viewed each other with mutual contempt. Vivian barely survived the war, having suffered a breakdown from overwork, while Dansey was appointed Menzies's official deputy in October 1942. Tales of their hostility to one another, and their intransigence when liaising with others, are legion, but in the notoriously difficult disciplines of managing technical and human sources each of the pair had particular skills which enabled SIS to gain the upper hand against its Axis adversaries.

The ability of SIS officers to think on their feet was demonstrated in December 1939 when Rex Millar, formerly of the Manchester Regiment, arrived in Montevideo to open a new station, and played a brilliant role in the sinking of the German pocket battleship, the *Admiral Graf Spee*. Like her sister ship the *Deutschland*, the warship had been sent on patrol into the Atlantic from Wilhelmshaven ten days before the outbreak of war and, having sunk or captured nine ships (with no loss of life), had been hunted by no fewer than twenty-two ships of the Royal Navy. When the *Doric Star* signalled on 2 December 1939 that it was under attack by a large German surface raider, Commodore Henry Harwood's Hunting Group G moved to the area where he anticipated the German would go next. They met off the River Plate as the *Graf Spee* prepared to maraud the rich trade routes off the coast of Argentina. Damaged in the resulting battle, the first major naval engagement of the conflict, despite having inflicted heavy losses on HMS *Exeter*, *Ajax* and HMAS *Achilles*, the *Graf Spee* was allowed, under international convention, seventy-two hours of sanctuary, but when the time came to put to sea, and face what Captain Hans Langsdorff had been led to believe, by Millar's spurious radio broadcasts, to be superior forces of up to nine Allied ships, he set off explosives on his command, and then shot himself a few days later. The hulk burned for a week before finally sinking, and Millar then arranged to buy the salvage rights – in order to examine the German radar equipment.

The episode was a triumph of deception on the part of Millar who had transmitted bogus signals to give the impression that Harwood's force included a battleship and an aircraft carrier, and Langsdorff, having intercepted the dummy wireless traffic, was convinced any further fighting would be futile. Recognising that any future change in Uruguay's neutral status might risk an interned *Graf Spee* falling into Allied hands intact, and accepting that it was impossible to reach Buenos Aires without venturing out to beyond the shallows, Hitler gave Langsdorff permission to blow up his own ship.

Menzies's consummate skill in Whitehall was to retain control over GC&CS and to use the ULTRA product to exercise influence over the Prime Minister. Churchill, always a great *aficionado* of intelligence, was entranced by the decrypts shown to him daily by the Chief. None of the services' intelligence directors enjoyed the same access, and word spread of the relationship. However, the disadvantage of mounting an undertaking as gigantic as SIS was the relative loss of control over the staff employed. Of the five major spies known to have penetrated SIS, four were wartime recruits. Kim Philby joined the Iberian branch concentrating on Abwehr intercepts because of his detailed knowledge of Spain acquired while he had served there as a war correspondent for *The Times* during the Civil War. John Cairncross was also transferred into Section V from Bletchley Park because of his linguistic skills, while George Blake, originally George Behar from Holland, was recruited from the Royal Navy because of his experience of the Dutch underground. Guy Burgess, a BBC producer, was briefly employed by an SIS offshoot, Section D in December 1939 to September 1940. All would inflict lasting damage on SIS, but were only able to infiltrate the organisation because the vetting procedures, such as they were, proved unequal to the task of checking on the backgrounds of so many wartime candidates. Blake, of course, did not betray his adopted country until after he had been captured by North Korean troops in June 1950, whereas Philby, Burgess and Cairncross deliberately manoeuvred themselves into positions where they could be of the greatest use to the NKVD. Considering that virtually every other British secret organisation was the subject of penetration by the Soviets, with two known spies inside MI5, and one SOE officer actually convicted of espionage, it is perhaps surprising that SIS did not experience even more extensive hostile penetration.

The extent of the penetration of SIS was, of course, completely unknown at the end of the war, and nor was there any evidence in the immediate postwar period of any loss of SIS secrets. Certainly there were severe operational losses in the Baltic and Albania, but these could have been explained away, and may even have been, as one of the occupational hazards of running high-risk operations completely reliant on emigrés. At that stage SIS had little clue of the NKVD's undoubted prowess at mounting large and complex double-agent operations, a skill that dated back to The Trust, the supposedly anti-Bolshevik organisation that had lured Sidney Reilly back to Russia. Similar operations had been developed in Poland, where the anti-Communist WIN resistance was actually an instrument of the secret police, and in Germany where the Ukrainian nationalists were effectively directed from Moscow.

It may well be that Menzies was the wrong person to undertake the necessary transformation of MI6 into the peace, but his position was unassailable and he canvassed opinions widely with a Reorganisation Committee which, unfortunately, included Philby among its members, so that all its deliberations were read in Moscow almost as quickly as they were circulated within Broadway. When the three armed services had complained about the quality of SIS's product he had agreed to the immediate secondment of representatives from each of them to supervise SIS's requirement sections, a solution reminiscent of Smith-Cumming's remedy that had silenced his critics two decades earlier. Having entered the war with a compromised structure with few assets abroad, C had ensured that SIS ended the conflict with the highest of reputations, complete with continuing control over the renamed Government Communications Headquarters (GCHQ), relocated from Bletchley to a dreary compound in the London suburb of Eastcote, and the pick of SOE, now dissolved.

Naturally, upon the cessation of hostilities there was a need to reduce the number of overseas stations and trim the staff, but Menzies was fortunate in that the incoming Labour administration's Foreign Secretary, Ernest Bevin, was a staunch anti-Communist and a firm believer in the clandestine options offered by SIS, including support of less palatable British policies such as the sabotage of refugee ships seeking to break the blockade of Palestine. This was the era of the so-called 'robber barons', C's men who had enjoyed 'a good war' and were willing to undertake the high-risk operations judged necessary to deter Soviet aggression. Covert stay-behind networks were organised and resourced across much of central Europe, sophisticated eavesdropping equipment was deployed against Soviet targets abroad, and plans were laid to fight the Cold War using the experience and contacts gained in the recent conflict.

Unable to match the funds available to the Central Intelligence Agency (CIA), created in 1947, SIS exercised maximum leverage by taking advantage of a continuing exchange of Sigint, supplying convenient intercept stations in far-flung corners of the Empire otherwise unavailable to the United States, and extracting the greatest possible American support for British objectives. This was achieved through Winston Scott who had served with OSS in London during the war and had been a member of the joint War Room run by MI5 and SIS in which certain selected OSS personnel had worked. This shared wartime experience had been the basis of Scott's relationship with SIS, and in January 1948 he accompanied the CIA's first Director of Central Intelligence, Admiral Roscoe Hillenkoetter, to Broadway to introduce him, and his two senior aides, Colonel Donald Galloway and Jim Angleton, to Menzies. In September that year C hosted a two-day conference, attended by Scott, Hillenkoetter and David Bruce, at which the entire British intelligence hierarchy was present, including GCHQ's Director Sir Edward Travis, Air Marshal Sir John Slessor, General Sir Kenneth Strong and the JIC Chairman, William Hayter.

Among SIS's potential assets in dealing with the Americans was Bevin's staunch anti-Communism, manifested not only in his stalwart support for SIS, but his enthusiasm for Christopher Mayhew's proposal for an intellectual attack on the Soviet Union, using covert means organised by a new organisation, the blandly-titled Information Research Department (IRD). Created in February 1948 under (Sir) Ralph Murray, IRD began with a staff of sixteen and in September of that year had a budget of £100,000, funded through the Secret Vote, to analyse Soviet policy and develop conduits to counter the Kremlin's propaganda. Unfortunately SIS's first effort to collaborate with IRD, to promote its first postwar Soviet defector, Colonel Grigori Tokaev, descended into farce. Tokaev was a top aeronautical engineer, a graduate of the prestigious Zhukovsky institute and Moscow's leading expert on jet propulsion and rockets. He had been coopted by Soviet Military Intelligence (the GRU) to supervise the abduction of key German scientists who could assist Soviet reconstruction, and provide valuable technical information, but when he learned that Dr Kurt Tank, the Focke-Wolf chief designer, had been selected as a target, he opted to escape to the West. Naturally, he was welcomed by SIS, which was anxious to exploit his propaganda value, and arrangements were made by IRD to publicise his book, *Notes on Communism – Bolshevism*. Unfortunately it seems that the newcomer to the capitalist West had acquired a better grasp of how Fleet Street works than the Foreign Office, and Tokaev leaked details of his book before the newspaper serialisation could be published. Tokaev went on to demonstrate his grasp of his importance by writing *Betrayal of an Ideal*, *Comrade X* and *Stalin Means War*, although the Foreign Office's own history of the origins of IRD refers to the 'considerable confusion' he had caused.[5] Nevertheless, despite an uncertain start, IRD was to play a significant role in the Anglo-American policy of confronting and challenging Soviet hegemony, and not simply following the passive line, as officially espoused, of 'containment'.

The bombshell that destroyed this burgeoning industry, and threatened to undermine the CIA's confidence in SIS, was C's decision in November 1951 to sack Kim Philby, then the SIS station commander in Washington DC, who had been implicated in the mysterious defections of Guy Burgess and Donald Maclean the previous May. Philby had known both men, but had been a close friend of Burgess who, incidentally, had never come under any suspicion until he had vanished with his old Cambridge colleague, Maclean. Burgess had lodged with Philby when they had both served at the British Embassy in Washington DC. However, Philby had been one of the small circle of insiders who had known that Maclean had become the principal suspect in a molehunt that had been conducted over seven years, and based on the cryptographic source codenamed BRIDE, to trace a spy in the Foreign Office who had appeared in intercepted wartime NKVD traffic as HOMER. Just as the net had tightened on Maclean, whose messages to Moscow from his contact in the New York *rezidentura* in 1944 had contained clues to a leak in the embassy, someone had warned him of the imminent danger.

Philby was the best candidate for 'the third man', and a detailed check on his background revealed numerous reasons why he should be dismissed. His SIS colleagues, almost all of them entranced by his captivating, easy charm, had overlooked his alcoholism, ignored his four (of five) children born out of wedlock, another illegitimate child born to his mistress, his marriage to a Jewish Communist from Vienna and his suspected prewar membership of the CPGB. For all these shortcomings, Philby had been a popular wartime recruit to SIS, with a beguiling sense of humour and crippling stutter that often attracted women, and one who had prevented his background as a war correspondent and university graduate from compromising relations with his SIS contemporaries, most of whom had naval or military backgrounds. He had also been viewed well by C who had hosted a dinner for him in September 1949, just before his departure for the United States, attended by the CIA station chief Win Scott, and a dozen other colleagues, including five SIS secretaries.

Under interrogation Philby fared badly and none of those who witnessed his behaviour believed he was anything other than guilty. He had certainly tipped off Guy Burgess to warn Maclean, but had he done anything worse? At that stage the whereabouts of Burgess and Maclean were completely unknown, for they had simply disappeared after they had landed from a ship in Cherbourg, and it would not be until a press conference held in February 1956 that they announced their presence in Moscow. Philby was later to bluster that he had baffled his interrogators, and some commentators have claimed that he had been in line for C's job, but the truth was that he could never have been considered as Chief. His father, after all, had been imprisoned in July 1940 as a Nazi sympathiser in India, shipped to England, and kept in detention until March 1941, and his Anglo-Indian ancestry would, in those racially bigoted times, have excluded him as a candidate. Certainly he had performed well during his postwar service at the Istanbul station, and his appointment to Washington DC was an important one, but he was never bound for the very top. Nor, for that matter, was he destined for prison, for he knew better than most that without any evidence, and probably without a confession, he could not be convicted of any crime. Philby continued to stutter his innocence, but there was no prospect of, and certainly no appetite for, a prosecution.

The certainty that Philby had been a traitor was not shared by all his colleagues, although they were all informed that he had been dismissed the service. Apart from those who had attended his interrogation, very few were privy to all the details, and some wartime friends preferred to believe he had been the victim of an injustice. The idea that he had been a dedicated Communist since graduating from Cambridge, and been in almost continuous contact with Soviet intelligence officers since 1934, simply did not occur to many of those who had worked with him and his sister in Section V where he had distinguished himself as an expert on Spain and a very capable analyst of the enemy's wireless traffic. The fact that he spent hours almost every day writing messages to the NKVD, and responding to lengthy questionnaires in which he compromised every facet of SIS, including all its operations, personnel and techniques, would not become known until after some of his file was declassified and released in Moscow in 1998.

Philby's departure from SIS was absolutely essential if American trust was to be restored, and in August Maclachlan Silverwood-Cope was sent to Washington DC to fill in until January the following year when John Bruce-Lockhart arrived as Philby's permanent replacement, with the difficult task of rebuilding the confidence of the CIA and the FBI. As a former head of the German stations, who had worked closely for years with the CIA and its predecessor, the Central Intelligence Group, Bruce-Lockhart knew many of the Agency's senior management, and was himself beyond reproach. His goal, of restoring SIS's tarnished reputation, was certainly achievable as C's stock in the United States was high, for Menzies had personally pulled off two important coups that would influence SIS's future for years to come. First there was the Sigint-sharing agreement of May 1943, known as BRUSA, which had been formalised after the war in 1947 with the United Kingdom – United Sates of America Security Agreement (UKUSA), a pact that had cemented the Anglo-American exchange of intelligence. The treaty provided for the division of Sigint collection and processing responsibilities between the two countries, and confirmed SIS and GCHQ as equal partners with their American counterparts. Menzies was also responsible for the agreements made with the foundling CIA on operational spheres, requiring approval for either service to run operations within each other's territories, and an understanding that each other's nationals would not be recruited or run as agents without prior consent. This became an issue in April 1951 when Hugh Redmond, a former D-Day paratrooper and now a CIA officer under 'non-official cover', was arrested in Shanghai, masquerading as a representative of Henningsen & Company, a food import and export company based in Hong Kong. Redmond's cover was back-stopped in the British colony, and it was SIS's responsibility to ensure that it was maintained without revealing his true role. Nineteen years later Redmond died in a Chinese prison, still protesting his innocence.

C's second great achievement was his unrivalled position as chief of

Britain's intelligence establishment, SIS having absorbed the remnants of SOE in June 1946 and seen off a further proposal to amalgamate SIS with MI5. While the Philby affair was an intense embarrassment, especially as he had participated in SIS's deliberations about its postwar structure and strategy, few could have realised its long-term implications, and none guessed its ultimate impact. Certainly Menzies himself did not for, when the scandal became public in 1968, and the former Chief attracted considerable adverse publicity, his protégé Nicholas Elliott telephoned him to commiserate about the bad news in papers, Menzies assumed Elliott had called to share his disappointment at having one of his horses narrowly beaten the previous afternoon! Evidently he had been entirely unmoved by the furore over Philby's treachery.

Whether the Philby debacle had any bearing on Menzies's decision to retire in July 1952, at the age of sixty-two, two and a half years after the mandatory retirement for his staff, cannot be ascertained. His wife Pamela, who had been in poor health for years, had died in March the previous year, and his relationship with the Hon. Audrey Chaplin, the daughter of Sir Thomas Latham, the chairman of Courtaulds, resulted in their marriage in December 1952, a few days after the death of his older brother Keith. Two years later Menzies attended the marriage of his only child, his daughter Fiona, and then returned home to Bridges Court, to a life of retirement spent hunting and racing until his death at King Edward VII's Hospital for Officers, of pneumonia on 28 May 1968. Two days later his obituary in *The Times* broke with tradition and announced the death of the 'former Head of the Secret Intelligence Service'.

The dozen or so years Menzies was Chief were later judged by critics to have been a period of cronyism, with C leaving a legacy of independent operations winked at by compliant foreign secretaries, but others acknowledged his extraordinary contribution, establishing SIS at the centre of informing, developing and executing British policy, and certainly perpetuating the SIS mythology into the postwar era. 'His successors benefited for at least a decade from his methods and influence', observed George Young, a future Deputy Chief. 'But it is doubtful whether the British intelligence interest is best served by maintaining the somewhat battered convention that SIS does not exist.'

Chapter IV

John Sinclair 1952–1956

> 'Sinclair, though not overloaded with mental gifts (he never claimed them) was humane, energetic, and so obviously upright that it was impossible to withhold admiration.'
>
> Kim Philby[1]

STEWART Menzies's chosen successor as Chief was General John 'Sinbad' Sinclair, so called because he had made the unusual career change from the Royal Navy to the Army. Born in Fulham, the son of the Archdeacon of Cirencester, Sinclair was seven years younger than Menzies, and until 1916 his career had been as a midshipman in the Navy. He had been educated at Osborne and Dartmouth, and had spent the first two years of the war in submarines, afflicted with chronic sea-sickness. After he participated in the landings in the Dardanelles, helping to land the Lancashire Fusiliers on the West Beach, his health collapsed and he returned to England to recuperate and, after just six years, leave the Navy.

In 1918, having taught briefly at the Downs School in Winchester, Sinclair had attended the Royal Military Academy at Woolwich as a cadet, uniquely winning both the Sword of Honour and the Pollock Medal (for academic achievement), before being commissioned into the Royal Field Artillery in 1919. He was to serve in the North Russia campaign at Murmansk, and then be posted to India before returning to Aldershot. Between 1929 and 1931 he was adjutant of the Honourable Artillery Company, and attended the Staff College at Camberley in 1932–3.

At the outbreak of the Second World War Sinclair had been an instructor at the Senior Staff College at Minley, and then served as a planner for the British Expeditionary Force. In 1941 he was appointed Deputy Director of Military Operations at the War Office, and then went on the staff of South-East Command before being promoted Deputy Chief of the General Staff, Home Forces. In 1944, having worked on the plans for the invasion of Normandy, he was named DMI, and in June the following year was appointed Vice-Chief of SIS upon the retirement of Claude Dansey, who had received a knighthood in July 1943, and had moved to Bathampton with his new wife, a 34-year-old divorcée. Whereas Dansey had established a reputation as a combative, irascible secret operator, Sinclair was his antithesis, a thoughtful, cautious soldier with a record of careful planning and an analytical mind, whom the Chief of the Imperial General Staff, Sir Alan Brooke, was slightly reluctant to lose to SIS, as he recorded in his diary on 15 June 1945: 'Dined with C who wanted to extract old Sinclair out of me. I am ready to let him go provided his health stands up to it.'[2]

Sinclair had always been Menzies's candidate as his successor. He was a straightforward military man, 'a tall lean Scot with the angular, austere features of a Presbyterian minister', according to George Blake, 'with no pretensions to intellectual prowess',[3] a view he would probably have agreed with. Despite his severe exterior, he also had a highly developed sense of humour and kept a toy missile on his desk, a gift from a subordinate who had 'received a severe rocket from his Chief'. He had married Esme Sopwith in 1927, the daughter of the Archdeacon of Canterbury, who had borne him two sons and two daughters. He possessed an inquisitive, analytical mind with a talent for analysing and solving difficult problems, and was never impressed by the Soviets, convinced that the Communists' inability to produce consumer goods would eventually lead to their economy imploding. Sinclair, who was always known to his family and close friends as Alec, and did not use the name John until he received his knighthood in 1953, had inherited his father's commitment to Anglicanism and remained involved in church affairs throughout his life. Philby admired him and in his autobiography expressed his regret at having lied to Sinclair when, at his final interrogation, he had been confronted by the Vice Chief and the Assistant Chief, Air Commodore (Sir) James Easton, and again had protested that the allegations against him were false.

Referring to them as 'bludgeon and rapier',[4] Philby had plenty of respect for Easton, who ran the 'R' or Requirements side of headquarters until his retirement in 1958, while Sinclair handled the 'P' for Production, which meant the world-wide network of stations overseas. Then, as now, the 'R' side was the more demanding, involving close liaison through the ten R sections with SIS's exacting clients, whereas the management of the stations was relatively untroubled, each station being largely autonomous and reporting through the appropriate regional controller. However, during Sinclair's tenure as Chief, the brinkmanship of the Cold War combined with the task of healing the wounds of world war and facing the challenge of independence movements across the globe, placed a greater burden on intelligence collection. Instead of accommodating the risk-takers, Sinclair brought what Maurice Oldfield would later describe as 'high moral standards and integrity of purpose' to SIS's operations. These Sinclair directed, living in 21 Queen Anne's Gate during the week, and spending the weekends at his country home in Sussex, which he had bought after having lived at Fernden Cottage, Haslemere, during the immediate postwar years.

He had a reputation for being somewhat austere and frugal, preferring to lunch on soup and cheese, occasionally going to his club, the Army & Navy in St James's Square and known as 'the Rag', but after he became Chief he preferred to avoid encountering friends there because he was uncomfortable about his inability to tell them what he was doing, his informal cover job being 'liaison between the War Office and the Foreign Office'. In 1953 David Boyle, who had been PA/CSS to Menzies, proposed Sinclair for membership of Brook's, in St James's Street, and he was an occasional visitor there for many years thereafter. Sinclair took a daily early morning stroll across St James's Park to keep fit and later recalled to friends that the only person he saw regularly on these walks was a tramp who slept on one of the park benches and, eccentrically, wore white cricket boots during the cricket season. Unusually among the other Chiefs, Sinclair always listed his home address and telephone number in *Who's Who*.

Of the problems Sinclair inherited from his predecessor the most lasting would be Kim Philby, who had taken himself off to Ireland to ghost a book for an old friend, the publisher Bill Allen. Matters might have been expected to stay like that but in April 1954 MI5 announced that a defector in Australia called Vladimir Petrov had confirmed that the missing diplomats Burgess and Maclean had been long-term Soviet spies who had been recruited while still at university. Although Petrov had no personal knowledge of the case, he had been friendly with another NKVD officer, Filip Kislytsin, who had handled some of their traffic in London. Petrov's defection to the Australian Security Intelligence Organisation had been a very public affair because the Soviets had attempted to hustle his wife aboard a plane to Moscow, and she too had defected during a refuelling stop in Darwin. Petrov's disclosures threatened to re-open the Burgess and Maclean affair and, when the *Sunday People* published an account of Petrov's revelations on 18 September 1955, the pressure for a government statement proved irresistible, and the task was given to MI5. The hastily drawn-up document, written by MI5's director of counter-espionage Graham Mitchell, and approved by the Director-General Dick White, was to prove a time-bomb, although when the final draft was sent to Sinclair for approval he did not know how flawed it was. He was unaware of how much MI5 had to conceal of its own part in the affair, and knew nothing of White's own role in the fiasco that had allowed Maclean to escape. Sinclair had been preoccupied with Philby's alleged involvement, which was then entirely unknown outside MI5 and SIS, and it must have been something of a relief for the Chief to learn that Petrov had said nothing about how Moscow had learned at the end of May 1951 of Maclean's imminent interrogation, or precisely how his escape had been orchestrated. Philby was called in for a further interrogation, but it was inconclusive. SIS had no new evidence with which to confront Philby, and he simply stuck to his well-rehearsed dogged denials.

Philby was not mentioned in the eight-page White Paper released in October 1955, so a Labour MP, Marcus Lipton, named him in the Commons and demanded an explanation, but the legal position was clear-cut. Whatever the private reservations of those who knew how badly Philby had performed under cross-examination, there was not a shred of proof that was legally admissible. Accordingly, a fortnight later, as the White Paper was debated, Harold Macmillan announced that he had 'no reason to conclude that Mr Philby has at any time betrayed the interests of this country'. With this endorsement Philby called a press conference to demand an apology and retraction from Lipton, who duly backed down. This left Philby in a curious, apparently disadvantaged position, so SIS agreed to help him find a job, and the following year he went to the Lebanon, where his father lived, as a Middle East correspondent for the *Observer* and the *Economist*, with a small retainer from SIS so he could submit reports to the station commander in Beirut. Once again, the Philby affair had been buried, but it was soon to emerge again.

Sinclair's short tenure as Chief was marked by one great success and three important disasters. The success was the overthrow of the nationalist prime minister, Mohammed Mossadeq, in Tehran, an operation masterminded by the Middle East Controller, George Young, and neatly executed by Norman Darbyshire. Codenamed BOOT, the objective was to protect Britain's large investment in the recently nationalised Anglo-Iranian Oil Company (AIOC) and install an administration that would be more pliant, thereby incidentally deterring any other challenges to British interests vulnerable elsewhere. The Foreign Secretary, Herbert Morrison, had proposed a scheme codenamed BUCCANEER to remove Mossadeq and seize the oil refinery at Abadan, but the Cabinet had baulked even though the SIS station commander in Tehran, Monty Woodhouse, formerly of SOE, had been confident of its success. The Cabinet had bowed to American pressure, the State Department fearing that British action in the south would be used as a pretext for the Soviets to occupy the north of the country. The alternative plan, prepared by the Foreign Office, was a coup, but on 17 October 1952 Mossadeq unexpectedly closed the British Embassy and expelled the staff, including the entire SIS station which had been preparing the ground for the insurrection when the government would be seized as thousands of demonstrators, paid by the station, took to the streets. The SIS officers decamped to Cyprus, leaving their agents in Tehran in wireless contact with RAF Habbaniyah, the British airbase in neighbouring Iraq, and then held a series of meetings in Washington DC to elicit the CIA's support.

By the end of February 1953 the CIA's Kermit Roosevelt had been placed in charge of a joint plan to replace Mossadeq with General Fazlollah Zahedi, who by then would have received a bribe of $70,000 (paid in equal shares by SIS and the CIA) and would be named as the new prime minister by the Shah, but when the coup began in August, it quickly descended into chaos. The Shah fled the country and the mob took over Tehran, urged by Mossadeq who had evidently been tipped off to what he termed 'foreign intervention'. However, just as the insurrection looked like ending in humiliating disaster, with Washington ordering a withdrawal of the CIA, SIS arranged a failure in communications at the wireless relay in Cyprus, which prevented the officers in Tehran from receiving the order to abort. At the final moment royalists loyal to the CIA gained control of the radio station and broadcast an announcement that Mossadeq had been deposed and the Shah was on his way back to the capital. This completely false news turned the tide, and within a week the Shah was back on his throne, Dickie Franks had re-opened the SIS station and calm had been restored. More importantly, a new agreement was reached with the AIOC to protect British interests in the future.

SIS's success with BOOT encouraged Eden, Selwyn Lloyd and George Young, to give further consideration to British strategy in the Middle East, and begin exploring the possibilities of replacing unfriendly regimes in Saudi Arabia, Syria and Egypt, using Iraq and Turkey as co-conspirators. This new policy was disclosed by Young at a conference held at Broadway in March 1956 and attended by Jim Eichelberger, the CIA's station chief in Cairo, and Wilbur Eveland, adviser to the Director of Central Intelligence (DCI) on affairs in the region, who recalled that 'what we'd heard was sheer lunacy'.[5]

Sinclair's relations with the CIA previously had been excellent, to the point that in October 1954 he had flown to Washington to see the DCI, Allen Dulles, and negotiate a global division of responsibilities, known as the Four Square Agreement. The emphasis had been the Far East, where the British Empire then still included Singapore, Malaya, Burma and Hong Kong, territories in which SIS collected intelligence and maintained an uneasy relationship with MI5's Security Liaison Officers through Combined Intelligence Far East (CIFE). SIS's objective was to retain its lead role in the region, where the CIA was escalating its presence in what had been French Indo-China. To help in the talks, Sinclair was accompanied by his station commanders from Singapore (Maurice Oldfield) and Saigon (Fergus Dempster) and readily accepted a plan to cooperate in Thailand, Laos, Vietnam, Cambodia and Indonesia to undermine Communist influence. Escorted by Winston Scott, the veteran CIA station chief in London who had known his guests since his wartime OSS X-2 service, the British group also included MI5's Dick White and Guy Liddell from the Atomic Energy Authority.

SIS also actively collaborated with the CIA in Operation WESTWARD HO, a guerrilla campaign conducted since 1947 against the Soviet occupation of Latvia, Lithuania and Estonia. Similar operations had been undertaken in Albania, codenamed VALUABLE and in the Caucasus, codenamed CLIMBER, but neither had achieved its objectives. VALUABLE had been the infiltration of partisans trained in Malta to undermine Enver Hoxha's regime in Tirana, but the environment proved so hostile that few of the agents survived long once they reached their native Albania. Similarly, CLIMBER had been intended to establish networks in the southern republics of the Soviet Union, but the presence of Kim Philby at the Istanbul station between February 1947 and August 1949 ensured their failure. Whereas Philby had been briefed in detail and had played an active role in CLIMBER, he knew only the outlines of VALUABLE and was probably not directly responsible for its demise, and the same can be said for WESTWARD HO, which was dependent on refugees from the Baltic being recruited from displaced persons' camps in Germany, trained in Britain and sent home by boat and by parachute. The entire organisation had been penetrated at the outset, and skilfully manipulated by the NKVD, although SIS failed to spot the telltale signs of Soviet interference and control.

WESTWARD HO had been run by a coterie of prewar anti-Bolsheviks headed by Harry Carr, the Russian-speaking Controller Northern Area who had spent fourteen years running the Helsinki station until it was closed in 1941, and then headed the Stockholm station for the rest of the war. A veteran of the North Russia campaign, Carr was subordinate only to the Director of Production, Kenneth Cohen who, until his retirement in 1953, enthusiastically endorsed the extension of SOE's wartime tactics to what was perceived as the Kremlin's most vulnerable flank. Carr's principal assistant was Sandy McKibben, a Russian-born former timber merchant from Tallinn who had been forced to abandon his business and flee to Stockholm in 1940, and was enrolled as an SIS officer after years of contact with the local station. Together, McKibben and Carr recruited the emigré agents, put them through a training course at Fort Monckton, an old SOE facility near Gosport, accommodated them in a safe-house in Chelsea's Old Church Street, and ran the entire operation from Biffy Dunderdale's Special Liaison Centre in Ryder Street. Dozens of candidates underwent the process and were despatched to the Baltic, either by the *S208*, a fast former Kriegsmarine E-boat operated from Bornholm and Kiel, or by air, but in every case the omnipotent local security apparatus took control of the network and worked their radios back without detection. The first infiltrators put to sea in Sweden, and landed by dinghy on a beach, while others made the journey by air, either to clandestine airstrips, or to pre-arranged drop-zones.

Some of the agents were executed, others served long terms of imprisonment and a few survived by collaborating with their captors but the Soviets were so confident of their mastery of SIS's organisation that they even risked sending their own nominees to London for additional training and new instructions. The scale of the deception only became clear accidentally when a water sample, supposedly taken from the River Tabor in the Urals in an effort to see if an atomic power station had been constructed upstream at Chadrusk, was discovered to be highly radioactive. The litre of water was so contaminated that it would have posed a danger to anyone in the vicinity of the river, and obviously the sample was not authentic. As the partisans certainly did not have the means, nor a motive, to pull off such a deception, presumably aimed at persuading SIS of the existence of some massive nuclear facility, it was assumed, correctly, that the entire exercise had been masterminded by the Soviets.

With suspicions raised, a review was conducted of all the agents sent to the three Baltic states, and when the radio traffic of the overlapping SIS and CIA-sponsored groups were compared they all looked anodyne, similar, and remarkably uninformative. Very reluctantly both agencies came to accept they had been duped, over a long period, and this was confirmed when an SIS agent, Janis Klimkans, was interrogated in London in July 1956. Codenamed VIESTUS, Klimkans was a Latvian, an official in Riga's Education Department whose father, a farmer cultivating land on the edge of the vast Baltic forests, had been shot by partisans at the end of the war. Klimkans had been collected by the *S208* in the autumn of 1952 and had spent a year undergoing training at a dedicated centre in Holland Park, West London, run by a former SOE officer, Peter Follis. When he was returned, carrying stores, radios, maps and money for the guerrillas, he was accompanied by two wireless operators, a Lithuanian and Heino Karkman, an Estonian.

Upon their arrival in Latvia Klimkans had assisted Karkman to return home and had continued to maintain contact with SIS, but Karkman had realised that the entire operation had been supervised by the Soviets, and at the first opportunity had returned to London to report his suspicions. Dismayed by his experience, Karkman moved to Sweden and found a job as a radio officer on a Swedish merchantman. Meanwhile, Klimkans made his own way to Sweden where he spent two months in detention at the hands of the security police before he completed his journey to London in September 1956. Having been tipped off by Karkman, SIS gave Klimkans a hostile reception and after four weeks of interrogation he confessed to his dual role for the Soviets. He then underwent a further two months of debriefing, and was flown to Stockholm where he was delivered to the Soviet Embassy with the fruitless plea that his Soviet controllers handle their prisoners as leniently. Of course, they did not, and most perished in the *gulag*.

When WESTWARD HO was exposed as a sham Carr went to run the SIS station in Copenhagen, where he remained until 1958, when he was replaced by Charles de Salis, and retired in 1961. Horrified by the scale of the deception, McKibben shouldered much of the blame and died eleven years later, a broken man, haunted by the agents SIS, powerless to extract, had been forced to abandon in their homelands. The whole operation was closed down, and no word of what had happened leaked. As for the Chief, he was probably too preoccupied with other concerns to order a post-mortem into the Baltic fiasco which had lasted more than ten years.

Of the two catastrophes to befall Sinclair, within a few days of each other in April 1956, the second, chronologically, was the loss of an SIS diver, Commander Lionel Crabb, but the exposure of Operation GOLD was, in intelligence terms, the more significant. However, there was a third debacle which only much later would be recognised for what it probably was, the very first sign of Soviet penetration of SIS. The foundations had been laid at the end of 1953 when the station commander in Japan, Maclachlan Silverwood-Cope, reported an approach from a senior member of the NKVD *rezidentura* in Tokyo. Silverwood-Cope had been in the Japanese capital since November 1952, when he had taken over from John Quine, and was an experienced officer, having worked at the Stockholm station from the end of the war until his return to London in April 1950. Silverwood-Cope reported that Major Yuri A. Rastvorov had indicated his wish to defect, but once the resettlement package had been negotiated and agreed in London, he suddenly changed his mind. The defection of Rastvorov was anticipated to be a very considerable coup because SIS had not received a significant Soviet defector since Colonel Grigori Tokaev in 1948. Various reasons for SIS's inability to attract defectors were advanced, but when Rastvorov switched to the Americans, in the airport at the very last moment during his exfiltration, his explanation was noted, but disbelieved. Rastvorov claimed to his delighted CIA handlers to have heard on the NKVD grapevine that SIS had been severely penetrated, and that therefore SIS could not guarantee his safety. As evidence, he cited the example of Lieutenant Vladimir Skripkin, an NKVD subordinate who he said had approached SIS somewhere in the Far East in 1947, but had been arrested in Moscow soon afterwards.

In fact Rastvorov's allegation had been entirely authentic, as SIS was to learn much later. Skripkin had made a tentative approach to SIS, but after his return to Moscow he had fallen for a classic entrapment technique involving two English-speaking NKVD counter-intelligence officers who called at his home and pretended to be SIS officers wanting to work out the details of his defection. Skripkin had fallen for the ploy and incriminated himself sufficiently to be arrested and executed, leaving the suspicion that word of Skripkin's offer must have leaked in London, and convincing Rastvorov that Washington was the less risky alternative for him. It was not until George Blake confessed to having spied for the Soviets that SIS realised that Rastvorov's fears had been entirely justified and, although he had probably not betrayed Skripkin, he had certainly compromised GOLD, a vastly expensive technical project in Berlin.

GOLD had its origins in a technical operation conducted in a tunnel dug under a street in Vienna to tap the telephone and teleprinter cables of the Soviet *kommandatura*, accommodated in the old Imperial Hotel. Altogether 81 speech circuits had been tapped, producing a daily total of 162 reels of tape, each with a duration of two and a half hours. The operation, codenamed SILVER, had been so successful that plans had been prepared to exploit other similar opportunities. After extensive surveys in Berlin, another site had been located, and a joint project, codenamed STOPWATCH by the CIA, was drawn up involving the construction of a tunnel almost half a mile long which would extend under the border at Rudlow into the Soviet zone and intercept a cable duct beside the Schönfelder Chaussee which carried traffic between the Soviet military headquarters in Zossen-Wunsdorf and Karlshorst to Moscow. The ambitious scheme was full of superlatives, and would require the tunnel to be dug undetected, the cables to be tapped unnoticed, and the product to be recorded, processed, translated and distributed without a leak.

This massive and very expensive undertaking was technically very challenging, but offered to supply the West with a trip-wire that would virtually guarantee that the Soviets could not mount a surprise attack on the allies. If the cables really carried the traffic they were believed to, it would enable the CIA and SIS to calculate precisely the Warsaw Pact's order-of-battle and give advance notice of every significant deployment. Careful monitoring and analysis of the intercepts would remove the continuing anxiety about Soviet intentions in Germany and act as a window into the daily activities of the Red Army's Central Group of Forces permanently based in East Germany. On the basis that Berlin would always be a likely flashpoint in any future conflict, the tunnel was to work in parallel with the huge radar and wireless intercept facility built atop the Teufelsberg in the British sector. Quite simply, it was thought impossible for the Soviets even to contemplate any significant movement or change in preparedness without the appropriate signs being detected.

With so much at stake, elaborate precautions were taken to isolate the CIA's Berlin base in the Clayalee, and the local SIS station in the compound beside the Olympic stadium, from the planning of the tunnel, and the first initial planning meeting took place over three days in London in December 1953, attended by George Young as SIS's Director of Requirements, Tom Gimson who headed the Y Section that had masterminded the Vienna tap, the project manager, Stewart Mackenzie, a future Controller of Operations, and John Taylor, a technical expert from the Post Office Research Establishment at Dollis Hill. The team having agreed the general principles, another meeting was held early in 1954 at the Y Section's office at 2 Carlton Gardens – only on this occasion the minutes of the discussion had been taken by a young Dutch-born SIS officer, George Blake, who the previous April had been released from captivity in Korea, and had joined the section in September 1953. By now the blueprints for the construction had been drawn up and there had been an agreed division of labour, with the processing to be shared in Washington DC, where a windowless building off the Washington Mall was prepared for the teletype, and a compartmented unit in Regent's Park with room for a staff of 300 linguists for the Russian and German voice traffic, working in shifts. Blake passed a copy of the minutes to his Soviet contact on 18 January 1954.

By August 1954 the surface building, ostensibly a radar station, warehouse and barracks, had been completed by a German contractor, and work began from the basement level to sink a shaft thirty feet, and then dig a tunnel six feet in diameter. The US Corps of Engineers completed the horizontal work on 10 March, and within three weeks had broken into the junction box housing the cables. At this point British telephone engineers were brought in to install twenty-five tons of pre-amplification equipment, voltage stabilisers and banks of tape recorders, together with the relay cables linking a specially fabricated tap chamber to sophisticated hardware under the warehouse building capable of handling up to 500 separate channels. The connections were made and on 11 May 1955 the first of many thousands of reels of tape were processed, revealing the 'take' to be a veritable intelligence bonanza. The raw material ranged from indiscreet conversations between officers and complaints about the frequent mechanical breakdowns that plagued the T-52 tank, to data that helped GCHQ solve some of the codes found in Soviet tactical wireless traffic. There were even sufficient references to a KGB operation to tap an American communications cable in Potsdam for the CIA to take the appropriate counter-measures.

The haemorrhage of Soviet traffic continued for eleven months and eleven days, until one o'clock in the morning of Sunday, 22 April 1956 when a team of team of Russian and East German engineers, apparently repairing flood damage to cable conduits across the city, uncovered the tap chamber and sounded the alarm. As the astonished men ventured into the main tunnel their conversations were picked up on ceiling microphones installed as a security precaution, and it was clear from the stunned amazement expressed by those that gathered that they at least had not been briefed on what to expect. They manifested complete surprise, mixed with grudging admiration for the sophistication of the undertaking. Two days later the Soviets held a press conference to express their indignation at the intrusion. Ironically, this particular propaganda exercise proved counter-productive, for the journalists invited on an underground tour to inspect the proof of espionage were all deeply impressed by what they saw. For Sinclair the loss of GOLD must have been a huge disappointment, especially as the operation fulfilled one of the major tasks set by the JIC, but after eleven years in SIS he must have been sufficiently experienced to have taken the setback philosophically, even if he had set so much store by the operation that he had kept a piece of the original Soviet cable on his desk as a reminder. Naturally he would have had to report the episode immediately to the Foreign Secretary, Selwyn Lloyd, and it may be that because of this incident, and the potential for political 'blowback' and adverse publicity, he omitted to mention his other embarrassment concerning SIS's veteran frogman, apparently missing in Portsmouth Harbour.

The news that the tunnel had been discovered reached Broadway while the senior management was taking steps to suppress any leaks about the disappearance of Commander Lionel Crabb. Known as 'Buster' after the prewar Hollywood movie star, he was always quite a character, instantly recognisable by his monocle, his pork-pie hat, the whiskers on his cheeks and his habit of carrying a Spanish swordstick. He had worked as a mine-clearance expert in the waters around Gibraltar during the war, and he had pioneered and perfected many of the techniques now associated with the sport of scuba diving. Crabb's role had been to inspect the hulls of Allied merchantmen and remove any limpet charges placed by underwater saboteurs, usually Italians working from Spain, and his exploits had led to the award of an OBE and the George Medal. Crabb ended the war in Venice, clearing the port of explosives and obstacles, and later he was to be attached to the Admiralty Research Laboratory at Teddington, and participated in dives on the wrecks of HMS *Truculent*, the submarine lost in the Thames estuary in January 1950, and on HMS *Affray*, four years later in the English Channel.

Despite being a heavy smoker and drinker and a weak swimmer, Crabb paradoxically was universally recognised as an exceptional diver and, after his official retirement from the Royal Navy in April 1955, he had been employed by SIS to undertake some particularly sensitive and hazardous operations, usually to inspect the sonar equipment and propulsion systems of Soviet warships, such as the *Sverdlov*, which had visited Portsmouth in October 1955. It was on just such a mission, in April 1956, under the Soviet cruiser *Ordzhonikdze* while the warship was on a goodwill visit to Portsmouth accompanied by two destroyers, that he disappeared, and generated one of the most enduring mysteries of postwar espionage.

Almost all the events of 19 April are shrouded in secrecy because Crabb's mission ended not just in disaster for himself, but led to a major domestic political scandal, an internal enquiry into SIS's activities headed by the former Cabinet Secretary, Sir Edward Bridges, and an international crisis because the cruiser had been carrying the Soviet premier, Nikita Khrushchev and Marshal Bulganin, to Britain on an official visit. The Prime Minister, Sir Anthony Eden, thought he had banned any potentially embarrassing clandestine operations for the duration of the visit, but through a set of bizarre circumstances SIS's Foreign Office Adviser (FOA), (Sir) Michael Williams, inadvertently gave permission to the head of SIS's London station, Nicholas Elliott, to conduct an underwater inspection of the *Ordzhonikdze*'s hull, a mission requested by the Admiralty. The Admiralty often requested such assistance, and it was not unusual for a ban to be placed on potentially embarrassing operations at moments of diplomatic sensitivity. For example, in 1953, when the *Sverdlov* had participated in the Coronation Review at Spithead, a photographic reconnaissance mission to be undertaken by the RAF had been vetoed on the grounds that such a venture would be a breach of the monarch's hospitality.

Williams should never have sanctioned the operation in defiance of the temporary ban placed on clandestine operations by the Prime Minister but, moments before Elliott had telephoned him for his official consent, he had received a call to inform him that his father had just died. Distracted by this news, Williams had allowed Elliott to proceed, and thereby set in train an extraordinary sequence of events that were to become a *cause célèbre* and have a disastrous impact on Sinclair. Having been given the go-ahead, Elliott authorised the head of SIS's naval section, Ted Davies, a Welsh RNVR officer, to hire Crabb and prepare for the assignment.

Davies had escorted the forty-six year-old Crabb to Portsmouth the day before the target ships arrived, and they both checked into the Sallyport Hotel, registering under their own names. During the course of the next day, however, Crabb suffered a minor heart attack, but insisted on being allowed to continue with his mission, and Davies appears to have acquiesced. Early on the morning of 19 April they had taken Crabb's equipment to the Gosport ferry slip and the experienced diver had donned his gear and swum towards the cruiser and one of its escorts, the destroyer *Smotriashchin*. A few minutes later he had returned to adjust the weights on his belt, and then disappeared from view, not to be seen again until a headless, handless body dressed in the frogman's distinctive, Italian-made two-part rubber dry-suit was recovered from the entrance to Chichester Harbour twelve miles away, in June the following year. The Soviets had registered a formal diplomatic protest when a sentry spotted a diver on the surface between the two Soviet warships, and this had made the matter public, forcing the Admiralty to acknowledge that Crabb had gone missing, allegedly three miles away in Stokes Bay while testing classified equipment, and Sir Anthony Eden to admit to the House of Commons on 9 May that 'What was done was done without the authority or the knowledge of Her Majesty's Ministers. Appropriate disciplinary steps are being taken.' He declined to make any further statement, insisting it was not in the national interest to do so, thus fuelling a frenzy of speculation. Behind the scenes, Eden was furious, not least because the relatively new Foreign Secretary, Selwyn Lloyd, had not been informed of what had happened until 3 May when the First Lord of the Admiralty, Viscount Cilcennin (the former James Thomas MP), had told the Foreign Office, and the Cabinet Office had not learned of the incident until the following morning when Cilcennin had walked over to speak to the Cabinet Secretary, Sir Norman Brook.

Shocked by Cilcennin's news, Eden asked Bridges 'to prepare a short report' which took just four days for him to draw up, and was presented to a Cabinet sub-committee consisting of the Prime Minister, Cilcennin, the Defence Secretary Walter Monckton and Selwyn Lloyd. After reading Bridges's conclusions, and his recommendation for disciplinary action, the committee asked him 'to look further into the question of Ministerial responsibility, and inter-departmental co-ordination of certain types of covert operation'. None of this, however, was Sinclair's fault but as he was anyway ready to retire, having only committed himself to SIS for ten years when he was originally persuaded to join, he announced his departure, leading many to conclude erroneously that Eden had sacked him, which was not true.

The other principal victims of the Bridges Inquiry were Michael Williams, Sinclair's Foreign Office Adviser who was transferred to the post of minister at the Embassy in Bonn, and Ted Davies who was sacked, leaving him to complain that he had been made a scapegoat. The Chief withdrew to East Ashling Grange, a large nine-bedroomed Georgian house north of Chichester, and became a non-executive director of the Universal Asbestos Company, and Chinnor Industries, firms run by former wartime friends. His contribution to the day-to-day management of the companies was minimal, but his colleagues took the view that his insightful comments during the board meetings more than justified his director's fee.

In his retirement Sinclair continued his lifelong interest in cricket and took an active role in the church as a member of the board of Bishop Otter College, a seminary in Chichester for those entering the Anglican priesthood. He was also chairman of the Diocesan Dilapidation Board, which dealt with housing for country parsons, and kept up his links with the Army as Colonel Commandant of the Royal Artillery, and for a few years ran the RA's charitable fund. In 1976, and a few weeks short of his eightieth birthday and his golden wedding anniversary, he went into St Richard's Hospital in Chichester for a check-up, and died there, to be buried at nearby Funtington Church. His funeral proved to be a large occasion as he had requested not to have a memorial service, and it was attended by Sir Maurice Oldfield representing the Service, as well as Stewart Menzies and Dick White. As was the custom at the time, Sinclair's obituaries omitted any reference to his service in SIS, where he was fondly remembered for having introduced some of the reforms of pay, conditions and pensions for staff that Menzies had neglected. Noting that Sinclair's obituaries had ended with his role as DMI, Oldfield rectified the omission by writing to *The Times* anonymously, and somewhat mysteriously mentioning his 'Government service for a further ten years', to set the record straight, recording Sinclair's:

> . . . determination to build an organisation which by its esprit-de-corps and fair conditions would attract the right type of young recruits. He laid the foundations which have stood the test of time and for which those who served with him are grateful. He expected of others the same high same standards he set himself; weakness was not for him nor for those who served with him.

Alluding to Sinclair's continued silence over the circumstances of his departure, and his refusal to record what really had occurred, Oldfield recalled:

> . . . his inability for security reasons to answer some of the criticisms made long after the event of happenings, during his period of office. Those who know the truth of such matters sympathised with him and are above all grateful for the memory of a dedicated upright patriot.

For those who knew C's true role, this guarded explanation was a fitting endorsement of Sinclair's clandestine career, but for anyone else the short article must have been quite a puzzle.

Chapter V

Dick White
1956–1968

> 'He was a nice and modest character, who would have been the first to admit that he lacked outstanding qualities. His most obvious fault was a tendency to agree with the last person he spoke to.'
>
> Kim Philby in *My Silent War*[1]

UNDER normal circumstances Sinclair could have expected to have retired at the end of May 1963, but he had indicated his desire, to his wife and four children, to take early retirement. Clearly he had not wished to leave Broadway under a cloud, and he would have liked to have ensured the succession for Jack Easton, but Anthony Eden was in no mood to accommodate him. Easton had been in Malaya during the Crabb affair, and therefore was completely untainted, and had also been groomed for the post, having been assured that he would be Sinclair's successor. He had graduated from Cranwell and been commissioned in 1928 and flown biplane bombers and amphibious aircraft before joining the Air Ministry's Directorate of Intelligence in October 1939. During the war he had been appointed Deputy Director of Air Intelligence, then Director, and had served on Churchill's CROSSBOW Committee to investigate the German V-1 and V-2 secret weapons. His arrival at Broadway had been prompted by the resignations of 'Lousy' Payne, the Deputy Director, Air, and Fred Winterbotham, the head of the Air Section, in 1945.

Having achieved so much, Easton was a natural, but the issue of the selection of the new Chief was not a simple one, for although technically the post was in the gift of the monarch, acting on the advice of her ministers, it had been the long-defunct Secret Service Committee which had selected Quex Sinclair, and it had been the Cabinet which confirmed the appointment of Stewart Menzies. He, of course, had stayed on beyond his proper retirement age and ensured a smooth hand-over to Sir John Sinclair who had been the obvious candidate. There had been no controversy, no debate and no alternative candidates, whereas with the sudden departure of Sir John, and in the absence of a planned succession, the choice was in the hands of Eden and Lloyd, doubtless listening to the Chairman of the JIC, Patrick Dean, and the Foreign Office PUS, Sir Ivone Kirkpatrick, and the Cabinet Secretary, Sir Norman Brook. Sinclair had lobbied for Easton, then aged forty-eight, who had been in SIS since 1945, and before that, as a Group Captain, had also spent two years supervising the RAF's Special Duties flights for SIS, but Brook had black-balled him; instead he received a knighthood.

Dick White never anticipated being asked to head SIS, and when Sir John Sinclair took early retirement before his forty-ninth birthday, at the end of May 1956, White's appointment as the first civilian Chief was highly controversial. Educated at Bishop's Stortford College, Christ Church, Oxford, and the Universities of Michigan and California, White had been an outstanding runner, and had been captain of rugby, cricket and athletics in his last year at school. Initially set for a career as a schoolmaster at the Whitgift School in Croydon, in 1936 White had been persuaded by Malcolm Cumming to be one of the first, if not *the* first, university graduate to join MI5. White had been accompanying a party of his pupils to Australia, and by coincidence Cumming was a passenger on the same ship, travelling to attend some Army exercises in the Far East. The two men had become friends, and upon his return to London Cumming had recommended White to his D-G, Sir Vernon Kell. At that time the Security Service was a tiny organisation, run from a suite of offices in Thames House, on the Embankment, still headed by Kell and his faithful deputy, Sir Eric Holt-Wilson, who had been with him since December 1912. When White transferred to Broadway, he was the fifth Chief, and the first with a degree.

White had achieved success quickly through his work as case officer for Wolfgang zu Putlitz, an anti-Nazi homosexual German diplomat. Putlitz had been recruited by 'Klop' Ustinov, himself a former press attaché at the German Embassy in London and was such an important source of information and documents from Ambassador Ribbentrop's office that much of it was taken personally by White to Sir Robert Vansittart, the Permanent Under-Secretary at the Foreign Office, and then the Prime Minister's Foreign Policy Adviser. The Putlitz case came to a conclusion when he was transferred to the German Embassy in The Hague and eventually had to be withdrawn and flown back to Britain. By the time Putlitz became friendly with MI5's Anthony Blunt, and eventually moved to East Germany after the war, declaring his life-long adherence to Marxism, it was too late to have any adverse impact on White's career. Although Putlitz was to fade from sight, spending much of the war in the United States, and then broadcasting for the Political Warfare Executive's 'black' radio stations from Woburn, Klop the consummate intelligence operator, was to remain a lifelong friend.

With his shrewd handling of Putlitz, White gained a reputation at the Security Service for quiet, thoughtful efficiency. He did not have rows, rarely appeared to disagree with anyone, and always advocated long-term advantages over short-term expediency. He seemed to get on with everyone he encountered, and in truth there was little competition inside MI5 to match his undoubted intellectual prowess. Counter-espionage was handled by a bluff military man, Brigadier Jasper Harker, although the real work was organised by the shy, retiring Guy Liddell, who came to rely heavily on White. On one occasion in 1940 a crisis arose when an anonymous staff officer attached to the British Expeditionary Force published *A Staff Officer's Diary* which included an indiscreet reference to the use of wireless intercepts. A controversy was averted when White simply called his older brother Alan, then working for Methuen, who had published the offending book, identified the author as a Major Gribble, and arranged for the problem passages to be removed from all future copies.

White had become Liddell's protégé, and few in Britain knew more about espionage than this sensitive cello player who, like his two brothers, had won the Military Cross during the Great War. Liddell had begun his counter-intelligence career in 1919 when he had joined Scotland Yard, and he had played a key role in every significant investigation conducted between the wars. Apart from a troubled family life, Liddell was handicapped by his choice of friends, exacerbated by his personal assistant, Anthony Blunt. Liddell would have been mortified to learn that Blunt had reported twice weekly to his NKVD contact throughout the war, but he would not live long enough to do so. White also got on well with Blunt, and inevitably came to know Guy Burgess and Kim Philby, who represented a new generation of clever young men drafted for wartime service into the intelligence world. While he did not deliberately outmanoeuvre his colleagues or take the credit for their achievements, White's posting to Montgomery's 21st Army Group in 1944 was based on his participation in the double-cross system, which had harnessed every Nazi spy sent to Britain, apart from those who were executed, and his shrewd handling of the signals intelligence sources codenamed ISOS and ISK which had given Bletchley Park a comprehensive insight into the enemy's intelligence activities. ISOS had been the Abwehr's hand ciphers, which had presented a relatively easy target for the cryptanalysts, and the ISK material had been derived from the machine-generated traffic. Since some of the controlled double agent messages had been relayed routinely over Enigma circuits to Berlin, MI5 had been able to offer the codebreakers a huge advantage on a daily basis, each time the German wireless operators reset their machines. The security of the Enigma machine's complex permutations was very dependent on the integrity of the original message, so if a potential adversary also had access to the cleartext, unravelling the enciphered version was much easier. The principle was simple, and therefore very sensitive and open to compromise, but White had exploited the flaw with skill and ingenuity. He was widely acknowledged to be clever, and those indoctrinated into ISOS and ISK knew him to be *very* clever.

At the end of the war, when the incoming Labour administration had appointed a former chief constable, Sir Percy Sillitoe, as Director-General, MI5 had been run by a triumvirate of Liddell, as his deputy, White, and a plodding bureaucrat, (Sir) Roger Hollis, a member of the prewar intake who had made himself an expert on Communism. Sillitoe had been completely out of his depth, and had even been persuaded to lie to the Prime Minister when MI5's competence was challenged in the aftermath of the Fuchs affair.

Since the end of the war the Americans and GCHQ had been working hard on a signals intelligence source codenamed BRIDE which offered occasional, fragmented glimpses into the NKVD's enciphered cable traffic. The first breaks had been achieved at the end of 1943 and the resulting decrypts had revealed the existence of a spy codenamed HOMER in the British Embassy in Washington DC in 1944 and 1945, and had given clues to the movements of another spy, codenamed REST and CHARLES, apparently a British scientist working at Los Alamos on the Anglo-American atomic bomb project. After four years of investigation, the net had finally narrowed on Klaus Fuchs, then a leading physicist at Harwell, and through a series of skilfully-conducted interviews the German-born scientist was persuaded to confess without ever suspecting that the original tip to his treachery had been a decoded Soviet message. MI5's triumph, in identifying Fuchs and persuading him to confess and plead guilty to breaches of the Official Secrets Act, for which he was sentenced to fourteen years' imprisonment, turned to ashes when MI5 was criticised for not having caught him earlier. When MI5's original Fuchs file was examined it was found to contain an entry dated 1945 which suggested he was probably a spy and merited an immediate investigation. This embarrassment was reported to Sillitoe who reluctantly agreed, under pressure from Liddell, White and Hollis, to conceal the true facts 'for the good of the Service' from Prime Minister Attlee, who then assured the Commons, based on a briefing from the D-G, that there had been no slip-up, and that MI5 had followed up every lead diligently. Appalled at his own behaviour, Sillitoe had gathered MI5's senior management together in the canteen on the top of Leconfield House, MI5's postwar headquarters, and explained what had happened, vowing never to mislead a prime minister ever again.

Stung by this very public rebuke, White had contemplated resigning, but had been persuaded that he would find it hard to find another job. Smarting with indignation and guilt, White had succeeded Guy Liddell as deputy D-G when the latter moved to head the Atomic Energy Authority's security division, and then had been appointed D-G when Sillitoe went into retirement in 1953.

For White, now married to the novelist Kate Bellamy, to whom he had been introduced by his brother who had published two of her books,

Jacaranda and *The Cage*, the promotion had been much needed. Always short of money, he had acquired two stepdaughters when he had married Kate, a divorcée, and they were to have two sons, one of whom would be mildly handicapped. It may be that the second of Kate's books, which was published in 1942, was somewhat autobiographical. It concerns a group of young Communists in London during the first year of the war, and a left-wing writer who is trapped in a marriage to a possessive husband who subjects her to domestic violence and kills her dog. Although she leaves him, and he joins the RAF, the melancholy tale ends with her travelling to his aerodrome to be reunited with him. While these events may have been entirely fictional, it is likely that the molehunters who subsequently investigated White may have taken an interest in his wife's political links during the war.

No sooner had the Fuchs controversy died down than White had been plunged into another debacle. The same source that had incriminated the physicist revealed in May 1951 that the spy codenamed HOMER was almost certainly the head of the Foreign Office's American Department, Donald Maclean. Once the Foreign Secretary had given his consent for Maclean to be interviewed, MI5 held a conference of case officers on Friday afternoon to discuss how the interrogation, set for Monday, 31 May, should be handled. Just as the meeting was breaking up, shortly before midnight, the night duty officer, Russell Lee, reported that an alert immigration officer at Southampton had spotted Maclean embarking on the *Falaise*, due to sail at any moment for Cherbourg. Instant action was required, and those assembled agreed that White should fly to France and intercept Maclean in the hope of persuading him to return home, but when White reached the airport to catch the first flight he discovered his passport had expired. Despite frantic efforts to revalidate it, White failed to make his flight and Maclean was able to escape unhindered. Embarrassed by this monumental blunder, White and his colleagues pretended that nothing had happened, and when Mrs Maclean telephoned on Monday morning to report the disappearance of her husband, they all acted as though this was the first MI5 knew of his departure two days earlier. This apparently inconsequential cover-up, to save a colleague's career, assumed much greater proportions four years later when one of the conspirators, Graham Mitchell, was set the task of drafting the government's White Paper on the affair. By then, of course, White had become D-G of MI5 and colluded in the deception when Mitchell prepared a version of events which both men knew to be completely untrue.

This Damocles' sword hanging over him must have been one of the reasons for White's initial surprise when his name was given to Anthony Eden as a suitable candidate for Sinclair's replacement, and his reluctance to take the post. While he was at the helm of the Security Service, surrounded by loyal colleagues like Hollis who knew the truth, White could have expected some protection from exposure, but what might happen if he was not around to manage events? Told by the PUS at the Home Office, Sir Frank Newsome, that his duty lay with whatever the Prime Minister requested, White accepted the appointment and took over Sinclair's office in the middle of July 1956, with Jack Easton staying on as his Vice-Chief.

Recognising the hostility to his appointment, White trod warily upon his arrival at Broadway, even when he discovered that Kim Philby was still on the books as an agent-runner, reporting to the Beirut station. In deference to Philby's many wartime friends, who were unaware of the volume of evidence against him, White allowed Philby's retainer and contact to be continued, although he personally never doubted his guilt. The only issue was when, or if, Philby had ever stopped spying for the Soviets. As it turned out, he had remained faithful to the Soviet cause for twenty-nine years, but White believed that to sack him for a second time would cause more problems than it would solve. The acerbic Peter Wright commented on White's early period as Chief that White:

> ... tried to introduce some line management. He was never entirely successful.
>
> Dick was not a particularly gifted administrator. His achievement in MI5 stemmed from intimate knowledge of the office and its personnel, and a deep knowledge of counter-espionage, rather than a flair for running organisations. Deprived of these, his first years in MI6 were, almost inevitably, marked by expediency rather than clear strategy.[2]

No sooner had White entered Broadway than the nationalistic threats of Colonel Abdel Nasser in Egypt turned from Arab rhetoric into action which had a direct impact on British interests. While Prime Minister Eden had been willing to withdraw British troops from the Canal Zone, he recognised the strategic importance of the waterway, the supply line for the Gulf's oil to Europe, and was highly suspicious of growing Soviet influence and an offer from Moscow to finance the ambitious Aswan Dam project. Nasser demanded control of the Anglo-French-owned and British-administered Suez Canal, and proceeded to seize it, sending Eden, already exhausted and in declining health, into paroxysms of rage, exacerbated by an SIS source, codenamed LUCKY BREAK, who reported that Nasser was falling under increasing Soviet influence and joining the Communist Bloc. Eden's first demand, which was to cause Selwyn Lloyd's Minister of State, Sir Anthony Nutting to resign, was for SIS to assassinate the troublesome Egyptian leader, and the second, which was to split the country and the Tory Party, was to collude with Israel and France to invade and regain control of the canal.

SIS's constitutional role in such circumstances is to provide the Cabinet with whatever clandestine support may be required, but White became acutely aware that SIS had few resources in Egypt. Although Cairo had been the regional headquarters for SIS's wartime cover organisation, the Inter-Services Liaison Department (ISLD), its operations had been conducted across the Middle East and not in Egypt, which had been the responsibility of MI5's regional branch, Security Intelligence Middle East (SIME). After ISLD and SIME had been dismantled, MI5 had retained a Defence Security Officer at the British base at Ismailia, but the belated decision to open an SIS station in Cairo meant that there had been no time to develop any local networks. Worse, when diplomatic relations had been severed, the SIS station, headed by Freddie Stockwell, had been withdrawn to Cyprus, leaving only SIS's commercial cover organisation, the Arab News Agency (ANA), but this had been closed down when its manager, James Swinburn, had been arrested by the ubiquitous local security apparatus, the Mukhabarat. While the ANA had fulfilled a useful function as a conduit for British propaganda, it was too transparent as a cover for intelligence officers posing as journalists, and certainly never fooled the

Egyptians who scooped up the entire structure, thereby leaving SIS dependent on intermittent reporting from neighbouring stations, and incidentally isolating LUCKY BREAK, supposedly a source in Nasser's immediate entourage with access to documents.

SIS's inability to report from Egypt may have been the reason for White's apparent acquiescence in STRAGGLE, the plan which culminated in MUSKETEER, the ill-fated amphibious landings at Alexandria in November. The Chief had been indoctrinated into Eden's plan by the Cabinet Secretary, Sir Norman Brook, and was informed of the scheme to have Britain and France respond to a surprise Israeli attack on Egypt by demanding a withdrawal and a ceasefire. The Anglo-French intervention would thus be given the cloak of respectability and legality, using the ceasefire, which Nasser would be bound to reject, as a convenient pretext. White soon learned that Eden had taken Selwyn Lloyd into his confidence, and had used the Chairman of the JIC, Sir Patrick Dean, as an intermediary to negotiate with the French and Israelis in Paris. Finally the Foreign Office PUS, Sir Ivone Kirkpatrick, had also colluded to keep those in the know to a bare minimum. SIS's intended role was to provide a secure communications channel between the SIS Israel desk, manned by Nigel Clive and Cyril Rolo, and Tel Aviv, where Nicholas Elliott was running the station temporarily, and to Cyprus where Godfrey Paulson was supervising the military component at the Nicosia station which operated under cover supplied by the British Middle East Office.

The key figure in SIS's contribution to STRAGGLE was Nigel Clive who had joined SIS in 1941 from the Middlesex Yeomanry, after his regiment had been chased out of Greece. Educated at Oxford, Clive been posted initially to Baghdad and then to Greece, where he remained until 1948 when he was sent to open a station in Jerusalem under all too transparent consular cover, a mission that was doomed and resulted in the almost immediate withdrawal of both himself and his deputy under direct threat from the Haganah. This was taken very seriously, not least because SIS's only postwar casualty had been Desmond Doran, the prewar station commander in Bucharest, who had been killed in September 1946 in Tel Aviv by a hand grenade lobbed onto the balcony where he was sitting with his Romanian wife and two other SIS officers, who were all badly injured.

In 1950 Clive was posted to Iraq, and on his return three years later was placed in charge of the Special Political Action section assigned the task of removing Nasser before, as LUCKY BREAK had predicted, Egypt fell under permanent Soviet influence.

White never flinched when he heard of Eden's request for Nasser's assassination, and Middle East Controller George Young had been quite willing to accommodate the Prime Minister, but in the event the opportunity never arose. SIS's choice for a replacement for Nasser, the deputy director of Egypt's air force intelligence, General Khalil, turned out to have acted as a double agent, pocketing SIS's bribe and reporting the attempt to the Mukhabarat. The invasion collapsed as soon as President Eisenhower's administration threatened to withdraw its support for sterling, and took seriously a Soviet threat to retaliate. Far from repeating the success of BOOT in Iran, STRAGGLE proved to be a costly failure, forcing the Prime Minister to stand down on health grounds.

As for SIS's relations with the CIA, the London station, then run by Chester Cooper, Dan Debardeleben and Cleveland Cram, continued to give unofficial assistance to SIS, including U-2 aerial reconnaissance imagery of Egyptian airfields, long after the State Department had issued its ultimatum. This may have been an act of reciprocity for helping the CIA in Tehran during BOOT, when a delay in passing on instructions from Washington had enabled the operation to succeed. Alternatively, the covert cooperation may simply have been a manifestation of personal loyalties of the kind that had made the symbiotic SIS–CIA relationship so enduring and so unique.

Responsible for liaison in Washington DC since the beginning of the year was Maclachlan Silverwood-Cope, on his second posting to America, having served in Stockholm for almost five years at the end of the war, followed by a posting to Tokyo in November 1952. His opposite number in London since the previous September, Chet Cooper, had been a former assistant to the DCI, Allen Dulles, and like his predecessor as Chief of Station in London, Win Scott, attended the weekly JIC meetings in Storey's Gate as an *ex officio* member. However, he and his deputy, Dan Debardeleben, had been deliberately kept isolated from the planning for the invasion, to the extent that on 24 October, the very night the JIC

Chairman, Patrick Dean, was in Sèvres concluding the secret deal with the French and the Israelis, his wife Patricia had been obliged to host a dinner alone at her home for Cooper and another CIA guest.

A week later RAF Canberras commenced the bombing of Egyptian airfields and the American ambassador, Winthrop Aldrich, was withdrawn from London. 'Diplomatic relations between Washington and London were virtually broken' recalled Cooper, who was, however, instructed that 'because the intelligence link to the British was too important to jeopardise [he was] to continue to maintain contact with British intelligence officials.'[3] This included dining with George Young, White's deputy, who was then heading a Special Political Action section intent on promoting STRAGGLE without alerting the committed Arabists of the CIA's Near East Division, led by Norman Paul and his deputy, Kermit Roosevelt, who had family connections in Damascus. Roosevelt's wife Lucky was a Druze Christian from the Lebanon and the Syrian Army's Chief of Staff, Shawqat Shukayr, was her mother's first cousin. Accordingly, while Cooper was regarded by SIS as a useful channel to the Eisenhower administration, few believed that the CIA could be relied upon to take an active role in stemming the tide of Nasser's brand of Arab nationalism, and so it turned out.

The full extent of the collusion between the British, Israeli and French governments, and the existence of the agreement signed by Patrick Dean at Sèvres, would remain secret for many years, with no public appetite to delve into the matter once Selwyn Lloyd had left the Foreign Office and been elected Speaker of the House of Commons. As for White, he would only entertain one further request for an assassination, when the elimination of General George Grivas, the elusive leader of the EOKA terrorists in Cyprus, looked like a potential solution to the crisis. In the event, although an SIS volunteer was dispatched to the island, a settlement was reached before Grivas could be found.

The Suez experience, so soon after the new Chief's arrival, confirmed to him that the Middle East Controller, George Young, had performed flawlessly throughout the crisis, and White replaced Easton with him as his deputy in March 1958. Easton, who had been given every reason to think he would succeed Sinclair as Chief, was appointed the British Consul-

General in Detroit, a post he was to fill for the next ten years without rancour.

A former *Glasgow Herald* journalist, Young was a big, ruddy-faced Scot who had served in Vienna and had masterminded the Tehran coup for Sinclair. He was also a man developing extreme right-wing political views, encouraged by his Dutch wife Geryke, who was from Batavia and had been interned in the East Indies during the war, enduring appalling hardships. Later, as Young grew increasingly anti-Semitic, White acknowledged that the appointment had been a dreadful mistake, and he encouraged him to take a post in the City with the merchant bankers Kleinwort Benson in 1961 so as to replace him with John Bruce-Lockhart. No sooner had Young left Broadway than his political views became more pronounced, and vocal. In 1962 he published *Masters of Indecision: An Inquiry into the Political Process*, and four books later, in 1972, he documented Soviet penetration of the British establishment with *Who Is My Liege? Loyalty and Betrayal in Our Time*. Although White was saved the embarrassment of any autobiographical disclosures from Young, who stood for Parliament in 1974, Young never concealed his contempt for politicians or sycophantic senior civil servants, and also complained that, although SIS's failures and scandals received full publicity, 'their successes go unrecognised'.

> When British governments are pursuing 'know nothing' policies, it is not easy to be their eyes and ears. Clear policy objectives aid purposeful and discriminating intelligence gathering. Muddled thinking means muddled intelligence work. When an army is unsure whether it is advancing, static or retreating, the generals can only guess what is on the other side of the hill. Nor are civil servants who are the first formulators of policy papers, necessarily looking for impartial evidence. They may be neutral in a political sense, but biased in matters when their own advancement clashes with the public interest.[4]

Young's final political contribution, *Subversion and the British Riposte*, published in 1984, would have caused White considerable discomfort, but by then he had long departed Whitehall. As well as advocating that Cabinet ministers should undergo positive vetting to weed out Communist recruits,

Young drew attention to the Israeli success in identifying Stig Bergling as a Soviet spy in 1977. Fortunately he restrained himself from speculating about how the KGB agent had been caught, but his remarks, though buried in the polemic, should have made the current Chief, Christopher Curwen, wince for the security of his star source, Oleg Gordievsky.

Under normal circumstances one might have expected White to have found himself impaled on the Suez debacle, but his protection was Geoffrey McDermott, the new Foreign Office Adviser appointed by Patrick Dean in October 1956. McDermott was a career diplomat who had begun World War II in Sofia and spent the rest of it in Cairo, after which he served in Santiago, returning to London in 1953. When Williams was removed after the Crabb fiasco there was a hiatus while White took over the Chief's reins, but Nasser's announcement of his nationalisation of the canal in July prompted Dean to order McDermott back from holiday in Switzerland to act initially as his deputy on the JIC, and then to work as White's FOA.

> Our instructions, passed down by word of mouth from Eden, were both clear and unusual. Firstly, only we three were to be in on all the intelligence and planning. The three were to be reduced to two at a later stage ... The task was to be given top priority as well as top secrecy. And the object of the plan was to topple Nasser, by force of course as this could not be done otherwise.[5]

McDermott recalled that 'Eden went to great pains to keep his intentions secret from our closest ally, the Americans', but in part because of this reluctance to draw in the Dulles brothers (John Foster, the US Secretary of State, and Allen, the DCI) the plan was doomed, although those most closely associated with the undertaking escaped relatively unscathed, apart from Eden who took off to Jamaica in ill health at the end of November. Newly knighted, Dean continued as Chairman of the JIC until 1960 when he was sent to New York as Britain's representative at the UN, and McDermott went to Cyprus at the end of 1958, at the height of the Emergency, to be replaced by (Sir) Robin Hooper, a former SOE 'Moon Squadron' pilot. On McDermott's final, round-the-world 'twilight tour' of SIS stations in the Far East he was given lunch by Allen Dulles in

Washington DC and 'was able to see for myself that in the intelligence world at any rate the treachery of Maclean and Philby, and Eden's offensive policy over Suez, had not permanently harmed our close relations with our American colleagues'.[6]

White, of course, could claim to have inherited a scheme of which he had little or no knowledge. Two years later, when SIS learned that Nasser was plotting a coup in Jordan, McDermott and White acted as a team and alerted Colin Figures in Amman. He in turn got word to King Hussein in time to have his Army commander, Ali Abu Nuwar, the main conspirator in Amman. arrested, thereby repairing some of the damage inflicted by Suez, and rebuilding SIS's status in at least that country where British paratroops also helped restore order.

Suez had undermined White's confidence in Easton, and had exposed two of SIS's other weaknesses. Firstly, SIS had provided no advance warning of Nasser's intentions and, once the canal had been seized, SIS had been ill-equipped to supply any meaningful support to the Chiefs of Staff. It had been the CIA that had provided the overhead imagery, and the plotting with Khalil had turned out to have been a waste of time and money. Worse, the Soviet intervention in Hungary, while Britain and America had been distracted in Egypt, had demonstrated the paucity of SIS assets in Eastern Europe. SIS maintained a station in Moscow, but it had never run an agent there. On the one occasion SIS had been given the opportunity to handle contact with a KGB illegal recruited in Canada by the Royal Canadian Mounted Police (RCMP) Security Service, the case had gone cold. The illegal, codenamed GIDEON, was the son of a Soviet official who had been employed by the Soviet trading organisation Amtorg in New York, and therefore had grown up almost more American than Russian, an ideal candidate for the KGB's 'Line X', supervising the insertion of illegals into the West. GIDEON had been recruited by the RCMP during his mission to Ottawa, and when he had been recalled to Moscow the RCMP had passed him on to SIS because the Canadians had no intelligence facilities overseas. Accordingly SIS had briefed the station commander in Moscow, the redoubtable Daphne Park, and sent Alan Urwick under supposedly 'deep' diplomatic cover to assist her. Unfortunately, when GIDEON was seen in the appointed place at the right time, he was not alone, and had not conformed to his other instructions, which prevented SIS from making contact with him. He was not seen again until 1993, when he was exfiltrated from the newly-created Russian Federation but, at the time of the planned Moscow street rendezvous, few had interpreted the episode as evidence that SIS had been penetrated.

It was on White's watch that SIS learned of a further traitor, beyond Philby, within its ranks. George Blake had served under three Chiefs but had only engaged in espionage, haemorrhaging SIS's secrets, while working for Sinclair and White. Born George Behar in Holland, Blake is probably best known as the spy who received the longest prison sentence ever handed out by a British criminal court, a total of forty-two years. He is equally as notorious for the fact that he served less than six years of his sentence before making a dramatic escape to the Soviet Union in October 1966. But in the intelligence community he is regarded as someone who changed history because he was the very first SIS officer to have been tried and convicted of having betrayed his country.

Blake's background was unusual. His father had been a Jewish businessman born in Constantinople who had served in the French Foreign Legion during the early part of the Great War and had subsequently transferred to the British Army during the Mesopotamian campaign. Evidently he had fought with distinction because he was decorated with the British Military Cross and the French Croix de Guerre. He also acquired British citizenship, and married a Dutch wife, Catherine, in London before settling in Rotterdam. Upon his death in April 1934, when young George Behar was thirteen, the boy went to Egypt to live with his aunt, his father's younger sister, and learnt for the first time of his Jewish origins. Those who know Blake say that his father's omission in not telling George of his Jewish heritage affected him profoundly. While in Cairo he also came to know his cousin, Henri Curiel, a left-wing activist eight years older than himself who was to be a founder member of the Egyptian Communist Party. Curiel was eventually to move to Paris, where he was murdered in 1978, in a political assassination linked to his enthusiastic support for the Palestine Liberation Organisation.

Blake's curiously cosmopolitan beginnings may have had some influence on his later development but he denies that Henri Curiel did any more than awaken a religious awareness within him. Indeed, Blake was to consider taking holy orders at one stage. The suggestion that Blake was indoctrinated by Curiel came about by an analysis of Blake's case by H. Montgomery Hyde in *George Blake Superspy* in which he incorrectly identified Curiel as Blake's uncle.

In 1939 Blake returned to Holland to complete his education but the war intervened and he was interned by the Nazis because of his British citizenship. After a month of detention Blake was released and he became active in the anti-Nazi resistance, working as a courier delivering messages and helping distribute underground newspapers. After the death of his grandmother in 1942 Blake decided to escape to Britain to join his mother and sisters who had already fled, and he made contact with the organisers of a route that guided *passeurs* from Paris to Lyons in the unoccupied zone, and then on to Spain. He crossed the frontier late in 1942 and, having been arrested by the Spanish police, was interned at the notorious Miranda del Ebro camp. His release came two months later, in January 1943, after the intervention of the British Embassy in Madrid, and he then completed his journey via Gibraltar and a sea voyage aboard the *Empress of Australia*. He underwent the routine four-day screening process at the Royal Victoria Patriotic School at Wandsworth and, once cleared by the security authorities, joined his family who had found a house in the London suburb of Northwood and went to work for the Dutch government-in-exile. After five months of unremittingly dull clerical work in the Dutch Ministry of Economic Affairs, Blake, together with his mother and two sisters, Anglicised his name by deed poll, and in October 1943 he joined the Royal Navy.

For the next year Blake underwent an officers' training course and had a spell at sea aboard the cruiser HMS *Diomede*. It has been suggested, originally by Rebecca West in *The New Meaning of Treason*, that Blake 'had been abstracted by SOE to work in their Dutch Section' but this is incorrect.[7] Nevertheless other authors have perpetuated this particular myth, with Cookridge claiming that Blake 'was seconded by the Royal Navy to the Dutch Section of SOE'.[8] In fact Blake remained in the Navy for almost a year before he was to enter the intelligence community and when he did so, it was to be SIS he joined, not SOE.

Blake's naval career was short. Assigned to submarine training, it was discovered that he had a medical condition which made him unsuitable for work underwater, and his name was passed to SIS as a potential recruit. A series of mysterious interviews in London followed, at the end of which Blake discovered in August 1944 that he had been enrolled as a member of the famed British Secret Service's Dutch Section, designated A2 and later P8. Although surprised by this unexpected development Blake apparently welcomed what he thought was an opportunity to return to Holland undercover, but he had not reckoned on the terms of an agreement that had been made by SIS with the Dutch intelligence service that precluded British subjects operating as agents anywhere in the Netherlands. Its purpose was to remove any fear that the British had any long-term interests in Holland, and avoid the bitter accusation made so often of SOE and SIS in France of meddling in an occupied country's internal politics. Accordingly Blake was to spend the first part of his SIS career as a conducting officer, escorting agents from one training school to another, and processing reports from SIS's networks in Holland. This was mainly office work in Broadway, where he was in close proximity to various very attractive secretaries who, he recalled:

> . . . were decidedly upper class and belonged to the higher strata of the establishment. There were among them daughters of Tory MPs and ministers, of bishops, of a Viceroy of India, of court dignitaries and some were even related to the Royal Family . . . They were mostly pretty, some very beautiful, but inclined to be vague and incompetent in varying degrees, though to this there could be exceptions. They were pleasant to work with and helped create a cheerful, friendly atmosphere in the office. I was a beneficiary of this as I spent most of my time there.[9]

Three of those who worked very closely with Blake, in the same room in Broadway, truly characterised the blue-blooded women who had been drafted into the wartime SIS by its equally well-born Chief, Bearing in mind that Blake had already acquired some sensitivity about the British class system, it can be imagined what effect their proximity had upon him. The three were Diana Legh, Guinevere Grant and the Hon. Iris Peake.

Diana's father was Colonel the Hon. Sir Piers Legh, then Master of the King's Household, while Guinevere's (now Dame Guinevere Tilney's) father was Sir Alfred Grant, the twelfth to succeed to a Scottish baronetcy that had been created in 1688. Iris was the daughter of a Tory minister, Osbert Peake MP (later Viscount Ingleby). These young ex-debutantes had been brought up on weekend house parties, country pursuits and the 400 Club. In contrast Blake, who was rather younger, had spent the past couple of years hiding his Jewish ancestry in a Nazi tyranny. According to Charles Seymour, then head of SIS's Dutch Section, Blake became infatuated with Iris Peake, and was to be very embittered when her father told him one evening after dinner at their mansion in Yorkshire that there was no chance of him ever marrying his daughter. Whatever the truth of the story, or the degree of tact exercised on this delicate subject, Blake remains to this day acutely self-conscious of his Jewish background and his heavily accented command of English.

After the liberation Blake stayed in SIS and was offered a permanent post. The alternatives were a job running pleasure cruises on the Rhine with an ex-SIS colleague with a wooden leg, or working as a buyer in a fashion house for a friend of his mother. Neither appealed, so he opted for a Russian language course at Downing College, Cambridge, and a future with SIS. Having learnt Russian it must have been only natural, following the twisted logic so typical of the Foreign Office, that he should have been posted to Seoul in South Korea in October 1948. Scarcely eighteen months later he was to witness the city being overrun by Communist troops as the North Koreans unexpectedly invaded at the start of what was to become the Korean War. The remaining employees of the British Consulate-General, including Blake, were taken into custody, and for the next three years he was to be a prisoner of the North Koreans. It was during this period of captivity which he shared with several other internees, including the *Observer* war correspondent Philip Deane that, according to Blake, he was to adopt the Marxist creed and volunteer to work for the Soviets.

By Blake's own admission, he returned to London in March 1953, having been released by the North Koreans, determined to work for the KGB. His contact was to be Nikolai B. Korovin, the KGB *rezident* who had been operating under diplomatic cover in London with the rank of first secretary, and then counsellor, since 1949. Korovin was to leave London in 1954, but returned from Moscow in 1956. In January 1961 he made a hasty departure following the arrests of the Portland spy ring, no doubt fearing that he might be implicated by Gordon Lonsdale, a KGB illegal. In fact he need not have worried because Lonsdale was to maintain his silence until he was swapped in April 1964 for Greville Wynne.

Blake's initial meeting with Korovin was in the customs building at Otpor, the frontier crossing point on the Trans-Siberian Railway between Peking and Moscow. 'He was a thick-set man of middle height aged about fifty' says Blake. 'He spoke English well but with a marked Slav accent.'[10] They arranged to meet again in The Hague in July 1953 and thereafter they met early in October outside Belsize Park tube station at seven in the evening and thereafter 'every month or three weeks'. Blake recalled:

> I cannot say that Korovin was the kind of man who naturally evoked very warm feelings in me. There was too much of the iron fist in the velvet glove about him for that, but I had a great admiration for his skill . . . Even though he was known to MI5 to be the KGB *rezident* in Great Britain and constantly followed by a highly experienced surveillance team, equipped with fast cars and modern radio communications, he always managed to get rid of his tail and meet me, punctually, at the appointed time and appointed place. He once told me how it was done. In order to meet me at seven o'clock in the evening, he left his house at eight o'clock in the morning and was on the move all day. The operation involved several people and cars and a few safe-houses. It was difficult and time-consuming, but it worked every time.[11]

There must have been a moment of disbelief when Blake revealed to Korovin in October 1953 that he had resumed working for SIS the previous month, and had been moved to one of the organisation's most secret departments, Section Y. Early in January 1955 Blake was transferred from what was essentially an eavesdropping post to the Berlin station, admitting that he 'had obtained all the operational intelligence which Section Y could provide'.[12] The KGB probably persuaded him that he should further his career by seeking a post abroad. Philby had observed that he 'could not reasonably resist a foreign posting without serious loss of standing in the service'[13] and the same was true for Blake. This move took him from processing the raw intelligence acquired from various clandestine microphone and telephone-tapping operations around the world to just one of the many centres where the work was actually conducted. Here the KGB assigned him a new case officer, a man he knew only as Dick. 'He was a thick-set man of about fifty with a pale complexion and a friendly twinkle in his eyes behind thick, horn-rimmed spectacles.'[14] For nearly the next five years Blake was to hold regular meetings with this man, handing over SIS's secrets on each occasion. Exactly what he betrayed during this period is known in part for he later confirmed to his British interrogators what he had provided. He admitted, for example, that he had disclosed the full details of GOLD and had ensured that the KGB had been alerted to it 'before even the first spade had been put in the ground'.[15]

Blake's career was unaffected by the premature conclusion of GOLD and he remained at the Berlin station, commanded by Peter Lunn, until he was posted back to London in the summer of 1959. On this occasion he was assigned to Production Research, based in Artillery Mansions, Victoria Street, which had the task of recruiting contacts among British businessmen travelling abroad. Of special interest were those developing commercial links in the Eastern Bloc, and the Controller of Production Research, Blake's immediate superior, was Dickie Franks who had been cultivating suitable agents for some years, and was a future Chief. Franks, of course, was also Greville Wynne's case officer, and during the period of Blake's work in Production Research, between mid-1959 and September 1960 Wynne was reporting to Franks, but had yet to meet SIS's future star source, Colonel Oleg Penkovsky. Simultaneously Blake had resumed contact with Nikolai Korovin, and another KGB officer whom he knew only as Vasili. He says that when Korovin 'was away . . . his place was taken by a younger man called Vasili, who differed from Korovin in that he had a much more cheerful disposition and looked typically English so that if he didn't open his mouth nobody would have dreamt of taking him for a foreigner'.[16]

In September 1960 Blake moved to the Lebanon where he started to learn Arabic on a Foreign Office language course at Shemlan, in the hills outside Beirut, and it was from here that he received a summons back to London at the end of March 1961. The apparently innocuous request was relayed to Blake by Nicholas Elliott, then head of the Beirut station but, as soon as Blake reported as instructed to SIS's personnel department at Broadway on Tuesday, 4 April, he was intercepted by Harold Shergold, a colleague from Germany who had spent his career operating against the Soviets and the East Germans, and Sir Ian Critchett. A baronet, Critchett had served in the RAF during the war and after postings to Vienna and Bucharest had been withdrawn in 1956 from the Cairo station where he had been Stockwell's deputy.

Blake was escorted across St James's Park to Carlton Gardens for interrogation. There he was confronted by Shergold supported by a panel of SIS officers who conducted a series of interviews which lasted until Thursday evening. The other three were John Quine, the former head of station in Tokyo and now head of SIS's counter-intelligence section, R5; Terence Lecky, another veteran of the German stations who had recently ended a two-year tour in Zurich; and Ben Johnson, an ex-policeman. Together the four men took Blake through his career and confronted him with the mounting evidence that he had compromised virtually every operation he had been given access to. In particular, he was challenged about the nature of his relationship with Horst Eitner, a German agent whom he had run in Berlin. Eitner had been arrested by the West German police as a Soviet spy and once in custody he and his wife had denounced Blake as a KGB asset. There was other evidence, albeit of a circumstantial nature, that suggested SIS had harboured a traitor. A Polish intelligence officer, Michal Goleniewski, who had defected from Warsaw in December 1960, had proved that SIS documents had been leaking to the KGB for years. One particular paper, an annual review of SIS's performance in Poland, was positively identified by Goleniewski as having reached the Soviets, and a trace had shown that it had been distributed to Blake. Taken with Eitner's damning testimony and the failure of GOLD and other technical surveillance operations. Blake had become a prime suspect.

There are two versions of what happened next. According to Blake he withstood the mounting pressure until Thursday afternoon when he was accused of having sold out to the KGB for money, and then having been the victim of blackmail. Blake says he was outraged at this suggestion and momentarily lost control, indignantly protesting that his collaboration with the Soviets had been ideologically motivated. That such a hardened professional should allow himself to be entrapped so easily sounds highly improbable, and it is not a recollection shared by the others involved. The other version is that Blake successfully resisted the growing weight of evidence against him until Thursday lunchtime when, as usual, the participants broke for a midday meal. On the previous two days Blake had been allowed to wander unaccompanied through the West End and eat alone in a restaurant. However, on this occasion he lost his nerve and decided to seek advice from his Soviet contact. He had an emergency telephone number for Korovin and a codeword to summon help, but at the very last moment, after he had approached and then circled a telephone kiosk, he decided against making the call. On his return to Carlton Gardens he was informed that his every move had been watched, and his interrogators demanded to know whom he had been thinking of telephoning. Not realising that he had been under surveillance Blake panicked and confessed he had thought of asking the Soviets to rescue him.

Whichever version is the truth, there is agreement about what happened next. He spent the weekend with his colleagues at a country cottage while a decision was reached about what action should be taken and on 10 April he was arrested by two Special Branch detectives, Louis Gale and Ferguson Smith. His trial at the Old Bailey, which the Chief attended together with other colleagues, lasted just one day, 3 May 1961, because he pleaded guilty to the five charges, and he was sentenced to a total of forty-two years' imprisonment.

It was only after Blake's appeal had been rejected that he was visited again by SIS, this time joined by MI5. Curiously Blake makes no mention of this important episode in his memoirs but this was the first chance the Security Service had been given to question Blake and extract whatever relevant knowledge he had still retained about his Soviet contacts. This was an entirely voluntary exercise, for Blake was under no obligation to receive Terence Lecky, representing his old service, and Tony Henley, MI5's principal interrogator (who habitually used the pseudonym Healey). He had passed into the criminal justice system and he had little to gain from helping his former colleagues. However, he cooperated to the full and together the two counter-intelligence experts made Blake reconstruct each meeting he had held with the KGB and identified his three case officers, including Nikolai Korovin, and Vasili S. Dozhdalev, a first secretary. The third turned out to be Sergei A. Kondrashev, first secretary at the Soviet Embassy since 1955, who was later to turn up attached to Soviet diplomatic missions in Austria and Bonn and, according to a KGB defector who confirmed his identity in 1962, was a key Soviet agent handler.

This unexpected source of knowledge about the KGB's First Chief Directorate (FCD) was Anatoli Golitsyn, formerly attached to the Soviet Embassy in Helsinki, who revealed for the first time that 'Nikolai Korovin', the case officer who had first met Blake on the Sino-Russian frontier, was actually General Nikolai Rodin. Golitsyn possessed an encyclopedic knowledge of the KGB's operations in northern Europe and in 1963 traveled to London to help MI5. He explained that Rodin was a skilled case officer who had been appointed *rezident* in 1949 in succession to Konstantin Kukin, an old-timer who had held the post since 1943. However, by the time Golitsyn made his revelation Rodin had already returned to Moscow.

During his long debriefing sessions held in Wormwood Scrubs prison, which continued until the end of September 1962, Blake admitted to having indiscriminately photographed everything that had passed over his desk for the Soviets. Considering that Philby had been fired from SIS in November 1951 the material supplied by Blake was of enormous value to the KGB as Blake represented, as far as is now known, its sole source of information from within SIS during the subsequent years. There is, nonetheless, some continuing doubt about exactly what intelligence disasters Blake could be held personally responsible for. He freely admitted his role in compromising GOLD in Berlin, but he had so comprehensively betrayed SIS's secrets that he himself was not entirely sure of the details or the scale of what he had done, and for which he showed no remorse – at his trial he even instructed his defence counsel, Jeremy Hutchinson QC, not to tell the judge during his plea for mitigation that he harboured any regrets. As a professional who had willingly betrayed his country, and had made a determined effort over a period of seven years to inflict maximum damage to SIS, Blake richly deserved his punishment. However, the severity of the sentence persuaded several other prisoners in Wormwood Scrubs that the Lord Chief Justice had been too harsh and three in particular plotted his escape. Sean Bourke, Pat Pottle and Michael Randle offered Blake their services and, following their own release, helped Blake to disappear on 22 October 1966.

Bourke was an Irish criminal who had served a seven-year sentence for mailing a letter bomb to a detective in Sussex against whom he had a personal grudge. Randle and Pottle were political activists who had been imprisoned with a group of others for eighteen months for their part in an anti-nuclear demonstration at RAF Wethersfield in Essex in December 1962. Together the three men had agreed to find and finance a safe-house for Blake, with whom they communicated by two-way radio, if he managed to scale one of the perimeter walls. Through a series of security lapses Blake was able to approach the wall under cover of darkness one wet Saturday evening and climb a home-made rope ladder thrown over the top by Bourke. According to *The Blake Escape*, the account subsequently published unapologetically by Randle and Pottle, which coincides in almost every respect with the version given by Sean Bourke in his *The Springing of George Blake*, the spy hid for the next two months in London, nursing the fractured wrist he had sustained in his fall to freedom from the prison wall. He was treated by a sympathetic doctor, and for five days was sheltered by a vicar, the Reverend John Papworth, at his home at St Mark's Church, St John's Wood. A former Labour Party parliamentary candidate, Papworth had been instrumental in persuading another sympathiser, the film director Tony Richardson, to finance the entire enterprise. Then Blake was driven by Randle and his wife in a concealed compartment of a Commer camper van to Berlin where he was welcomed to the Eastern Bloc by one of his KGB contacts, Vasili Dozhdalev, who happened by coincidence to be in the Soviet zone at the time, and was therefore available to confirm Blake's identity. Having dropped Blake off in Berlin, Randle and his wife (and two young children, brought along as additional cover) motored back to London via Ostend and resumed their lives.

Blake's audacious escape prompted a major review of prison security, conducted by Earl Mountbatten with a panel of three assessors and given expert advice in secret by a veteran intelligence officer, Tony Brooks. He was especially well-qualified to help Mountbatten, having parachuted twice into France to work for the wartime resistance, for which he was decorated with the DSO and MC. Aged not yet twenty, he had been the youngest agent sent by SOE into the field, and he had worked continuously in the underground between July 1942 and the Liberation, apart from a period of ten weeks spent in England for briefing, and three days spent in prison. Since the war he had operated for SIS in Sofia, Belgrade, Cyprus and Paris, and more recently had transferred to MI5 where he was to score some impressive achievements, which were to include the recruitment of the KGB's Oleg Lyalin. Brooks's contribution was to go deliberately unacknowledged in the report, which was drawn up by the inquiry's secretary, (Sir) Philip Woodfield, so as to protect his identity. Woodfield's report, published in December 1966, just as Blake was settling into his new life in Moscow, cast no fresh light on exactly how Blake had managed to elude the police but it did highlight several flaws in prison security which, too late, were tightened up.

Blake's incredible escape baffled both the police and the Security Service and their inability to solve the mystery led to any number of rumours about his possible role as a double or triple agent. Certainly those SIS officers privy to the case had been dismayed that a decision had been taken on the very highest level to prosecute Blake, and that no offers or inducements were made to him to extract a confession. His statement, made under caution to Detective Superintendent Ferguson Smith, was to be the basis of the charges preferred against him. Those who would have opted to keep this embarrassing case out of the courts did not fully appreciate the political implications of suppressing such a matter, following as it did only a month after Gordon Lonsdale and the other members of the Portland spy ring had each received substantial sentences in a well publicised prosecution. Indeed, in that case Lonsdale, the KGB's illegal *rezident* in England, had been meted out a sentence of twenty-five years by the same judge, Lord Parker, so Blake ought to have known what to expect, even if he had not anticipated that the prison terms would be consecutive and not concurrent. Although SIS certainly did not conspire with the KGB to free Blake from a sentence perceived to be savage, such rumours circulated. One unforeseen consequence of this interesting but misguided speculation was the caution with which Blake was eventually welcomed to Moscow. Apparently even the KGB found it hard to believe that their man could have engineered his own escape with just £700 and the help of a wealthy film director, a clergyman, a pair of naive peace campaigners and a hard-drinking Irishman.

White had calculated that, with most of the evidence against Blake being heard *in camera*, and the imposition of a D Notice to prevent press speculation, his embarrassment value to the government would be kept to a minimum. No expulsion of Soviet diplomats was necessary, Nikolai Korovin having already slipped out of the country, and Blake's wife, who had herself served in SIS as a secretary, could be relied upon to maintain a discreet silence about the nature of her husband's work, even if the Prime Minister had a little disingenuously distanced the Foreign Office from her husband by assuring the Commons that Blake 'had never been an established member of the Foreign Service'. However, Blake's true function quickly leaked to Fleet Street and word spread that Blake had received a year of his sentence for every British agent he had betrayed. The government must have been further irritated when it was alleged in 1964 that Blake had not been segregated from Gordon Lonsdale in C Hall, one of five prison wings in the Scrubs. The Home Secretary, Henry Brooke, denied the allegation in response to a parliamentary question, but Blake (and some other ex-prisoners) are adamant that Blake and Lonsdale met regularly each afternoon while taking their half-hour daily exercise in the yard.

The reality was that both SIS and the Security Service were keen to find out how Blake had left the country and who had been involved. Their initial list of suspects included Sean Bourke, who had been discharged from the Scrubs just three months before the escape, Michael Randle and Pat Pottle as all three had been friendly to Blake in prison, and Randle had sent Blake a Christmas card after his release. When MI5 obtained a pre-publication copy of Bourke's book, *The Springing of George Blake* the conclusion was reached that the two central co-conspirators referred to as 'Pat Porter' and 'Michael Reynolds' were Pat Pottle and Michael Randle. Both men exactly matched Bourke's descriptions. They both had an Irish mother and English father, and Reynolds had a wife called Anne and two small children, and lived in Camden in a 'modest house' with a 'modest income'. Pottle was indeed 'a couple of years younger than Michael', lived in a flat and had 'recently started a little business' with some friends – in fact it was an antique business. Although MI5 and Special Branch recognised the implications of Bourke's story no attempt was made by the police to interview either of his fellow plotters. A warrant was issued for Bourke's arrest but he successfully fought an extradition hearing in Dublin in February 1969, and died in 1982, refusing to the last to name his helpers even though he had long since fallen out with Blake.

There the matter rested until 1987 when Harford Montgomery Hyde published his biography of George Blake and disclosed that Pat Porter and Michael Reynolds 'had belonged to the Committee of 100, the nuclear disarmament group formed by Bertrand Russell'. He stated that the pair had been imprisoned from 1961 to 1963 because they had 'helped to organise the civil disobedience at Wethersfield RAF base in December 1961'[17] and thereby effectively identified their real names because only six people had been tried for the incident at Wethersfield. They were Helen Allegranza, Terry Chandler, Ian Dixon, Trevor Hatton, Patrick Pottle and Michael Randle. There could be little doubt who 'Pat Porter' and 'Michael Reynolds' were meant to be. As a former lawyer, Member of Parliament, wartime SIS officer and distinguished author, Hyde's confident assertion carried great weight. Confronted by newspaper journalists, the pair admitted their involvement, Pottle was still in the antiques trade in north London while Randle had moved to Bradford where he had been appointed a lecturer in peace studies. Responding to the sudden media interest in what they had done nearly a quarter of a century earlier they wrote their own account, and thereby forced the authorities to prosecute them. Clearly, declining to follow up newspapers and authors who had named them was one thing, but allowing them to boast openly of what they had accomplished was quite another.

The trial, held in 1990, was delayed by legal wrangles over the lengthy delay in bringing proceedings, with the defence arguing that a decision had been taken more than twenty years earlier not to pursue Randle and Pottle even though their complicity had become known to Special Branch and the Security Service. Retired officers of both organisations gave evidence and during the course of the hearings it was disclosed by ex-Commander Rollo Watts of Scotland Yard, but not explained, that no further inquiries had been made of Randle and Pottle even though they were believed to have been responsible for aiding Blake's escape. Nor, for that matter, has anyone suggested why Bourke chose to incriminate his two friends in his book. Blake was among those who was appalled when he read Bourke's story and realised how easy it would be for the British authorities to identify Randle and Pottle.

Blake's original autobiography, entitled *No Abiding City*, was written at much the same time as Bourke's book, but no western publisher who examined it was prepared to buy the manuscript. The literary agent Robin Denniston recalls accompanying an American colleague, Hal Schalatt, to Moscow in 1968 to read it, but they found it dull fare. Instead Denniston wrote a brief report on its contents for SIS upon his return and was entertained to lunch by MI5's long serving Legal Adviser, Bernard Sheldon, in a private room at St Ermin's Hotel with a party of interested SIS officers. Their objective was to determine whether Blake had the capacity to inflict further damage on SIS from behind the Iron Curtain. Their conclusion was that he had probably already done as much mischief as he could and, although publication of Blake's book might well offend the public, it would be unlikely to have any operational relevance to the Service. Since that very subjective assessment a further Official Secrets Act has been passed to prevent former security and intelligence officers from capitalising in print on their experiences, but no attempt was made to prevent the release in 1990 of an up-dated version of *No Abiding City*, entitled *No Other Choice*, although the Crown succeeded in sequestering the royalties.

Blake's career as a spy lasted for seven years, from the moment of his first interrogation in Korea in 1951 by Colonel Nikolai Loyenko, to his arrest nearly ten years later. However, his value to the Soviets probably extended beyond that period for he would certainly have had useful information to impart after he had escaped to Moscow, either filling in the inevitable blanks in the messages he had conveyed earlier, or helping the KGB to spot previously unidentified SIS personnel overseas. From the

Soviet standpoint Blake must have been able to supply a wealth of information to which Philby had never gained access. Blake says that while he was in SIS he never met, and had never even heard of Philby. 'This is not so strange if one bears in mind . . . we had worked in quite different fields; he in counter-espionage and I in espionage.'[18] His offer to work for the KGB came at a time when Philby had not long been excluded from SIS so the Soviets could double-check his material against what Philby had already provided, and give the continuity in the flow of data which is the ambition of every case officer.

SIS's damage assessment into Blake's betrayal concluded that he had played a part in betraying at least two GRU officers who volunteered to help the West. Piotr Popov was caught as a result of Blake's tip in 1957, having learned from his office colleague that the CIA had acquired a good Soviet intelligence source. He may also have been instrumental in Colonel Oleg Penkovsky's arrest in October 1962, even though that event took place while he was in Wormwood Scrubs. The head of the Moscow station, who had run Penkovsky in 1961, and whose wife had relayed messages from him, was Ruari Chisholm. When the Chisholms had been posted to the Soviet Union in May 1960 SIS believed that he had survived his tour of duty in Berlin without having been identified as an SIS officer. Blake's interrogators realised too late that for four years Chisholm had worked alongside George Blake who confirmed that he had told the KGB of his role. Thus the Chisholm family had been under intensive surveillance from the moment they had arrived in Moscow, which in turn had made it very unlikely that Penkovsky could escape detection.

Blake's treachery had a profound impact on White and SIS, and represented eloquent proof that the organisation's security procedures had been deeply flawed. Why had Blake been posted to one of SIS's most sensitive sections upon his return from captivity? Why had the many clues indicating penetration, which emerged when Norman Mott, and Terence Lecky undertook the damage assessment, been given other interpretations, such as one of the consequences of a break-in at Guy Bratt's station in Brussels? Any explanation except hostile penetration had been accepted until the proof had been supplied by a defector. Even then the certainty that Blake had been a spy had not amounted to sufficient evidence to convict him, and it was only when Blake had given a confession, under caution from a Special Branch officer, that a criminal prosecution became possible. White had played a continuing role, advising the Attorney-General, Sir Reginald Manningham-Buller MP, on the sensitivities of the case. Blake pleaded guilty before the Lord Chief Justice, Lord Parker, and received five maximum sentences, to be served consecutively. Instead of facing a manageable fourteen years inside, as he had anticipated, and maybe had been led to expect, he was instead given an unprecedented forty-two, causing the defendant to collapse in court, and stay in a state of shock for several days.

White's willingness to be ruthless with Blake, who cooperated in the damage assessment, was rewarded the very day that he was driven to Wormwood Scrubs, for later the same evening the Chief went to the Mount Royal Hotel in Marble Arch to meet Colonel Oleg Penkovsky, codenamed HERO, the GRU officer who would 'pay the rent' for SIS. Although Penkovsky proved to be the outstanding source of White's tenure as Chief, his case is much more closely associated with Dickie Franks, the officer who recruited his courier, Greville Wynne, and later was to be appointed Chief (*see Chapter VIII*). For White, the need to protect HERO was an all-consuming preoccupation, and when he was arrested, in October 1962, at the height of the Cuban missile crisis, the Chief was particularly anxious about precisely how the Soviets had caught him. Had this been an example of textbook counter-intelligence techniques and intensive surveillance, or a tip from another traitor? With the Blake debacle so recent an event, it was essential to know exactly what had led to the loss of SIS's star agent, and his courier. Clearly the Soviets had set a skilful trap, for Wynne had been in the safety of Austria when Penkovsky had been arrested, and then had ventured into Hungary for a trade exhibition, where he had been detained and flown to Moscow for interrogation, trial and imprisonment.

White had good reason to fear penetration because one of his former colleagues in MI5, Arthur Martin, had come to see him secretly to voice his suspicions. Martin, formerly a wartime wireless intercept operator and GCHQ's liaison officer at Leconfield House when Klaus Fuchs had been identified in the BRIDE traffic (later designated VENONA), was the consummate counter-intelligence specialist who had been among the first to express his doubts about Kim Philby. Martin was the epitome of the quiet, reserved, analytical MI5 molehunter who viewed facts dispassionately and wrote succinct, compelling reports. It had been his idea to offer Philby an immunity from prosecution approved by the Attorney-General, Sir John Hobson, but at the last moment White had been persuaded to send Nicholas Elliott to the Lebanon to make the offer, in January 1963. Elliott and Philby had been old friends and White thought he would have more impact than the former Royal Signals NCO. Peter Lunn, the station commander who had just replaced Elliott in Beirut, was instructed to invite Philby over to his secretary's apartment for a private meeting, but when Philby knocked on the door, his head swathed in bandages after an accident during a heavy drinking session the night before, it was opened by Elliott who pitched Hobson's offer and explained that SIS had now acquired irrefutable proof, but did not spell it out, nor say it was from a Soviet defector, Anatoli Golitsyn, combined with testimony from Flora Solomon, Aileen Philby's close friend who had come forward to denounce Philby as having attempted to recruit her for the Soviets before the war. An ardent Zionist, she had been dismayed by the anti-Israeli tone of Philby's newspaper reports from the Middle East in the *Observer* and through her friend Lord Rothschild had approached Dick White, who had introduced her to Arthur Martin. Taken together, the accumulation was damning, although it fell well short of evidence that could be placed before a court in a criminal trial. However, what struck Elliott was Philby's apparent total indifference to the nature of the evidence against him. He never asked what it was, so Elliott had no need to disclose it.

In addition to this evidence, there was soon to be other material, from GCHQ's BRIDE/VENONA cryptographic project, which would be found to contain six references to a spy operating in London in September 1945 codenamed STANLEY. This only became available after Elliott's confrontation because MI5 had ceased work on BRIDE in 1953, but the intercepts were to be re-examined, with even greater vigour, in the months ahead. From the context of one message, indicating that STANLEY had access to SIS files on Mexico and was well-informed about the as yet unannounced defection of a GRU cipher clerk, Igor Gouzenko, in

Ottawa, it was obvious that Philby was the spy, and had been handled by an NKVD officer, Boris Krotov, who was also running HICKS, now identified as Guy Burgess. Since Philby had known of the BRIDE project since his arrival in Washington DC in September 1949, he may well have assumed that sooner or later it would compromise him.

Apparently brought to a low ebb by his chronic alcoholism, Philby accepted the immunity, admitted that he had spied since 1934, and promised to return the next day with a complete, typewritten confession. This he did, but when Martin had examined the signed two-page document in London, as Elliott completed a tour of sub-Saharan Africa stations, he realised Philby had duped his old friend. Philby's statement incriminated his oldest SIS colleague and schoolfriend, I. I. 'Tim' Milne, and named other equally implausible officers as his fellow conspirators. Nevertheless, it did contain admissions regarding his betrayal of Konstantin Volkov, an NKVD officer who had attempted to negotiate his defection to the British in Istanbul in August 1945, and CLIMBER, SIS's ill-fated postwar attempt to infiltrate agents into the Caucasus. Also authentic, although disbelieved at the time, was Philby's identification of his first NKVD contact in London, known to him as OTTO, as an Austrian postgraduate student, Dr Arnold Deutsch. Later, in April 1964, John Cairncross would be questioned by Arthur Martin in Cleveland, and confirmed that he too had been run by a mysterious handler, known to him only as OTTO.

By the time Elliott was sent back to Beirut to confront Philby ten days later, he had disappeared. Tim Milne, then at the Tokyo station, was investigated and cleared, although his brother Antony, who had been at the Montevideo station between 1961 and 1965, was fired for failing to have declared a past relationship with Litzi Friedman, Philby's first wife. A British diplomat, Michael Stewart, who also had shared Litzi's favours, was rather more lucky, and was appointed to Washington DC before going to Athens as ambassador, and receiving a knighthood.

As Martin scrutinised Philby's confession he came to realise that the document had been skilfully crafted, and deduced that Philby must have been tipped off in advance, a suggestion initially made by Elliott who recalled that Philby had shown no surprise at his unexpected appearance, and had even remarked that he 'had half thought it would be you'. Based on these clues, and the fact that he had spent five months preparing the brief on Philby's guilt, Martin became increasingly convinced that Philby's confession had been made under Soviet control, suggesting that MI5 had been penetrated at a high level. It was also a plausible explanation for the strange contradiction of Philby's cooperation, followed swiftly by his defection. The odd lack of logic in Philby's behaviour, and his uncharacteristic willingness to surrender without a fight, had troubled others too, who had wondered why Philby should have changed his mind. In addition, MI5 suspected that the unexpected appearance of a senior Third Department KGB officer in Beirut shortly before Elliott's arrival may not have been a coincidence. Accordingly, Martin had turned to White because he dared not confide his fears to those above him, and C had listened to him with much more than professional respect. They had known each other for more than sixteen years and Martin had married Joan Russell-King, White's MI5 secretary.

Martin had compiled a catalogue of incidents, intelligence failures, losses, odd coincidences, tips from defectors and other events that, when listed together, looked quite shocking and had even cast doubt on some of the operations that MI5 had hitherto regarded as successes. The bottom line was that the Security Service had probably harboured a spy for a long time, and the cast of suspects was depressingly short and senior. According to Martin's analysis, the spy had to be one of three people: Malcolm Cumming, then Director of A Branch, Sir Roger Hollis, the D-G recommended by White, or his deputy, Graham Mitchell. White also knew Mitchell as an MI5 colleague who had joined the office, and concentrated on the study of fascists, just two years after him. A Wykehamist who had overcome childhood polio to excel at tennis and yachting, Mitchell acted as MI5's link with the Prime Minister's office during the Profumo affair. News that such a senior MI5 figure had fallen under suspicion might completely undermine the little confidence left in Hollis's Security Service, after a series of debilitating security scandals and tribunals of inquiry. Having heard the evidence White agreed to contact Hollis, omitting to mention that he too was a suspect, and obtain his consent to a surveillance operation on Mitchell, to be undertaken by SIS personnel unknown to him. The task was assigned to Stephen de Mowbray who recruited newcomers like Michael Oatley to maintain a discreet watch on Mitchell as he commuted to and from his home close to Chobham Common.

Thus began one of the most controversial periods in the history of either service, with SIS seeking to catch MI5's Deputy D-G engaged in espionage for the Soviets. From White's perspective, the prospect of entrapping Mitchell must have been fraught, for he knew only too well how he had colluded with Mitchell to conceal the truth about his botched attempt to intercept Donald Maclean in France back in May 1951. Whatever his personal fears, White supported Martin, up to the point when Mitchell unexpectedly requested early retirement in the beginning of September 1963 and the operation, codenamed PETERS, was abandoned. In April the following year, when Martin extracted a confession from the wartime MI5 officer Anthony Blunt, and exposed him as the fourth man in Philby's Cambridge ring, Hollis lost patience with Martin and requested White's intervention. The solution was a swap, with Martin joining SIS, eventually to become head of the Registry in 1967, and Terence Lecky moving to MI5, but it left the question of penetration unresolved, and much resented by some in the Security Service. At White's suggestion the issue was then examined by a joint, six-member MI5–SIS committee, codenamed FLUENCY, with Geoffrey Hinton representing SIS, that was to review the investigation under a rotating chairman, the first of whom was an MI5 molehunter, Peter Wright.

FLUENCY would study no fewer than 270 suspicious incidents, all regarded as evidence of penetration, of which seventy could easily be attributed to Anthony Blunt. The remaining 200 were then narrowed down to twenty, eventually leaving three episodes for which there were no obvious explanations. Firstly, there was the assertion by Konstantin Volkov in August 1945 that a Soviet spy in London was 'the acting head of a department of the British Counter-Intelligence Directorate'. Secondly, there was Igor Gouzenko's reference to a spy codenamed ELLI who had worked for MI5 at its headquarters, then accommodated at Blenheim Palace, in 1942. Lastly, there was an allegation from the Polish defector Michal Goleniewski that MI5 had harboured a spy with a profile that at one point seemed to match an officer called Michael Hanley. After an investigation codenamed HARRIET, 'Jumbo' Hanley was cleared and in 1972 was appointed D-G, a post he was to hold for seven years.

Finally, the FLUENCY members concluded, by a majority, that MI5 had suffered penetration and that Mitchell had been the best candidate. There the matter remained, with Mitchell effectively immune to further enquiries, and Hollis going into retirement as expected in 1965, to be succeeded by his deputy, (Sir) Martin Furnival Jones, until the work of the FLUENCY committee was disinterred by the former Cabinet Secretary, Sir Burke Trend. His final verdict, which studied a two-day interrogation of Hollis who had been called back to London to answer the allegations, was equally inconclusive, indicating that there was no reason to believe he had been a spy.

Leaving the issue of hostile penetration unresolved was a nightmare for White who knew the game, and many of the players, all too well. The molehunts had almost paralysed the Security Service and according to Hollis had come close to undermining MI5's cohesion and discipline. The worst of all worlds was the impasse in which the Chief found himself, beset by those who remained convinced that the Soviets had planted as yet undetected moles in both organisations. Certainly Stephen de Mowbray and Arthur Martin never lost their faith in the high priest of Angletonian counter-intelligence, Anatoli Golitsyn, and even after their retirement collaborated together on editing his masterwork, *New Lies for Old*, which was published in March 1984 by Barney Blackley of The Bodley Head, one of de Mowbray's old friends from Lymington.

White's own wartime friendship with Blunt and Burgess remained a continuing source of embarrassment for him and awkwardness for others, and in fairness to him it should be noted that he never attempted to restrict the molehunts whenever their research encroached on his personal connections. He kept up his friendship with Tess and Victor Rothschild, both of whom had served with him in the wartime Security Service, and were regarded by the molehunters as walking encyclopedias of the Cambridge Communists and intellectuals of the 1930s. Nevertheless, White's past connections did cause problems, such as the occasion in 1966 when White nominated (Sir) Stuart Hampshire to undertake a review of GCHQ's operational effectiveness and future. Hampshire had been a wartime cryptanalyst for the Radio Security Service, but after a brief postwar career in the Foreign Office had taken up academic life as Professor of Philosophy at Princeton. The Cabinet Secretary, Burke Trend, had asked White to recommend a suitable candidate to undertake a review of GCHQ's performance so the new Labour administration, anxious to cut costs, could consider its role in the future. The National Security Agency (NSA) was pressing for a commitment from GCHQ to participate in the development of the next generation of Sigint intercept platforms, the satellites which threatened to gobble up at large proportion of the Secret Vote. The huge Rhyolite system, scheduled for insertion into geostationary orbit at the equator over Indonesia in June 1970 would be dependent on a ground station at Pine Gap in Australia and would collect telemetry, radar and VHF microwave traffic in prodigious quantities and give UKUSA a tremendous advantage, but at a price that the precarious Labour-managed economy could barely afford.

Bearing in mind Hampshire's wartime experience in signals intelligence, White had put his name forward, failing to mention that MI5 had accumulated quite a dossier on Hampshire, who had been named as a spy by Goronwy Rees in June 1951, days after the defection of Burgess and Maclean. A mercurial Welsh academic and wartime military intelligence officer, Rees acknowledged having spied for the Soviets until 1938, although MI5 later suspected he had remained in touch with the KGB until 1964. Whatever the truth, Rees had denounced Hampshire, who was an old friend of Guy Burgess and before the war had travelled in France with Anthony Blunt, but White had ignored the allegation. When he was interviewed in 1967 Hampshire recalled that in 1938 he had been pitched by a drunken Burgess at his flat in Chester Square 'to undertake dangerous but exciting work for peace', but had never bothered to report the incident. Nor had he mentioned an earlier drunken dinner party in Paris at which James Klugmann had sounded him out about the strength of his left-wing politics. An overt Communist, and later the CPGB's official historian, Klugmann was known to MI5 as a talent-spotter who had recruited John Cairncross. When the MI5 molehunters interviewed Hampshire about his contacts with so many known Soviet spies, Hampshire had replied that he had not given any thought to the matter because he knew they were friendly with White!

MI5's subsequent investigation of White turned up another potentially awkward fact. White had done nothing about other allegations made by Goronwy Rees, whom he had disliked even though he had been close to his mentor, Guy Liddell, and had failed to act on Rees's charge that Robin Zaehner also had been a spy. An Oxford don and skilled linguist, Zaehner had joined SIS during the war and had operated among the hill tribes of northern Persia before transferring to Greece to help run SIS's disastrous postwar attempts to infiltrate guerrillas into Albania. Later he had returned to Oxford, and his last service for SIS had been a mission he had undertaken to Tehran in 1951. However, what the molehunters found inexplicable was White's failure to follow-up Rees's charge, especially as Zaehner had fitted the description of a spy in August 1945 given by Konstantin Volkov. Zaehner was interviewed at All Souls and cleared, but the episode tended to illustrate White's somewhat haphazard approach to counter-espionage, contradicting his image in Whitehall as a truly intelligent intelligence officer.

While it would be unfair to assert that White left SIS in turmoil in March 1968, his twelve years as Chief had not been marked by overwhelming success. He had attempted to modernise the service by introducing proper salaries, vetting, pensions and terms of employment, to get rid of the old hands from prewar, isolate the robber barons, and in 1964 had supervised SIS's transfer from Broadway to the hideous modern concrete twenty-storey Century House in Westminster Bridge Road, and C's office from the elegance of 21 Queen Anne's Gate to the tenth floor of the sterile tower block overlooking Waterloo Station. Since 1961 his deputy had been John Bruce-Lockhart, the former head of the German stations who had rescued SIS's reputation in Washington DC and then replaced the irascible George Young. Internally, as a reflection of the government's interest in the emerging, newly independent countries in the dark continent, and the conflict with Rhodesia, White separated Godfrey Paulson's combined Middle East and Africa Controllerate and in 1963 passed responsibility to Allan Rowley for providing intelligence on Rhodesia within John Debenham Taylor's new Africa Controllerate. Major Rowley had joined SIS in November 1948, having won the Military Cross in Burma at the end of the war, and had served in Egypt, Addis Ababa,

Turkey, Rangoon and Singapore. Most recently he had returned from a three-year secondment to the Australian Secret Intelligence Service.

With John Briance, who had spent twelve years in the Palestine Police, as his PS/CSS wielding his axe, White transformed the upper reaches of SIS by promoting Tim Milne, back from Japan, as Controller Middle East; Stevenson Mackenzie, after four years in Buenos Aires, as Controller Western Hemisphere; and Ellis Morgan, formerly of Rangoon, Bangkok, Hong Kong, Singapore and, most recently the New Delhi station, as Controller Far East. The objective was to invigorate the Service, move the Chief's pawns around the board so as to protect those individuals compromised by Philby and Blake, and establish new stations manned by experienced personnel. This was a constant juggling act, balancing scarce resources against the best calibre of new recruits, and deploying the right men in the field, and White was especially handicapped by the knowledge that, from the safety of Moscow, both Philby and Blake would be scouring the Foreign Office's *Green Book* to spot the SIS officers working overseas under diplomatic cover, and then listing them for the KGB. The result could be benign, or maybe harassment or worse, but in an organisation dependent on personal relationships and plenty of overseas postings, the challenge of covering the world's trouble-spots in time to provide useful CX should not be under-estimated. If that is not a full-time occupation, the Chief also has to negotiate with the Treasury, cultivate the Cabinet Secretary and maintain harmonious relations with the Foreign Office PUS and Secretary of State. And all at a time when the public had come to believe, through novelists and newspaper reports, that the intelligence community was populated by double-dealing traitors and incompetents who routinely abandoned their agents, betrayed their sources and lied for a living.

White's relations with his foreign secretaries during Harold Wilson's premiership, briefly Patrick Gordon-Walker, Michael Stewart (twice) and George Brown, were always coloured by SIS's ambivalence over Rhodesia. As a colony, Rhodesia's Special Branch had an established liaison relationship with the Security Service, through Bill Magan's E Branch, but the prospect of conflict, and the Prime Minister's demands on the JIC required a renewed collection effort. This was easily achieved in the sense that SIS's man in Salisbury, Jack Beauman, was declared to his opposite number, Ken Flower, the emigrant from Cornwall who ran the Rhodesian Central Intelligence Organisation. When the CIO had been created in October 1963 Flower had taken White's advice on its structure, and Beauman's attitude was that, whatever the dispute with Wilson's Labour government in London, SIS's role was to keep open a line of communication to the rebels. The precedent, of course, had been the Chief's determination to maintain good relations with the CIA during the Suez Crisis, whatever the disagreement between their political masters. In consequence, SIS's reporting from the front line failed to alert the JIC to the likelihood of a Unilateral Declaration of Independence, which took place in November 1965, and then neglected to show how sanctions were being systematically evaded by Ian Smith's illegal regime. Because of reliance on the liaison relationship, SIS somehow missed these two major events.

The task of monitoring Rhodesia within Taylor's Africa Controllerate fell to John Main, an SIS officer since 1952. Thereafter he had served in Stockholm, Vientiane and Djakarta, and he sifted the CX for the JIC Chairman, Sir Bernard Burrows, until his transfer to the New York station in 1966. Taken by surprise by Smith's coup, Wilson found the JIC's assessments on Rhodesia to be thoroughly unhelpful and demanded action from SIS, preferably to replace Smith. The task eventually fell to John da Silva, who returned from the Washington DC station in September 1969 after a long SIS career in the Middle East, but there were no suitable candidates for recruitment in Salisbury from where Neville French was expelled in 1966, followed by Anthony Freemantle in January 1969. Freemantle had joined SIS in 1961 after national service with the RAF and had been posted to Mogadishu and Basra before going to Rhodesia in December 1967. Having unwisely predicted in January 1966 that Smith's regime would collapse in 'weeks rather than months' Wilson became increasingly frustrated at SIS's apparent inability to influence events in Rhodesia, and would not learn for years of the scale of the sanctions-busting. Although the Royal Navy ran a Beira patrol to blockade oil deliveries to Lonhro's oil pipeline terminal at Umtali, Rhodesia received continuous supplies through Mozambique, Zambia and South Africa, to the extent that petrol rationing was abandoned in 1971. All United Nations restrictions were circumvented with ease by the South Africans and Portuguese, and SIS reports from Pretoria, detailing the Rhodesian countermeasures and written by Robert Sloan and John Quine, were ignored. Similarly, a new station was established at the Consulate-General in Lourenço Marques, manned by Paul Homberger, formerly of the Caracas Station, with John Pilkington watching the trains in Beira. SIS's other principal station in the region, Dar-es-Salaam, was opened by W. J. R. P. G. (Bill) Dawson in April 1964, who was transferred from Lomé, and Daphne Park was sent to Lusaka in 1964 where she was joined by MI5's Tony Crassweller. As SIS's focus shifted to Africa, the stations in Lima, Montevideo and Rio closed, another manifestation of the Chief's strategy.

The CIO found plenty of willing collaborators who offered to help Smith's economy. The Chief of the French SDECE, General Eugene Guibaud, had once worked on a farm in Rhodesia and was keen to assist. Similarly, SISMI's General Michelli harboured fond memories of prewar Italian Somaliland and knew that Smith had been sheltered by Italian partisans when he had been an RAF fighter pilot on the run from the Nazis. The large Greek expatriate community in Rhodesia mobilised their political connections at home, and the CIO found friends in Zaire, Biafra, Chad and Togo, all countries that were anxious to trade with the supposedly beleaguered regime. In reality, it was SIS that was isolated within the international intelligence community, half-heartedly attempting to enforce the UN sanctions which were being undermined or ignored by much of the rest of the world.

When one of SIS's enterprises, a propaganda scheme run by 'Interform Great Britain Limited' from an accommodation address in Dover Street, was exposed in December 1966 by Ian Colvin of the *Daily Telegraph*, nobody in Whitehall made the connection between the veteran journalist and his oldest friend, Nicholas Elliott, then promoted as White's new Controller Western Europe. When he left Century House in March 1969 no objections were raised when he joined the board of Lonhro, a public company managing huge investments in Rhodesia.

Harold Wilson was later to complain that he was never told about the scale of the sanctions-busting schemes devised by the CIO, or even that

British Petroleum was one of the principal offenders, but the information featured in the JIC assessments. However, SIS chose not to highlight the issue because Ken Flower, who continued to travel to England regularly to see his family, continued to act as a link to the Smith regime. Although Flower was never on SIS's books formally as an agent, he was regarded as an exceptionally helpful communications channel, and played a key role whenever, periodically, negotiations were opened to reach a settlement. Indeed, Flower was still directing the CIO in 1979 when Mrs Thatcher's administration reopened discussions and, after three months, reached an agreement after talks at Lancaster House, which he attended. Thereafter Robert Mugabe, the new Prime Minister of Zimbabwe, invited Flower to continue as the CIO's Director, a post he filled until the death of his wife in November 1981.

White's other experiences in Africa were not dissimilar to the frustrations of Rhodesia, although in strategic terms only Nigeria and Kenya were to be of any economic significance to Britain. However, the KGB's interest in the newly independent countries showed them to be vulnerable, and reluctantly SIS embarked in 1960 on a programme to establish stations in parallel to MI5's network of Security Liaison Officers spread across key members of the Commonwealth. Frank Steele, who had served in the Colonial Service in northern Uganda before he had joined SIS in 1951, was commissioned after three years in Tripoli to advise on a structure for SIS in Africa, but it would take years for his recommendations to be acted upon. Until Steele's survey, conducted in 1956, SIS's sub-Saharan presence had been non-existent, but thereafter Bunny Pantcheff moved to Lagos in October 1958; (Dame) Daphne Park reached Leopoldville in 1959; Stephen Longrigg went to Dakar and Ivor Rowsell and Sandy Goschen to Mogadishu in 1960; Michael Oatley was posted to Nairobi and Craig Smellie to Khartoum in 1961, and Robert Dawson to Lomé in 1962. The result of SIS's belated effort to establish a presence was a paucity of CX in respect of either the Rhodesian crisis, or the civil war in Nigeria which erupted without much advance warning in 1967.

With postwar service in Austria and Berlin, Goschen had been sent from the Baghdad station in December 1966 to Lagos where he operated under cover in the High Commission until June 1969, with his deputy,

Charles Gardner, declared to his hosts, the MI5-trained Nigerian Intelligence Service. In that same year Gardner, a life-long bachelor who had been born Israel Gold in Kalusz, Austria, in the First World War, was transferred to Nairobi at the request of Jomo Kenyatta to build a local intelligence agency, the Directorate of Security Intelligence, in addition to the Special Branch that had been nurtured for many years by MI5's Walter Bell. This was a post that, most unusually, with assistance from Desmond Harney who had been in Kenya since 1964, Gardner was to fill continuously until his retirement in 1980, and provide SIS an invaluable window on East Africa, even though other officers continued to be posted to Nairobi to run the station. Whereas White would authorise the creation of new stations in Pretoria, Accra and Kinshasa, none would make a significant contribution to the prosecution of the Cold War, or inhibit growing Chinese, Cuban, Soviet or East German operations across the region.

White possessed great personal charm and modesty, but although he was a member of the Garrick Club, which has a reputation for frivolity and indiscretion, with a membership drawn from the law, the stage, journalism and politics, he always kept his reserve and was regarded as slightly isolated and aloof by his staff, in contrast to Menzies who had enjoyed frequent informal conversations over drinks in the evening with his senior, blue-blooded staff, such as David Boyle, Count Fanny Vanden Heuvel, Peter Koch de Gooreynd and Wilfred ('Biffy') Dunderdale. Even the junior personnel, who referred to the Chief as 'the August Presence', were ushered in to see him for a pep-talk and a chat before taking up a new post.

When Desmond Bristow had been seen off to the Madrid station by Menzies in May 1947, to replace an SIS officer given a silent *persona non grata* after an incident in which one of his agents had been compromised, he had been impressed:

> As a result of that chat, C took on a completely different hue for me. He had given me a very wide latitude, certainly much wider than the one I had formulated in my own mind, about my job in Spain. The chat definitely elated me.[19]

White, however, had been cut from different cloth and rarely saw the need to offer any personal words of support to his station commanders. Unlike all his predecessors, he had never led men into combat and, with his modest, lower-middle-class background, his father having owned an ironmonger's shop in Tonbridge, he was mildly socially insecure, a certain shyness that manifested itself as diffidence. He never had the ability to mix easily with the 'other ranks' and at the same time was ill at ease with the aristocratic plutocracy that Menzies had surrounded himself with so naturally. White's hesitancy in such circles was interpreted by others as an attitude to his colleagues approaching contempt but he nevertheless saw himself as a gentleman, if not one from the top drawer. This concept is not unimportant in the intelligence community. Professor R. V. Jones recalled that the Danish physicist Niels Bohr had confided to him that 'He had been happy to cooperate with the British Secret Service because he found that it was run by a gentleman.'[20] White was indeed a gentleman, but one from a high street in Kent, not the rolling countryside of Leicestershire so enjoyed by the Quorn with which Menzies had hunted.

White's lasting contribution to the intelligence community was undoubtedly his alliance in 1968 with Denis Greenhill and Burke Trend to reform the JIC by giving it greater independence. The JIC had been moved away from the Foreign Office in 1957, following the Suez disaster, and had been replanted firmly within the Cabinet Office, now with its own Assessment Staff divided into Current Intelligence Groups, and no longer reporting to the Chiefs of Staff. These sub-units, manned by personnel on secondment from other departments and services, had provided a separate filter for the interpretation of intelligence offered by the various collection agencies, and represented the largest single reform of the JIC since its creation in 1936. Furthermore, White's system would remain in place until it was dissected by the committee chaired by Lord Franks following the Falklands Conflict of 1982.

While White's reform gave responsibility to a separate, independent organisation for the scrutiny of CX and the preparation of assessments, one of the consequences was a reduction in the capacity of Century House to conduct its own expert analysis. Some of White's critics saw the erosion of this core function as an attempt by the Chief to marginalise the Soviet Bloc elite, men like Frank Rendle and David Peck, who had become highly professional Kremlin watchers. Rendle had served in Indonesia, and Peck had completed a tour, almost certainly betrayed by George Blake, at the Moscow station in 1957. According to the Australian journalist Brian Crozier, who had been recruited as a source by SIS's Donald Lancaster in Singapore, Peck 'was, in the view of some leading experts, the best Sovietologist in the country, although the least known by the nature of his career'.[21] However, like so many others compromised by Blake, they could not hope to operate under cover abroad again without attracting the attention of the KGB, so their future lay at head office. By reducing SIS's analytical capacity White was perceived by some as attempting to shift the balance of power within the organisation, which effectively was split between those with Far East, Middle East and Soviet interests. White himself had never served overseas, apart from a spell in Europe with the 21st Army Group at the end of the war, and various visits abroad, and knew nothing of the disciplines and pressures of running a station in a foreign environment. However, he clearly understood, from his experience in MI5 where the so-called 'Malayan Mafia' wielded extraordinarily disproportionate influence, of the camaraderie and cohesion of officers who have together faced common adversaries. In such circumstances, as happened in the Security Service, the subtleties of office politics and personal loyalties developed in the field can prove surprisingly strong, especially in a crisis. Under his predecessors the Soviet specialists had been SIS's driving force, but White saw a wider picture, and the concentration on Moscow diminished to move the emphasis onto the Labour government's preoccupations in Aden, Oman and Borneo where British troops were engaged, sometimes in a clandestine role, in unpublicised regional conflicts.

When White finally retired from Whitehall in 1972 he lived in a modern, timber-frame house he had built himself at Burpham, near Arundel in Sussex, with his wife Kate, leading a vegetarian existence and writing poetry. By then his sons Stephen, a television film producer, and his mildly handicapped elder son Adrian, had left home, giving him the opportunity to meet and talk to writers expressing an interest in the history of the Security Service.

This was an odd departure for the man who had opposed the

preparation of the official history *British Intelligence in the Second World War* and had protested vehemently when Sir John Masterman had sought permission to release a sanitised version of *The Double Cross System of the War of 1939–1945*, even if his brother had been chairman of the Publishers Association. It may be that White was troubled by the unresolved issues of Soviet penetration and sought to use other researchers as surrogates, or maybe he simply could not resist meddling. Either way, he gave strong hints to the BBC journalist Andrew Boyle, who was writing *Climate of Treason* about the Cambridge spies, that Professor Sir Anthony Blunt had spied for the Soviets and betrayed his country. Boyle, who disguised the true name of the spy to avoid legal action, got only part of the story, asserting that 'Maurice' had been granted a royal pardon soon after the defections of Burgess and Maclean, whereas in fact Blunt had accepted an immunity from prosecution in April 1964. White had known the full details of Blunt's confession, but why he chose to open that Pandora's box in 1979 remains a mystery. Whatever his reasons, he later cooperated with Andrew Boyle on his own biography, although the project had to be completed by Tom Bower after the death of both men.

White died on 22 February 1993, of cancer, and at his memorial service held at the Guards Chapel, Wellington Barracks, the lessons were read by the current heads of the two services he had led: Dame Stella Rimington for MI5, and Colin McColl for SIS.

Chapter VI

John Rennie 1968–1973

> 'The high point of FO/FCO control was probably reached in 1968 with the appointment as head of SIS (known as "C") of a Deputy Under-Secretary in the FCO.'
>
> Robert Cecil in *British and American Approaches to Intelligence*[1]

THE only Chief, apart from his predecessor, to have been appointed from outside the Service, Rennie had no background in intelligence, although he had spent five years, 1953–8, running the Information Research Department, the Foreign Office's propaganda arm created by Christopher Mayhew early in 1948 to counter Soviet mastery in the field. Rennie's appointment, by the Labour Foreign Secretary Michael Stewart, was a surprising choice, but was supported by the PUS, Sir Denis Greenhill. The fact that White had not groomed a successor, and was unwilling to recommend either of the two obvious internal candidates, Christopher Phillpotts and Maurice Oldfield, and had left the matter entirely to the mercurial George Brown, or his successor Michael Stewart, was not to his credit. Indeed, Oldfield had served as White's deputy since 1966, following the early retirement to Warwick University, at the age of fifty-one, of John Bruce-Lockhart, so White's reluctance to recommend him in particular was inexplicable, and a subject White never addressed.

Born in Marylebone in January 1914 to a match manufacturer, Rennie had been educated at Wellington and Balliol College, Oxford, and, after graduating with a third-class degree in modern history, had spent four years in New York as an advertising executive, where he had married a Swiss, Anne-Marie Godat, who bore him one son. A talented painter, he had been exhibited at the Royal Academy in 1930 and 1931, and at the Paris Salon in 1932. A week after the outbreak of war he had joined the Consular Service in Baltimore. In September 1940 he transferred to the British Press Service in New York and then moved to the British Information Service before returning to London in January 1946, when he formally joined the Foreign Office. Three years later, in March 1949, he had been posted to Washington DC with the rank of First Secretary (Commercial), and in June 1951 went to Warsaw. Following his unusually long stint in IRD, where Nigel Clive (who himself ran IRD for three years) says he was 'widely admired for his skill and ingenuity', Rennie was posted to Buenos Aires as Minister (Commercial) in April 1958, and then in November 1960 went straight to Washington DC where he served alongside Maurice Oldfield and Denis Greenhill. In 1964, having returned to London to take a year off to nurse his terminally ill wife, he was promoted to Assistant Under-Secretary in charge of the Americas, concentrating on the dispute between Guatemala and British Honduras. He spent the following year on loan to the Civil Service Commission, chairing the interview board. In October 1966 he was back at the Foreign Office, having been promoted to Deputy Under-Secretary for Defence, and having married a widow, Mrs Jennifer Rycroft, by whom he had two more sons. The following year he was knighted.

At the time of his appointment Rennie was hardly on a fast track to the top of the Foreign Office. He had served as a lacklustre diplomat, but had the advantage of a long friendship with Greenhill, the influential PUS. His other advantage was having Oldfield as his deputy, doubtless to the irritation of Phillpotts who took early retirement in 1970, at the age of forty-five, after an impressive career in SIS that had included the stations at Copenhagen, Athens, Paris and Washington DC. Having served in Royal Navy gunboats in the English Channel during the war, Phillpotts, who was the son of an admiral, had made his mark in Greece where he had played a key role in intercepting weapons destined for the EOKA terrorists in Cyprus, work for which he had been decorated.

Phillpotts's handicap was that he had been appointed Director of Counter-Intelligence in succession to Geoffrey Hinton at a time when molehunts were being conducted to root out officers who had concealed past membership of the CPGB. Phillpotts had latched on to Andrew King and Donald Prater, and had challenged their assertions that their prewar adherence to the Party had been declared years earlier, and was of no significance. Both men had held key positions in SIS, and if they had been Soviet sources the implications would have been catastrophic.

A graduate of Magdalene College, Cambridge, King had joined the Z Organisation under London Films cover to undertake missions in Austria and Germany before the war. Once hostilities had begun King had joined SIS formally and had worked in Switzerland throughout the war, successfully running an important Polish agent, Halina Szymanska, who was in touch with the Abwehr chief, Admiral Wilhelm Canaris. This link was of considerable significance and by the time King had returned to London in 1946 he had acquired an enviable reputation as a skilful case officer, having handled one of the most sensitive sources of the war. In October 1950 he went to Vienna as head of station, and in 1953 handed over to George Berry. In 1958 he had been posted to Hong Kong for three years. When Phillpotts reviewed King's case, he thought it likely that King might have been vulnerable to blackmail by the Soviets, and King accordingly left SIS in 1967, aged fifty-two, to spend half his retirement in the Philippines where his open homosexuality went unremarked.

Phillpotts was equally concerned about Prater, who was recalled from Stockholm, where he had been head of station since 1965, to undergo interrogation. Born in Australia and a graduate of Corpus Christi, Oxford, Prater had been badly wounded in North Africa in 1942, and had joined SIS in 1946. He served at postings in Singapore, Düsseldorf, Vienna and Beirut, where he had handled Philby, and agreed to resign before his fiftieth birthday to take up an academic appointment, lecturing in German at the University of Canterbury in New Zealand. In later years Prater was to build an impressive reputation as a scholar and biographer, and retired to Geneva before finally returning to Cambridge. While Phillpotts could prove only that King and Berry had failed to declare their prewar CPGB membership, he remained suspicious of them.

Having spent two years in Washington DC at the height of the CIA's ruthless molehunts, Phillpotts took the view that SIS must be entirely cleansed of all potential contamination and his subordinates there, successively Stephen Longrigg and Stephen de Mowbray, were indoctrinated into James Angleton's labyrinthine theories of Soviet penetration. The discovery of George Blake had forced a general acknowledgment that there was nothing obsessive about the belief that SIS had been one of the KGB's prime targets, and that the security procedures needed to be tightened up. Others saw the entire process as corrosive, and at times ludicrous, such as the moment when Theo ('Bunny') Pantcheff toured the Africa stations seeking evidence of penetration, confiding in his subordinates that he had identified the redoubtable Daphne Park as a suspect. Such preoccupations struck some of the old hands as idiotic, but the senior management, conscious that another George Blake could ruin the Service, opted for the ruthless approach.

Both King and Prater were dismissed, and others, like Tony Milne who had been close to Philby's first wife Litzi Friedman, chose to depart voluntarily, leaving some colleagues with the impression that a witch-hunt had been conducted, thereby making the ebullient Phillpotts few friends in an organisation where trust is an essential and valued commodity. He had also been the bearer of bad tidings over Dick Ellis, SIS's Australian-born postwar Controller Far East, who confessed in 1966 to having sold secrets to the Germans from the Paris station before the war. While admitting that he had betrayed much of the information found in Nazi files which had been attributed mistakenly to Sigismund Best and Richard Stevens, the two SIS officers abducted at Venlo in November 1939, Ellis insisted that he had never spied for the Soviets. By that time Ellis had long retired, but had been re-employed by SIS to weed the files in anticipation of the move from Broadway, and his protests had been disbelieved by his interrogators, Bunny Pantcheff and MI5's Anne Orr-Ewing, and by Phillpotts. Ellis had joined SIS in Paris after graduating from the Sorbonne and, after a brief stint in Istanbul, had been attached to the PCO in Berlin until 1938 from where he had been recalled to supervise technical coverage of the German embassy's telephones in London. Soon after the tapping had begun, the Germans had inexplicably become uncharacteristically discreet, as though they had been tipped off. After the war, which Ellis had spent in New York with British Security Coordination, he had been Controller Far East and Controller Western Hemisphere, until his retirement in 1953 to help develop the fledgling Australian Secret Intelligence Service. As a spy for the Germans, Ellis had obviously done immense harm; if he had been a spy for the Soviets, the ramifications were incalculable.

A lengthy investigation, codenamed EMERTON and conducted by William Steedman, formerly head of the Bonn and Berne stations, concluded that Ellis most likely had succumbed to Soviet pressure after the war, but the matter was never resolved, and he died in July 1975, still in contact with a characteristically forgiving Maurice Oldfield. Peter Wright, who participated in the Ellis interrogation, described Oldfield as:

> . . . a shy and a good man. But he was a poor judge of character.
>
> Even though we had uncovered a traitor of major proportions, I sometimes felt as if it were I who was being blamed. Oldfield despised the climate of fear engendered by Phillpotts' vetting purge, and campaigned hard to change Dick's mind. The fact that Ellis had confessed seemed to weigh hardly at all on his thinking. As far as he was concerned, it was all a long time ago, and best forgotten.[2]

Wright disapproved of Oldfield's forgiving nature, but there can be no doubt that Oldfield remained on good terms with Ellis. Indeed, after Ellis had died and the first disclosures emerged of Ellis's treachery, his family and supporters pointed to his correspondence with Oldfield, which remained cordial until the end of his life. In fact, of course, this was simply another example of Oldfield's kindness, even if it was misguided. However, the greatest surprise to those who were indoctrinated into Ellis's confession was that the evidence against him had been available since 1945 when the Sicherheitsdienst chief, Walter Schellenberg, had stated under interrogation that the Germans had received information from a certain Captain Ellis before the war. When the relevant report was checked, it was discovered that it had been annotated by none other than Kim Philby, who had scrawled in the margin 'who is this Ellis?' At the time, Ellis's office was a few doors away, in the same corridor in Broadway Buildings. As for the evidence that Ellis had sold out to the Soviets too, there seemed to be just two items. Firstly, it was known that the German section running Ellis before the war had been penetrated by the Soviets, so there was a good chance that they had become aware of his role for the Nazis. Secondly, it was known that after Philby's recall to London in 1951 and his dismissal, Ellis had flown back to see him. If they had plotted together, Ellis refused to admit it, even under the most persistent questioning by Steedman who had pursued the case through the German files since 1949, with gaps for his three-year tours of duty in Bonn and Berne in 1953 and 1960 respectively. Rewarded with a CBE and a second, final posting to Bonn in September 1966, Steedman went into retirement in December 1969. According to him, Ellis could have been caught twenty years earlier if successive SIS Chiefs had devoted sufficient resources to checking on Schellenberg's allegation. To Phillpotts's disbelief, he had been reprimanded by Oldfield for using 'Gestapo methods' to extract Ellis's confession. However, by the time he retired Phillpotts had fired another of Philby's close friends, and had uncovered a scandal in Egypt where a member of the Cairo station had been conducting a homosexual affair with his East German source.

Some in SIS believed the molehunts had gone too far, but only a very few indoctrinated officers knew the full implications of the KGB's continuing efforts to penetrate the British establishment. MI5, where only a few officers were aware, for example, of Blunt's confession in 1964, believed that there were clues to current penetration to be found in the relationships forged among undergraduates immediately before the war. Research into events that had taken place more than thirty years earlier, aided by the cryptographic window offered by the VENONA decrypts, showed that the NKVD and GRU had been tremendously active in London during and after the war, and that there were dozens of spies referred to in the partially-broken texts who had not been identified completely. How many had gravitated, with expert advice from the notorious Cambridge spies, towards SIS and GCHQ?

Within four months of taking office, having complained he had been kept isolated for much of that time, Rennie learned the hard way how thin on the ground his officers were in Eastern Europe. When Soviet tanks rolled into Czechoslovakia in August 1968, SIS was taken completely by surprise. There had been no advance warning and no reports from the Prague station to indicate that an invasion was imminent. As the Warsaw Pact troops tightened their grip on the country, and brought to an end Dubcek's flirtation with democratic socialism, SIS was devoid of sources. Fortunately GCHQ was able to provide hour-by-hour commentaries, based on intercepted radio conversations exchanged between Prague's taxi drivers, monitored at the NSA's base on top of the Teufelsberg in Berlin, but Rennie was conscious of SIS's shortcomings.

The reason for the lapse was in part the shift of emphasis developed by White when he had responded to the Labour government's demand for information from Africa, long regarded in SIS as a career backwater. Prior to independence, responsibility for security had been in the hands of MI5 Security Liaison Officers, but as Ghana, Nigeria, Sierra Leone and the new countries in East Africa established their own administrations, SIS saw the need to gather intelligence, especially when Biafra attempted to break away from Nigeria, and Ian Smith declared Rhodesia's unilateral independence. White had authorised the opening of new stations across the continent, but without additional funding inevitably there had been a cut in the coverage in Central Europe, with actual closures in Central and South America.

At home, the publication of Philby's mischievous memoirs, *My Silent War*, with a foreword written by Graham Greene, caused much irritation at Century House, although the traitor's remarks about White and Oldfield were entirely laudatory. From an operational standpoint, the book was far from damaging, and the principal victim seemed to be Philby's wartime adversary, Felix Cowgill, who was shown an advance copy of the galley proofs at his home in Wiltshire to gauge his reaction. Now long retired, Cowgill was not particularly interested, and the decision was taken to maintain a discreet silence on Philby's disclosures. The sting of much of them had been removed the previous year when the *Sunday Times* had publicised Philby's defection in January 1963 and shown the hollowness of Harold Macmillan's statement in 1955.

The other unwelcome development in the early part of Rennie's period as Chief was the thorny issue of Northern Ireland, where Ted Heath became frustrated by the inability of the local administration, the Army and the Royal Ulster Constabulary (RUC) Special Branch to cooperate and collect intelligence on the Provisional Irish Republican Army (PIRA). Even MI5's new Director-General, Michael Hanley, had been reluctant to get his organisation embroiled in the province, but had agreed to second David Eastwood to act as a security adviser; Eastwood was later to be followed by Denis Payne.

Heath had demanded that SIS play a role in Belfast, but Rennie and Oldfield had been very reluctant to commit their personnel to the quagmire. Internment, always opposed by the Army as counter-productive, had failed, not least because the RUC had relied on out-of-date information, and the province suffered from quite enough overlapping jurisdictions, but Heath was convinced MI5 did not have the political skills required to address the many issues raised by the paramilitaries. The Army had been called in to keep the two communities apart, but whereas the RUC was widely distrusted by the republican, Roman Catholic minority who saw the predominantly Protestant police as too closely associated to the loyalists, they did have confidence in the military. MI5, on the other hand, had made no headway, and Heath believed SIS could have a role, despite SIS's position that, constitutionally, Ulster was not a foreign country or somewhere it should be operating. However, there was one awkward and potentially sinister development that undermined the stance initially taken by Century House, which was a sudden interest in Ireland by the Soviets who in 1971 upgraded their mission in Dublin to the status of an embassy. At the time the only link between Dzerzhinsky Square and the IRA was a vague allegation, made by General Jan Sejna, former chief of the Romanian intelligence service, the DIE, who had defected in February 1968 to the CIA. During his debriefing Sejna had alleged that the KGB had funded the IRA and that his own organisation had acted as surrogates, providing training to IRA terrorists. No evidence had emerged at the time to support these assertions, although Sejna's credibility, as the most senior Warsaw Pact officer ever to defect, was not in doubt, but the influx of Soviet journalists and diplomats to Dublin certainly suggested Sejna had been on the right track.

Of course, the Prime Minister's view prevailed finally, and Frank Steele arrived at Laneside, a quiet villa overlooking Belfast Lough in October 1971 as deputy to the UK Representative, Sir Howard Smith. Steele had served in Basra, Cairo, Tripoli and Beirut, and had just returned from three years in Nairobi when he went to Northern Ireland, initially on attachment to the Home Office, but after the imposition of direct rule from London. in March 1972, to the Northern Ireland Office. Steele's task was to develop a line of communication to the Provisional IRA, so a truce could be negotiated, and this he achieved. The first Secretary of State for Northern Ireland, Willie Whitelaw, wanted to speak directly to the PIRA leadership, and Steele arranged the meeting, first having obtained agreement to new conditions for the republican detainees in prison in the province, the so-called 'special category status', and the freedom for the PIRA delegation to choose its composition. When the names were submitted, they included a young Gerry Adams, a former barman widely regarded as the commander of PIRA's Ballymurphy battalion in the Belfast brigade, and then a prisoner in the Long Kesh internment camp. Adams was released for the preliminary talks held at the end of June 1972, in which a teacher, David O'Connell, represented PIRA's Southern Command, and Steele was accompanied by (Sir) Philip Woodfield of the Northern Ireland Office. O'Connell had been imprisoned on both sides of the border, having served six years in Crumlin Road prison for his part in the ill-fated IRA campaign of 1962, and six months in the Republic after a raid in January 1957 on the RUC barracks in Brookeborough. On that occasion O'Connell had been badly wounded in the stomach, and had lost a knuckle on his right hand. More recently, O'Connell had been implicated in an attempt to smuggle a cargo of weapons from Czechoslovakia to Ireland, in October 1971. On that occasion a Belgian DC-3, loaded with four tons of mortars, bazookas and grenades, had been impounded at Schipol, but O'Connell and his girlfriend had evaded capture.

Terms for a temporary truce were agreed between the two sides, and plans were made for a further meeting, to be held in London, with Whitelaw. The RUC noted that Adams was collected from Long Kesh by two sisters, Dolours and Marion Price, who were later to be convicted of terrorist offences in London.

The delegation, apart from the PIRA founders Adams and O'Connell, consisted of Sean MacStiofan, Martin McGuinness, Ivor Bell and Seamus Twomey. According to the RUC, MacStiofan, born John Stephenson, formerly an RAF corporal, was PIRA's director of intelligence;

McGuinness had been a butcher; Bell was a mechanic; Twomey a bookie. The seventh man was a Dublin solicitor, Miles Shevlin who, though billed to act as a note-taker, was to take a leading role in the discussions. The group was met by Steele at the border with Donegal on the morning of 7 July 1972 and flown in a helicopter to RAF Aldergrove where an Andover was on the tarmac for a flight to RAF Benson. From there Special Branch cars drove them to 92 Cheyne Walk, the home overlooking the Thames of Whitelaw's junior minister, Paul Channon, where the Northern Ireland Secretary was waiting for them.

The talks proved completely unsuccessful, with MacStiofan announcing that his conditions were a British withdrawal from Ulster, recognition of Eire's sovereignty and an amnesty for all prisoners, detainees and fugitives. Whitelaw, who had been led to expect an atmosphere of conciliation, was shocked by MacStiofan's bizarrely misguided, aggressive attitude but listened to what he regarded as an unrealistic rant. No agreement was reached apart from a proposal to hold a further dialogue, and Steele accompanied the PIRA men back to Londonderry, noting that Bell and Twomey seemed the most intransigent, whereas McGuinness and Adams had been relatively quiet and thoughtful. On the flight back Steele attempted to explain some of the political realities of the parliamentary process in London, asserting that successive British governments would exercise unlimited patience in the future to contain Republican violence, and that any prospect of a military victory against the British Army was a mere pipe-dream. In casual conversation he discovered that McGuinness had never visited England before, and had only once been to Scotland, to indulge his passion for fly-fishing. His first trip to London had a profound effect on him and had also served to sow the seeds of doubt in Adams. However, PIRA security was very leaky, and word of the secret meeting at Cheyne Walk spread, placing Whitelaw in such an impossible position that he considered resignation, but instead, with the support of Heath and the Cabinet, made a statement to Parliament acknowledging the stories circulating in Dublin, that confidential talks had taken place.[3] While the Commons was understanding, the Unionists reacted with fury at what they perceived, after the concessions to republican prisoners, to be further signs of betrayal.

Within two days of the PIRA delegation's return the cease-fire collapsed during a sectarian confrontation on a housing estate in West Belfast. Steele remained at Laneside, and SIS concentrated on O'Connell. In March 1973 he only narrowly escaped arrest when the crew of a tramp steamer, the *Claudia*, was arrested off the coast of County Waterford. The *Claudia* had been loaded with five tons of weapons in Tripoli, the first of several PIRA attempts to smuggle Libyan guns and explosives into the Republic. This particular operation had been masterminded, not by PIRA, but by SIS, which had monitored the movement of the ship and its crew from the moment it had sailed to the Mediterranean from Hamburg. In overall command, in close contact with Rennie, was an SIS officer who had served in Paris, Warsaw, Singapore and, most recently Santo Domingo.

In September 1972, two months after the London talks, Seamus Twomey, by then PIRA's chief of staff, was arrested in Monaghan after a bank raid and charged with possession of £3,500 in stolen notes. He was convicted, but was rescued from Mountjoy prison at the end of October 1973 by a helicopter. Of the other visitors to Cheyne Walk, Martin McGuinness was to be arrested in Buncrana, convicted of PIRA membership in the Republic and serve a twelve-month sentence; Ivor Bell, a Long Kesh escapee and now commander of PIRA's Belfast brigade, was caught in Belfast in April 1974. As for MacStiofan, effectively PIRA's leader, he was imprisoned in Dublin in December 1972, and was to lose influence over the organisation, leaving it to McGuinness and Adams to take the political initiative and eventually to be elected to Westminster. While it may have been 'the long game' and taken twenty years, the Cheyne Walk meeting was unquestionably the very start of the Irish peace process.

In July 1973 Steele returned to London and was replaced by Craig Smellie, a pipe-smoking Arabist with experience in Alexandria, Baghdad, Rome, Khartoum and Tripoli, who was sent to Belfast for an unsuccessful two years to sort out the inter-agency rivalries. As Oldfield and Rennie had predicted, the exercise served only to compound the muddle, although in later years Michael Oatley, another Africa hand with experience in Nairobi, Kampala, Lomé and Accra, was to accomplish far more by opening a clandestine line of communication to the Provisional IRA leadership.

While on the one hand Rennie was attempting to make headway in the fog of Northern Ireland, PIRA had become a key target for SIS, but in December 1972 Patrick Crinnion, a member of the Gardai's Special Branch was arrested in Dublin with his SIS contact, John Wyman, and both men were charged with breaching Ireland's Official Secrets Act, together with another SIS officer, Andrew Johnstone, who was never apprehended. At their trial they were sentenced to six months' imprisonment, and released immediately because of the time they had spent in custody on remand. The incident highlighted the occupational hazards of cultivating 'unofficial assistance' from friendly governments, and Rennie was obliged to take the political flak for an operation mounted to gain access to the Gardai's very extensive files on a common foe.

Probably the most memorable event during the period of Rennie's tenure was the defection of Oleg Lyalin, the culmination of a recruitment achieved by a joint MI5–SIS group which had targeted potentially vulnerable suspected KGB and GRU professionals. SIS's man on the team was Tony Brooks, a former SOE agent in Lyons who had won the DSO while still a teenager. After the war Brooks had been absorbed into SIS and had organised stay-behind networks in Eastern Europe, working from the Sofia and Belgrade stations.

During routine surveillance Lyalin had been spotted conducting an illicit relationship with his secretary, Irina Templyakova, and had agreed to trade information in return for eventual resettlement in Britain, but in August 1971 his defection had been forced when he was arrested on a drink-drive charge by the traffic police in London's West End. This unexpected development prompted Operation FOOT, the expulsion of ninety Soviet diplomats known to be KGB or GRU officers, mostly already identified by Lyalin, who were working under commercial or other covers in London, and the refusal to readmit a further fifteen who happened to be out of the country. Among the later group was Yuri Voronin, the KGB *rezident*, an exclusion which forced a very junior subordinate, a security officer at the Trade Delegation in Highgate, to assume his duties temporarily. It later years SIS learned from Soviet defectors that this dramatic, unexpected reaction had severely disrupted the Third Department of the KGB's FCD, and had an adverse impact on dozens of intelligence careers. In contrast, the only significant loss among those expelled from the British Embassy in Moscow in retaliation was Hal Doyne-Ditmass, an MI5 officer seconded to the SIS station.

The plan to act against the Soviets had been in preparation since a meeting held at the Foreign Office by the PUS Sir Denis Greenhill on 25 March 1971 attended by C, the Chairman of the JIC Sir Stewart Crawford, the Cabinet Secretary Sir Burke Trend, Sir Martin Furnival Jones of MI5, and the permanent under-secretaries at the Home Office, Ministry of Defence and the DTI. The initiative for removing about a hundred Soviets came from MI5's D-G who complained that:

> In the last fifteen years there had been evidence of penetration of the Foreign and Commonwealth Office, the Ministry of Defence, the Army, Navy and Air Force, the Labour Party, Transport House and the Board of Trade. It was difficult to say exactly how much damage was being done. But it was equally difficult to believe that the Russians maintained such a large establishment for no profit. At least thirty or forty Soviet intelligence officers in this country were actually running secret agents in government or industry.

Following Furnival Jones's presentation, Rennie added that 'the Russians attached high priority to acquiring scientific and technical secrets, and to commercial information with military overtones'. Advocating a mass expulsion, C confirmed that:

> Our Allies in western Europe, far from viewing our action badly, would probably welcome it. It was clear that the French were concerned about the numbers of Russians in their country. They might emulate our action. This would make it difficult for the Russians to switch their trade.

Having examined a table displaying the numbers of Soviet personnel engaged on diplomatic duties in Western Europe, the USA and Japan, which indicated that there were more posted to Britain than anywhere else, the meeting closed with agreement to draft a minute on the subject. Once the Foreign Secretary, Sir Alec Douglas-Home, had been convinced of the necessity to restrict the size of the Soviet Embassy in London, and get rid of the disproportionately large KGB and GRU *rezidenturas* which were draining MI5's limited resources, his task was to persuade the Prime Minister, who was less enthusiastic. However, on 30 July Heath received a memorandum from Home Secretary Reginald Maudling and the Foreign Secretary, in which they pressed the case for action:

> Soviet intelligence officers operate under cover of the various Soviet establishments in this country. Apart from the Soviet Embassy (189) there are the Soviet trade delegation (121), contract inspectors (73), and other organisations such as the TASS news agency, the Aeroflot airline and the Moscow Narodny Bank (134). The total is higher than the Soviet establishment in any other country of Western Europe.[4]

Having reluctantly accepted the need for action, but uncertain over the appropriate timing, Ted Heath agreed to have the matter raised privately with the Soviets, who were anticipated, correctly, to be unresponsive. On 4 August Sir Alec wrote to his Soviet counterpart, Andrei Gromyko, drawing his attention to the problem and illustrating it with a complaint about 'an application for a visa from a man named B. G. Glushchenko, together with the statement that he had been nominated to the post of First Secretary at the Soviet Embassy in London'.

> This man was in Britain from 1964 to 1968. At that time he was described as the representative of *Aviaexport* at the Soviet trade delegation, Mr Clushchenko's activities however had little to do with the sale of aircraft. He came to our notice on various occasions; for example, he offered a large sum of money to a British businessman if he would obtain details of certain British military equipment.[5]

Gromyko failed to reply, so it was decided that the announcement would be made on Saturday, 24 September when the Commons would not be sitting. However, the news of Lyalin's defection leaked, and was published in the *Evening News* on Friday, 24 September, so Operation FOOT was advanced by twenty-four hours, and handled by Greenhill, as Sir Alec had left for New York. Moments after the Soviet chargé had returned to the embassy, after his painful interview with Greenhill, the MI5 watchers were amused to see an unidentified KGB officer sprint across Kensington Palace Gardens from the KGB *referentura* opposite, to the chargé's office in the main embassy building.

Rennie had not been entirely alone in coping with the FOOT crisis, for the firm government response had been supported by the PUS, MI5's Director-General, and of course Dick White, who was still pacing the corridors of Whitehall. Quite simply, White had not been able to afford to retire, and he had persuaded the Cabinet Secretary, Burke Trend, to authorise the creation of a new post, that of Intelligence Coordinator to the Cabinet, to act as a bridge between the Joint Intelligence Committee, the Permanent Under-Secretaries' Committee and the Prime Minister. Some believed the appointment had been made to retain White's unrivalled, encyclopedic knowledge of MI5 and SIS operations over the previous thirty years; others interpreted the move as a lack of confidence in Rennie, and maybe concern about Harold Wilson's Labour government.

Rennie's tenure as Chief was brief, and after just five years he retired, the catalyst being the embarrassment caused when his eldest son Charles and daughter-in-law were arrested in a squat for possession of Chinese heroin and tried at the Old Bailey. Despite the protection of a D Notice, which requested discretion on the identity of SIS's Chief and his personnel, the inevitable publicity in *Stern* and elsewhere in the foreign press, which spilled over to Britain, was too much for Rennie to endure, especially as he had become the first Chief to be a target for terrorists, and he handed over the reins to his deputy, Maurice Oldfield, a few months short of what would gave been his official retirement date, January 1974.

Whereas past Chiefs had probably never been in any physical danger, or subject to direct threats of assassination or abduction, Rennie's position and loss of anonymity had placed him and his family at very considerable risk. Nor was this some vague, unquantified hazard, as was proved in July 1976 when the British Ambassador to Dublin, Christopher Ewart-Biggs, was assassinated. Although widely misidentified as an SIS officer, Ewart-Biggs had always been a regular diplomat, but had acted as SIS's Foreign Office Adviser between 1966 and 1970. As for Rennie, who was to spend his retirement painting and sailing, and occasionally chairing the English

Speaking Union's current affairs committee, he was to remain under close protection until his death in September 1981 at St Thomas's Hospital in Lambeth.

The concern over the disclosure of the Chief's identity may seem anachronistic by today's standards, but even in 1973 newspaper editors deferred to the voluntary code known as the D Notice system. The only book to have described SIS's modern existence was *The Espionage Establishment*, by the American journalists David Wise and Thomas B. Ross, which in 1968 had given a detailed account of Dick White's career and had identified Century House as the current headquarters, and in October 1967 had been serialised in the New York *Saturday Evening Post*. A year later, when Richard Deacon released *A History of the British Secret Service*, arguably the first of a genre, he omitted Rennie's name entirely. Indeed, it was not until 1983, and the publication of *Through the Looking Glass: British Foreign Policy in the Age of Illusions* by an Oxford academic, Anthony Verrier, that Rennie's name gained a wider circulation, Verrier commenting that:

> [Rennie] lacked that close connection with and understanding of SIS which distinguished many of his colleagues. The appointment was not welcomed in Century House, partly because Rennie's heart was not in the intelligence business, but also due to a belief of the men on the tenth floor that a professional SIS could find 'Cs' from its own ranks. Rennie did his best to work amicably with his new confrères but the appointment inevitably meant that relations between the Foreign Office and SIS changed still further from the mutual suspicions of the 1950s and the cautious cordiality of White's years as 'C'. Rennie did not consciously intend to weaken SIS or subordinate it to the Foreign Office. But Rennie's advent as 'C' meant that the Foreign and Commonwealth Office collectively came to regard SIS as part of Whitehall rather than as an independent service.[6]

No doubt there is more than a little truth in Verrier's observation, which is somewhat harsh on Rennie, for SIS was indeed already on its way to becoming a mere adjunct of Whitehall, following the determination of Dick White to create a modern Service relevant to the tasks set by the JIC.

Chapter VII

Maurice Oldfield 1973–1978

'Intelligence is about people and the study of people.'
Maurice Oldfield at a school speechday[1]

ALWAYS recognised as immensely bright, Oldfield had gained a commission in Egypt while serving in Security Intelligence Middle East (SIME) as a sergeant in the Intelligence Corps during the Second World War, and had been invited by Brigadier Douglas Roberts to transfer to SIS in London at the end of 1946, together with a group of others, among them Alistair Horne, Myles Ponsonby and Harry Shergold. Having established his reputation, according to Kim Philby as 'Brig's Brains',[2] Oldfield joined R5, the requirements section dealing with counter-intelligence, as Roberts's deputy. He spoke fluent French and German, having travelled widely on the Continent before the war, and was well liked. The eldest son of a Derbyshire tenant farming family, with ten younger brothers and sisters, from the village of Over Haddon, Oldfield had taken an MA in history at Manchester University on a scholarship and excelled as an organist, specialising in church music. With a first-class honours and elected to a fellowship, he had intended an academic life, but he settled for the world of intelligence.

Oldfield served at Broadway as a counter-intelligence specialist until his first overseas posting, to CIFE in Singapore in 1950 as deputy to James Fulton, a future Controller Far East. In 1953 he was back in London, but in 1956 he returned to Singapore as station commander, in charge of several others in the region.

Between 1960 and 1964 Oldfield undertook his last overseas posting, as SIS's station commander in Washington DC, replacing John Briance. During this crucial period of the Cold War he handled the RUPEE intelligence from Oleg Penkovsky, which was categorised as CHICKADEE, being his subjective reporting on political issues and personalities, and IRONBARK, the missile manuals he copied, so allowing Oldfield a ring-side seat during the Cuban missile crisis of October 1962. This was also the period when an FBI surveillance team reported having observed homosexual activity on the part of Oldfield, but the matter was not raised in London. The four years Oldfield spent in Washington DC enabled him to develop many lasting friendships in the American intelligence community at a time when the CIA had received valuable information about Soviet spies in Britain from Anatoli Golitsyn, Michal Goleniewski and Yuri Nosenko. In addition to tips from these three sources, who were all to defect to the United States, Oldfield acted as a conduit for GRU leads originating from Dmitri Polyakov, providing the basis of numerous important investigations subsequently conducted in London. Thus Oldfield found himself in daily contact with the CIA's Counterintelligence Staff, then headed by James Angleton who shared his interest in medieval history, and spent much time with Angleton's deputy, Ray Rocca. On one memorable occasion, during an after-dinner discussion about McCarthyism at Oldfield's apartment, Rocca almost came to blows with Jim Bennett, then the deputy head of the RCMP Security Service's Soviet desk.

Some of Oldfield's colleagues, particularly Nigel Clive, later expressed surprise that someone of his undoubted intellect could have been 'led up the garden path'[3] by the Macchiavellian interpretations placed on the debriefs of successive KGB defectors, but during the four years that the pudgy, rotund Oldfield was in the United States he knew better than most that such counter-espionage successes as had been achieved against the Soviets had come exclusively from defectors. There had been a series of celebrated counter-intelligence coups in Britain, and all had originated with information received by the CIA from renegade KGB personnel. The first to fall had been Harry Houghton, identified by Michal Goleniewski, a Polish intelligence officer working for the KGB who had learned that the former Royal Navy petty officer had been recruited while at the British Embassy in Warsaw in early 1952. Surveillance by MI5 had led to the arrests of his co-conspirator Ethel Gee, also employed at the Admiralty's Underwater Weapons Research Establishment in Portland, the KGB illegal *rezident*, Gordon Lonsdale, and two other illegals, Morris and Lona Cohen, alias Peter and Helen Kroger. This investigation was considered a tremendous achievement, and the same source had fingered George Blake. His case was followed by the arrest in September 1962 of an Admiralty clerk, John Vassall, who had been blackmailed in Moscow by the Second Chief Directorate. Caught in a homosexual honeytrap while attached to the British Embassy in 1955, Vassall had been compromised by Yuri Nosenko, a KGB officer anxious to negotiate a new life for himself in the United States. In addition, in 1962 the FBI had managed to recruit a disaffected GRU officer, Dmitri Polyakov, who was to supply a mass of secrets, including the identity of Frank Bossard, a spy in the Air Ministry in London.

Although MI5 maintained the pretence that all these spies had been captured by the efficient application of skilful counter-intelligence, Oldfield knew that the tips had come from Soviet line-crossers cultivated by the CIA, and was deeply conscious that neither MI5 nor SIS had attracted a single defector since Grigori Tokaev in 1948. There could be several reasons for this apparent failure, but one was the possibility of hostile penetration, a theme peddled convincingly by Anatoli Golitsyn, who had defected to the CIA from Helsinki in December 1961.

Always fascinated by counter-intelligence, and appointed Director of Counter-Intelligence upon his return from Washington DC, Oldfield was drawn into Angleton's 'wilderness of mirrors', which so consumed his successor in Washington DC, Stephen de Mowbray, a Sovietologist who succumbed to Golitsyn's labyrinthine, corrosively self-destructive theories. Although never an adherent on the same scale as the younger man, Oldfield eventually was to renounce his commitment to Golitsyn's theories, but their friendship was to prevent him, when he was Chief, from exercising any discipline over de Mowbray. In any event, Golitsyn's sternest critics could not deny that he had been responsible for tipping off the CIA to the clues that eventually led to the arrest of the NATO spy George

Pacques, and to the identification of Hugh Hambleton as another long-term Soviet mole inside NATO's headquarters. Whereas Pacques made an abject confession, and acknowledged having spied since he had been recruited by a Russian in Algiers during the war, Hambleton evaded the molehunters for a couple more decades until he was arrested in London in June 1982 and imprisoned.

Oldfield's appointment as Chief in 1973 by Ted Heath, was uncontroversial as he had served as deputy to both White and Rennie and, having been passed over once, was the obvious choice. According to Heath, he enjoyed a good relationship with Oldfield, and others have noticed the similarity between the two men. Both had attended grammar schools, were the same age, had served in the Army during the war and reached the same rank, lieutenant-colonel, were bachelors, and were both organists. There the similarities ended, for Oldfield had a reputation for an impish sense of humour, was a great raconteur, and was a popular member of the Athenaeum where he served on the house committee and came into contact with plenty of journalists for whom he was discreet but accessible. One of reasons why Oldfield got along with Heath was the quality of his CX, especially on the European Economic Community, one of the Prime Minister's preoccupations. Oldfield not only collected good intelligence through the regular stations, in Paris, Bonn and Brussels, but when Britain's application to join the EEC was finally accepted he was allowed to place some of his personnel on the personal staffs of the British commissioners, making George Thomson's private office in Strasbourg a useful source of information about the Community. A former Labour minister, Thomson (later Lord Thomson of Monifeith) willingly consented to the enterprise.

Oldfield was also a devout and regular churchgoer, worshipping at St Matthew's, Westminster, where he played the organ, and claimed to read St Augustine's *Confessions* every year. He had intended an academic career, but one in the church would not have been improbable, and he would not have been the first SIS officer to have considered taking holy orders. Indeed, Anthony Coombe-Tennant MC, a wartime Guards officer who escaped from a German prisoner-of-war camp and literally walked across much of Europe to be repatriated, headed the Copenhagen station after the war, and later served in The Hague and Baghdad, in 1961 became a

Benedictine monk at Downside Abbey. Similarly Francis Aiken-Sneath, who joined SIS from MI5 at the end of the war and served under consular cover in Indonesia, had also become a priest.

The Chief's deep commitment to Anglicanism occasionally conflicted with his role as Chief, and according to Harold Wilson and David Owen both received short shrift when they suggested to Oldfield that Uganda's President Idi Amin might be a suitable candidate for assassination. Similarly, when in February 1973 the Littlejohn brothers, Kenneth and Keith, were arrested in England and extradited to Dublin to face bank robbery charges, Oldfield gathered his staff in the canteen on the top floor of Century House to deny their claims that their criminal activities had been sanctioned by SIS to discredit the Provisional IRA. In fact, although the Littlejohns had been in contact with SIS, to offer information about PIRA operations that they had encountered, and had been assigned a case officer and encouraged to submit further reports, they had never been given a licence to commit armed robbery. Clearly affronted by the assertion, Oldfield gave his personal word that there was absolutely no truth in the tale; this inevitably received wide publicity, and gained even more when Kenneth Littlejohn escaped from Mountjoy Prison and granted several newspaper interviews while living as a fugitive in Amsterdam. Such episodes are embarrassing for any intelligence agency, which cannot afford to turn down potentially useful tips from dubious sources, but it would be an error to judge a service's performance by the headlines it attracts, often unfairly.

Nevertheless, it is clear that the need to acquire intelligence about the Provisional IRA led SIS to forge links with some risky individuals, among them the Oxford-educated drug dealer Howard Marks, who ran a dress shop in Amsterdam as a front for his international trading. Originally from Wales, Marks had been up at Balliol with an SIS officer, Hamilton McMillan, and he volunteered information about PIRA personalities in Holland. His intelligence had been accepted gratefully, but when, in November 1973, he was arrested in Suffolk on charges of importing and distributing fifteen tons of hashish, his involvement with SIS emerged as a central plank of his defence. Marks claimed that his drug-smuggling and his boutique had been covers for his real job, working against Irish terrorists, and he was acquitted. Later Marks was to be arrested in Majorca by the Drug Enforcement Agency and imprisoned on federal charges in Florida, but even though he had by then become, as he eventually admitted, the world's largest dealer in marijuana, he managed to negotiate his early release. However, Marks's first acquittal had been an embarrassment for SIS, a further example of how the unscrupulous could misrepresent their relationship with SIS to personal advantage. The dilemma for SIS, of course, like any other intelligence agency, was that valuable information did not come exclusively from Mother Theresa.

SIS's tangle with Marks demonstrated the organisation's determination to tackle the Provisional IRA, as the need to deal with escalating Irish terrorism became a priority. Heavy-handed Army tactics had proved counter-productive, internment without trial had been an affront to justice, and SIS's second representative in Belfast, Craig Smellie, had not been a success. Whereas the republicans had anticipated a major breakthrough at Cheyne Walk, judging talks at such a high level to indicate a weakness in the British position and maybe the start of a withdrawal, Willie Whitelaw had explained that PIRA could never win a military victory and would never be allowed to do so, by any British government. He found the terrorists unreasonable and unrealistic, with absurdly high, unachievable expectations, just as some on the republican side had been bitterly disappointed, convinced that future political goals could only be accomplished through further violence.

The result of the breakdown in the talks had been renewed terrorism, some of it conducted on the UK mainland, although one of Steele's later successors, Michael Oatley, continued to maintain a discreet line of communication to Gerry Adams and Martin McGuinness, PIRA's new leadership. Even Oldfield himself was drawn into the conflict when, on 13 October 1975, a thirty-pound bomb containing anti-personnel steel bolts was found hanging on the railings outside the entrance to Marsham Court where Oldfield lived. Had Oldfield himself been the target, or had PIRA been aiming for Lockets, the neighbouring restaurant so popular with members of parliament? This was a question that was never answered, but the Chief's personal security was increased, and thereafter he was permanently accompanied by two armed bodyguards.

In the years since Frank Steele had established SIS's reluctant presence in Belfast more evidence had emerged of the KGB's interest in PIRA activities. It had been a tip to the Irish authorities from SIS that had led to the expulsion of the local TASS correspondent, Vladimir Kozlov, in December 1975, but the issue of the precise role, if any, being played by the KGB in Ulster, was to remain unresolved for some years until, as we shall see, two defectors, Ilya Dzhirkvelov and Oleg Gordievsky, clarified the situation.

Oldfield was much liked within SIS, and widely admired in Whitehall, but his one weak spot was over the spectre of hostile penetration so apocalyptically described by Anatoli Golitsyn. Golitsyn's dire warnings of KGB manipulation and deception had been swallowed by Stephen de Mowbray and Bunny Pantcheff to the point that SIS had participated in a worldwide molehunt conducted by the CIA through a highly secret international counter-intelligence exchange created in 1967 and codenamed CAZAB after the five English-speaking countries which sent representatives to the occasional meetings. CAZAB-cleared officers who shared Golitsyn's labyrinthine vision of the Kremlin's plots inspired numerous investigations in Langley, Ottawa and London, and when an inquiry, conducted by a joint committee codenamed FLUENCY, into Soviet penetration of MI5 appeared inconclusive, de Mowbray took his suspicions direct to Downing Street, with the reluctant consent of Oldfield, thereby prompting a further review by the recently-retired Cabinet Secretary, Sir Burke Trend. The very existence of the FLUENCY committee, and its apparent inability to resolve the many debilitating allegations of a high-ranking mole inside the Security Service, was to act as a ticking time-bomb, waiting to detonate under a future administration with devastating consequences.

Although Oldfield had become an apostate when it came to genuflecting to Golitsyn and Angleton, he had made no attempt to rein in de Mowbray who immersed himself in Soviet history, and after his retirement in 1979 published *Key Facts in Soviet History*. In 1971 Oldfield exercised his authority as Deputy Chief to remove de Mowbray from Century House, where he had been since his return from Washington in June 1968, and post him out of harm's way to Malta for two years, but when he returned in 1973 he was as committed as ever to pursuing the counter-intelligence leads indicating hostile penetration, and obtained Oldfield's consent to approach Downing Street on the issue.

De Mowbray's objective was to persuade the Cabinet Office to authorise a major review of security policy and clear up all the loose ends left by FLUENCY. The reaction of MI5's D-G, Sir Michael Hanley, to the news of this initiative was close to apoplectic; he resented Oldfield's unwillingness to impose discipline on his staff, however recalcitrant, and interpreted de Mowbray's behaviour as a direct attack on the integrity and efficiency of the Security Service. When de Mowbray had reached Downing Street for his appointment he was seen by the Cabinet Secretary, Sir John Hunt, who had very little idea of the blood-letting that had occurred inside MI5 and SIS during the molehunts, and he took the expedient of commissioning his predecessor, Burke Trend, who had retired to be Rector of Lincoln College, Oxford, to undertake a thorough review of FLUENCY to reach some judgments about de Mowbray's concerns. The result was that Hanley assigned an office to Trend in MI5's headquarters and turned over to him all the FLUENCY files so he could make an independent assessment of what precisely had occurred, and what measures had been taken to counter the danger of penetration. The fact, of course, that such a senior mandarin had been engaged for nearly a year in such a sensitive task was a potential bombshell, which was eventually to detonate when a disaffected MI5 retiree, Peter Wright, revealed some details of the inquiry to Chapman Pincher in 1981. Wright mistakenly believed that Trend had found evidence of penetration and had been persuaded of Hollis's guilt, but when Mrs Thatcher described the Trend Inquiry in her Commons statement in April 1981, prompted by Pincher's book, she said he had come to the opposite conclusion, thereby effectively demolishing Wright's theorem. Far from satisfying Wright, her statement prompted him to co-author *SpyCatcher*, an explosive exposé of MI5's molehunts.

The seeds of the *SpyCatcher* affair were certainly sown in 1973 when de Mowbray, for entirely proper motives, pursued the unresolved issue of Soviet penetration of MI5, but his impact on Downing Street was not what he could have anticipated. Hunt's strategy of calling Trend in from his retirement to take a fresh look at the issue was also perfectly correct, but the real problem after Harold Wilson's return as prime minister in 1974 lay in his paranoia about security matters. While Wilson trusted Hunt, and got on well with Oldfield he was always very sceptical of MI5 and believed the organisation was scheming against him. His fear of plots knew no bounds and was fuelled by his political secretary, Marcia Williams, who was equally suspicious of the Security Service and was convinced the South African Bureau of State Security (BOSS), was actively engaged in subverting the Labour government. There was some evidence to support her anxieties, for her sister had been courted by a suitor who turned out to be a BOSS agent and was placed under surveillance by MI5.

During his first administration Wilson had used George Wigg, as Paymaster-General, to keep an eye on MI5 and protect Downing Street from security scandals, but during his second premiership Wilson had no similar individual to liaise with MI5, so he came to depend heavily on Sir John Hunt and avoided dealing directly with the Director-General, Sir Michael Hanley. In contrast, his relations with Oldfield were always good, and in 1975 he had called in C to discuss rumours of disloyalty within the Security Service. However, Wilson was not so much concerned with Soviet penetration, but rumours that certain MI5 officers had been undermining the government. Later Wilson was to confirm that Oldfield had said 'there's a section of MI5 which is unreliable'[4] and had named Charles Elwell, the former Director, F Branch, as a possible conspirator. Once a naval officer and prisoner of war at Colditz, Elwell held strong views about political subversion and had been briefed on OATSHEAF, an investigation conducted into the possibility, initially floated by Golitsyn, that Hugh Gaitskell had been murdered so he could be replaced by someone controlled by the KGB. To protect Wilson, his name had been concealed behind the codename WORTHINGTON, and eventually the matter had been dropped for lack of any proof. Nevertheless, the very fact that MI5 had undertaken such an investigation was political dynamite, and Oldfield took Peter Wright to dinner in early August 1975 in an attempt to learn how far the smears had been taken. Wright had promptly reported Oldfield's approach to Hanley, which only served to poison the inter-agency relationship even further. The net result was that Wilson remained convinced an MI5 plot had existed, and Oldfield had appeared to have corroborated it.

Wilson was later to give the impression that he had rarely encountered the Chief during his second premiership, whereas Oldfield had in fact played a significant role throughout the first foreign policy crisis to engulf the new Labour government in mid-July 1974 when the Greek junta overthrew the President of Cyprus, Archbishop Makarios, forcing him to flee to the British Sovereign Base at Akrotiri for evacuation to Malta. The Greek Army colonels, who had seized control of their country in 1967, and were controlled by the Interior Minister, George Ioannides, had long funded the EOKA movement in Cyprus, committed to union with mainland Greece, through the intelligence service, KYP, which enjoyed very close ties to the CIA station in Athens headed by Richard Welch. Acting on instructions from KYP, the predominantly Greek-officered Cyprus National Guard had mounted a coup with EOKA to remove Makarios, who narrowly escaped the presidential palace with his life. Knowing of the American administration's support for his regime, and the strategic importance of the US Navy's bases in Greece for the Sixth Fleet, Ioannides had counted on at least tacit approval from Henry Kissinger's State Department. However, the colonels had overplayed their hand and the Americans, on balance, were slightly more in favour of Turkey, where the NSA maintained a string of vitally important listening posts along the Black Sea coast to monitor Soviet missile tests at Tyuratam and Kapustin Yar. Distracted by the domestic political crisis surrounding President Nixon, the Americans declined to intervene or join the British in attempting to moderate a Turkish reaction.

These events had taken SIS completely by surprise, leaving the new Foreign Secretary, James Callaghan, in a quandary but with a treaty obligation, as the British guarantor of Cyprus's independence, of preventing a Turkish invasion. All the reporting from Nicosia, Athens and Ankara proved completely unreliable, as did the CIA's interpretation of Turkish intentions when, on 20 July, some 30,000 Turkish troops began landing on the north coast of the island and by the end of August had occupied a third of it. President Nixon, on the point of resignation following the Watergate scandal, was powerless to intervene and in any event the CIA link with KYM, Welch's deputy Gust Avrokotos, was altogether too close to the colonels' junta, leaving Callaghan hopelessly exposed and impotent in the eastern Mediterranean, operating with minimal reinforcements for the Sovereign Bases and only a single assault carrier, HMS *Hermes*, carrying 700 Royal Marine Commandos, available to deploy against the Turks. By the time the Royal Navy could be brought to the scene the invasion had been completed and Britain's guarantee exposed as worthless.

As a member of the Commonwealth, Cyprus had been under Britain's influence since independence had been negotiated with Makarios in 1959, and the Sovereign Bases and GCHQ's intercept station at Agios Nikolias represented important regional assets for the UK, even if Harold Wilson had undertaken an as-yet-uncompleted secret study, as part of his swingeing defence cuts, to determine whether they really needed to be retained. While the base areas and the listening post were to be confirmed as extremely valuable, they did not accommodate sufficient military strength to preserve the island's independence from Athens, nor stop Turkish regulars from taking control of a territory stretching from Kyrenia to Nicosia. SIS's failure to warn the JIC of either the coup or the imminent Turkish reaction highlighted the need for good intelligence, a view expressed by an investigation conducted by the Foreign Affairs Select Committee, to which Callaghan and his minister of state, Roy Hattersley gave evidence, which published a report concluding that 'If it is true that the three stages of the Cyprus crisis came as a surprise to the British Government, this argues deficiencies in Government intelligence which ought to be remedied.' The select committee had expressed astonishment that there had been no advance warning, but as SIS did not officially exist, C escaped all censure. In reality, Callaghan's room to manoeuvre was severely limited, and the only ships available to him were two frigates, HMS *Rhyl* and *Andromeda*, led by a guided missile destroyer, HMS *Devonshire*, a task force that was unlikely to have much impact on Turkey's huge naval presence.

Callaghan's bitter experience with Cyprus left him scarred by the speed with which crises could develop within Britain's sphere of influence, so he was extremely alert when, in November 1977, SIS reported a threat from the Argentine junta to invade the Falklands, a tiny, distant British dependency under constant threat from Buenos Aires, which required an instant response from the government. At the time Argentina was considered to be on the brink of war with Chile, over a long-standing territorial dispute in the Beagle Channel, and use of the deep anchorage at Stanley was considered to be a potential motive for an invasion so an Argentine naval force could sail south, down a coastline devoid of harbours, to enforce the claim in Tierra del Fuego. Tensions had heightened in March 1977, during ministerial negotiations with the Argentines in New York, and the established British strategy had been to delay talks beyond each 'invasion season' and deal with the pressures from one year to the next, relying on the JIC's Latin America Current Intelligence Group to produce occasional threat assessments.

SIS was represented in Buenos Aires by Simon Butler-Manning, and by chance the Governor of the Falklands was an SIS retiree, Neville French, who had been expelled from Rhodesia for spying in 1966, so Oldfield was at the apex of an intelligence triangle. The new Prime Minister James Callaghan, who well understood the use of the naval deterrent, sent the nuclear submarine HMS *Dreadnought* down to the south Atlantic as part of a task force codenamed JOURNEYMAN, with the intention of persuading the Argentines to change their mind. No invasion took place, but controversy surrounds the exact circumstances in which the junta abandoned the plan, if indeed there really was one. According to Callaghan's version, Oldfield was instructed to leak the deployment of JOURNEYMAN in Buenos Aires, and others have suggested that *Dreadnought* deliberately compromised her presence in the area by surfacing close to an Argentine merchantman, confident that the sighting would be reported to Buenos Aires. This is disputed, and it has been pointed out that a Royal Fleet Auxiliary tanker, the *Olwen*, had spotted the submarine's periscope, and had reported it to the Admiralty by radio, receiving in reply confirmation that the submarine was a friendly. Such traffic would have been monitored by the Argentines, so one way or another the news of *Dreadnought*'s arrival on station off the Falklands would have become known in Buenos Aires. In Argentina the official view is that there never was a real plan to invade in 1977, but there was a deception scheme to draw

Chilean attention away from a firm intention to seize the disputed Beagle Channel. Ultimately the dispute was resolved by the Pope's intervention and his binding arbitration, and no public admission was ever made regarding JOURNEYMAN, so details of the operation were consigned to the classified archives, and were not available when Mrs Thatcher's administration faced an almost identical challenge five years later.

This episode, which was to have considerable repercussions later, demonstrated Callaghan's willingness to use intelligence to protect British interests overseas, and he had another opportunity to project British forces in Belize, by flying carrier-launched Buccaneer fighter-bombers along the Guatemalan frontier when Oldfield reported an imminent threat to invade the former British colony. Such incidents, of course, went unreported outside the JIC, and demonstrated SIS's continuing, unsung value to successive governments.

Unusually, Oldfield served under four foreign secretaries, being Sir Alec Douglas-Home, Tony Crosland who died suddenly in office in February 1977 of a stroke, David Owen and James Callaghan, and three prime ministers, but he seems to have enjoyed the closest relationship with Owen who, uniquely, later wrote affectionately about him. Although Owen had always opposed the anachronism of SIS's official lack of status, he had found the deniability very convenient when he was appointed Crosland's successor. Callaghan had then circulated a memo proposing that the government 'should break with precedent and formally avow the existence of MI6'.[5] Initially sympathetic, Owen had consulted Oldfield who had:

> . . . produced compelling arguments for continuing the convention. Admittedly it was absurd, even risible, but the protection afforded by not admitting it existed was absolute; whereas once it was acknowledged there would be a constant attempt to make Ministers answerable and a progressive erosion. While one could imagine Ministers initially holding the line on a blank refusal to discuss any detail, there was a reasonable fear that gradually, as had happened in the US Congress with the CIA, more important information would be divulged under parliamentary pressure.

Owen observed that 'the crucial question is how a democracy can have confidence in the operation of the Secret Services without risking intelligence being compromised'[6] and he conducted a study to examine all the operations that had been referred up for approval since Labour came to power in February 1974. At the end of the exercise he concluded that Oldfield had been scrupulous in obtaining the Secretary of State's consent for operations rightly judged to have required it. He had half-expected an organisation with a tendency to freelance, exercising more independence than was appropriate, but in fact he found this simply was not the case. 'I grew to respect of the work of MI6, particularly in Southern Africa, where they provided me with a lot of intelligence',[7] he recalled. Naturally, the Foreign Secretary was never told every detail of every operation, but where there was an element of political risk or blowback Oldfield had always applied for the necessary sanction. Among those was a briefing given on an approach made to a Soviet diplomat in a European country who looked like a potential defector. Owen was consulted because the offer had come from an identified, middle-ranking KGB officer working under diplomatic cover, and there was every chance that the man was simply part of an elaborate provocation intended to flush out the local SIS personnel, maybe plant a double agent peddling disinformation, or perhaps cause an international incident. Oldfield had already consulted the host country's security service, which had given its approval in principle, so the potential downside looked minimal, and Owen granted his consent, thus initiating one of SIS's most successful penetrations ever.

The potential defector had been Oleg Gordievsky, a 'Line PR' political reports specialist of the Third Department of the KGB's elite FCD which covered Scandinavia and the UK. Disillusioned after the Soviet invasion of Czechoslovakia, and warned of his future behaviour because of an affair with his secretary, Gordievsky had been a member of Mikhail Luibimov's *rezidentura* in Copenhagen since October 1972, on his second tour of duty in Denmark as press attaché. He had been pitched by the SIS station commander, Robert Browning, whom he had encountered casually at a local squash club. Educated at Marlborough and Corpus Christi, Cambridge, Browning had spent eight years in the Colonial Administration Service before joining SIS in 1961 and being posted to the Geneva station in October the following year. Declared to the Danish security police, the Politiets Efterretnigstjenestre (PET), Browning had worked with them to establish a safe-house in an apartment in Skovelunde, and had relied on PET support for counter-surveillance to ensure his meetings with Gordievsky were undetected by the local KGB.

Although there were some initial doubts Gordievsky eventually appeared to be the genuine article, and was not interested in an instant defection, being willing to maintain contact with SIS, supplying high-grade information from inside the KGB, until the right moment. If there was a single worthwhile investment made by Oldfield during his tenure as Chief, it was the successful recruitment of Gordievsky, an event that was to pay dividends into the future as the case would run for nearly a dozen years, until August 1985. Quite apart from producing a veritable bonanza of highly relevant information from the very heart of the Third Department, Gordievsky's survival gave testimony to SIS's essential integrity, proving that the organisation could run a successful penetration into the KGB with fear of compromise. The betrayals of Philby and Blake were ancient history, and the modern SIS was shown to be able to run a good case (a feat that SIS had never accomplished abroad) without endangering the source. Gordievsky's recruitment and safe management provided a steady flow of excellent intelligence and heightened SIS's status in the eyes of the CIA, which was allowed only to know that a successful penetration was in progress. Oldfield's achievements as Chief were recognised by his award of the KCMG in 1975, which he had received at Buckingham Palace, accompanied by two of his sisters, on the same day that Charlie Chaplin was invested, and a GCMG three years later, making him the first and only Chief to have been promoted to that coveted most senior rank of the order.

On the issue of his successor, Oldfield had been keen to recommend Theodore 'Bunny' Pantcheff, the son of a naturalised Greek who had adopted Alderney as his home. A Cambridge graduate, where he had taken a first in German in 1941, Bunny Pantcheff had investigated Nazi war crimes in the Channel Islands immediately after the war, and had joined SIS from the Intelligence Division of the Control Commission for Germany in 1948. He was to remain in Munich until 1956, and then was posted to Nigeria to open a station in Lagos in 1958 and after independence in 1960, when Desmond Parkinson relieved him, moved the following year to Leopoldville. His subsequent career was to include command of MI5's British Security apparatus in Germany for two years and a return to Century House in June 1971 as Controller Africa. Oldfield's offer to Pantcheff, who was five years younger than the Chief, of a promotion coincided with his inheritance of a house in Alderney, and the offer of a post on the local bench as Jurat. Once described as 'having an intellect of steel, the appearance of a country tobacconist, the name of a Soviet spy and a heart of gold',[8] Pantcheff declined Oldfield's offer and took early retirement at the end of 1977 to write books, the first of which, *A History of Alderney under the Nazi Occupation*, was published in 1981.

After his retirement at the end of March 1978 Oldfield moved into Brentwood House in Iffley and embarked on a research project, initially intended to be on medieval history at All Souls, Oxford, but when he discovered the amount of scholarship that had been undertaken on his chosen subject since he left Manchester he decided to study another topic, and embarked on a study of the diaries of the first Chief, Mansfield Smith-Cumming. Unfortunately this idea also had to be abandoned, partly because of the apparent disappearance of all but two volumes of the first C's diary, but mainly because, in September 1979, he was asked by the new Prime Minister, Margaret Thatcher, to take up the appointment of Intelligence and Security Coordinator in Northern Ireland where the many overlapping security and intelligence agencies seemed more adept at combating each other than the Provisional IRA. MI5, the RUC Special Branch and the Army all ran competing organisations in the province, and Oldfield's task was to direct their activities against the common target, and restore the tense relations between the RUC and the Army, as personified by the mutual hostility of the uncompromising GOC Northern Ireland, General Sir Tim Creasey, and the Chief Constable, Sir Kenneth Newman. When Oldfield's appointment was made public, on 2 October, by the Secretary of State, Humphrey Atkins, Newman had gone to the Police Staff College at Bramshill as Commandant, and his deputy (Sir) Jack Hermon was named as the new Chief Constable, Soon afterwards Creasey was replaced by Lieutenant-General Sir Richard Lawson, and the

Commander Land Forces in Northern Ireland, General Sir James Glover, returned to London as Director of Defence Intelligence. Oldfield also arranged to have two deputies, Brigadier (Sir) Robert Pascoe from the Army and Assistant Chief Constable John Whiteside of the RUC, and this arrangement, embodied as the Planning Staff, ensured closer liaison between the two services which had been in conflict for the past two years.

Despite a complete lack of any formal executive powers, Oldfield's formidable reputation ensured cooperation and within six months, remaining ensconced in his quarters at Stormont Castle for weeks at a time, he was able to transform the intelligence environment. During his infrequent visits to London Oldfield lived at his flat in Marsham Court, which was conveniently located directly above Locket's restaurant, and his meals were often brought up to him by a waiter. On one evening, when a waiter was delivering his dinner, an incident occurred which was the subject of a report by Oldfield's Special Branch personal protection officer. This resulted in an interview in March with the Cabinet Secretary, Sir Robert Armstrong, at which Oldfield was challenged about his homosexuality, and he was forced to acknowledge that over the past two decades he had lied on his positive vetting questionnaire which specifically requested a declaration of any sexual proclivities that might leave him vulnerable to blackmail. His security clearance was revoked immediately and he resigned his post attached to the Northern Ireland Office in June, to be replaced by Sir Brooks Richards, the Cabinet Intelligence Coordinator since mid-1978.

This sad episode brought to an end a very distinguished intelligence career and was the source of much dismay among his many friends who found it hard to believe that Oldfield was homosexual. Some preferred to believe that he had been the victim of a smear campaign orchestrated by Ulster loyalists and, although the conspiracy theorists had a field-day, the unpalatable truth was that he had been picking up young men for casual sex for some years undetected. This had been known to a few very close friends, including Jimmie James, who had joined SIS in 1947 and later had served in Rangoon and Hong Kong. Finally, after a year in Berlin, he had returned to London and for a time had shared a flat with Oldfield, who suffered mild psoriasis which made him self-conscious about his appearance. James knew many of Oldfield's secrets, and was probably his closest friend in the office, but he had retired from Century House in 1972.

Among those dismayed by what he termed the 'shattering news', David Owen in particular felt betrayed:

> I was impressed by Maurice Oldfield as were most of the few politicians who dealt directly with him. Parliament was, however, now being told that we had been wrong to trust his word as Head of MI6 and that the positive vetting procedures had been totally ineffective. I enjoyed talking privately with him on world problems, often without even my Private Secretary present, and I asked myself, should I have spotted something? He had implemented the policy that had led to many people's lives being blighted, either by being dismissed from their job or having their promotion prospects blocked, because of the security doubt about homosexuals . . . I had challenged the need to apply the policy so rigidly and had even spoken to Maurice Oldfield about it. Margaret Thatcher's announcement made me wonder not only whom I could trust but also whether I should have guessed. I had known Maurice Oldfield was a bachelor. He seemed well-adjusted, though I noticed that after a chat in the evening he was reluctant to go, leaving an impression of loneliness.[9]

The strange circumstances of Oldfield's departure were to be complicated not only by sectarian suspicions in Northern Ireland, but also by the fact that his secretary, Eileen Streather, had married an Army information officer, Colin Wallace, in August 1975, a couple of months after he had been dismissed for leaking a classified document to a journalist. Wallace had claimed that the leak had been part of his covert role in a psychological warfare campaign directed against the Provisional IRA. Wallace and his wife had then moved to Arundel in Sussex, where he was convicted in March 1981 of the manslaughter of the husband of his assistant, with whom he had become infatuated. He was sentenced to ten years' imprisonment, and was released in December 1986, to continue a campaign to prove his innocence of the charge. Many of his supporters believed he had been framed, and that his arrest was not unconnected with the Ulster conflict and his links to clandestine operations in Ulster.

Oldfield's resignation was quickly followed by a diagnosis of diverticulitis, a condition to which he succumbed in March 1981. He was buried in the Oldfield family plot at St Anne's, Over Haddon, and his memorial service was held at the Royal Naval College at Greenwich on 12 May, and was conducted by a former SIS colleague, the Reverend Halsey Colchester, who had taken holy orders in 1972 following a career that had included service at the Istanbul, Athens and Paris stations.

Many of Oldfield's friends, who knew nothing of the circumstances in which the former Chief had lost his security clearance, were appalled as details of his private life emerged and relieved that he had died just nine months after his resignation, and before he had been obliged to endure any public humiliation. Even after there had been confirmation of the tragedy, some loyally refused to believe any of it and preferred to remember the donnish, shambling 'Moulders', who had once taken the trouble to send a personal letter of encouragement and an extract from Sun Tzu's *The Art of War* to Steven Donoghue, the nine-year-old son of the head of Wilson's Policy Unit who had written to him for advice on how to become a secret agent.

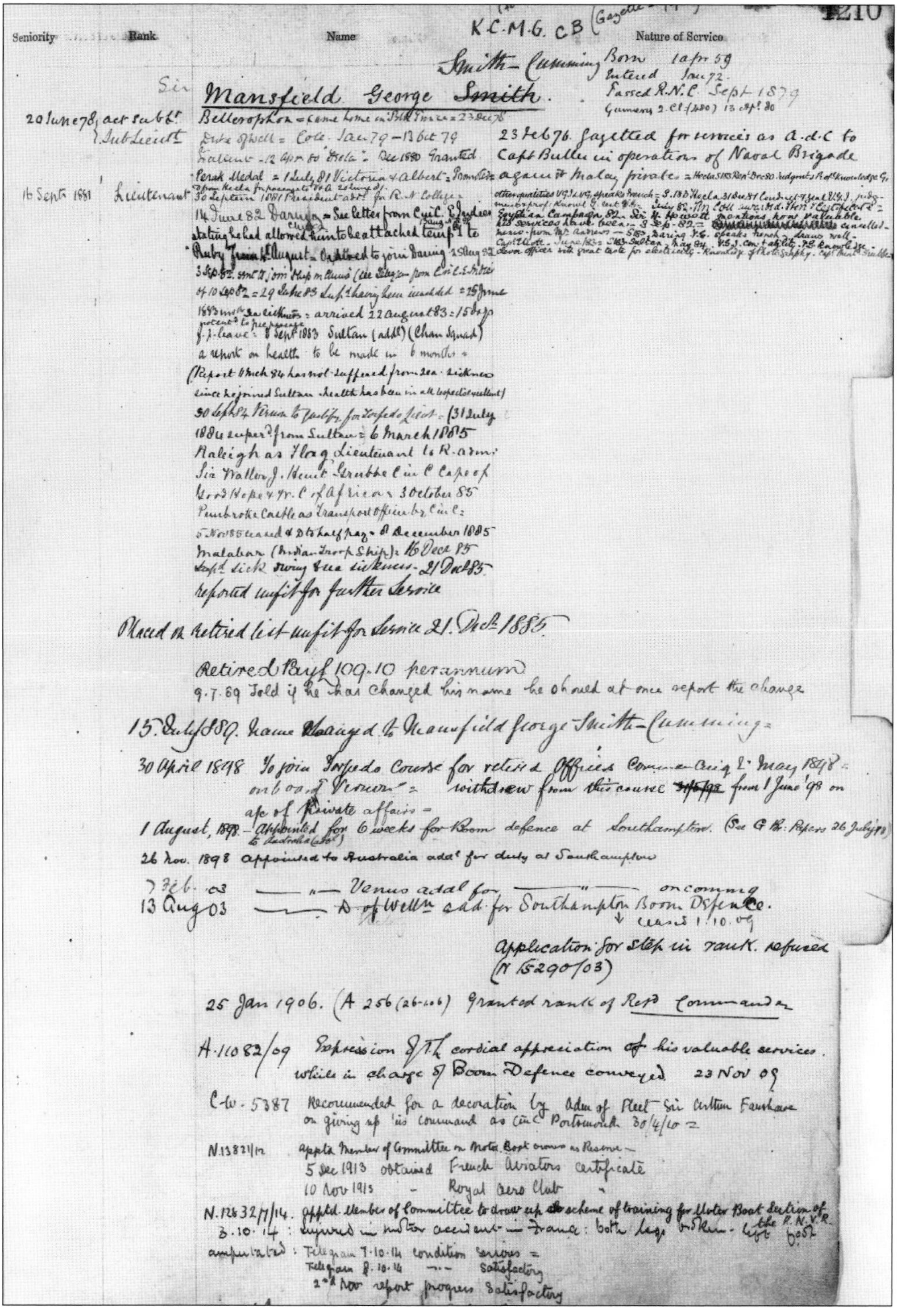

Seniority Rank Name Nature of Service 1210

K.C.M.G. C.B.

Smith-Cumming

Born 1 Apr 59
Entered Jan 72
Passed R.N.C. Sept 1879
Gunnery 2 Cl. 13 Apl 80

Sir Mansfield George Smith.

20 June 78, act. Sub Lt. Sub Lieut. Bellerophon = came home in Fifth Tirza = 23 Dec 78

Duke of Well = Cole. Jan 79 – 13 Oct 79

Sultan – 12 Apr 80 "Hecla" – Dec 1880 Granted

Perak Medal = 1 July 81 Victoria & Albert = Promoted

16 Sept 1881 Lieutenant 30 Septem 1881 President addl for R.N. College

14 June 82 Daring = See letter from C in C. E. Indies stating he had allowed him to be attached temp to Ruby from August = Ordered to join Daring 25 Aug 82

3 Sep 82 sent to join ship on Sums (see letter from C in C E. Indies 4 10 Sep 82) = 29 Feb 83 Supd having been invalided = 25 June 1883 sea sickness = arrived 22 August 83 = 15 days

f. p. leave: 8 Sept 1883 Sultan (addl) (Chan. Squad.)

a report on health to be made in 6 months =

(Report 6 Mch 84 has not suffered from sea sickness since he joined Sultan. Health has been in all respects excellent)

30 Sept 84 Vernon to qualify for Torpedo Lieut. = (31 July 1884 superd from Sultan) = 6 March 1885 Raleigh as Flag Lieutenant to R. Adm: Sir Walter J. Hunt Grubbe C in C Cape of Good Hope & W. C. of Africa = 30 October 85 Pembroke Castle as Transport Officer by C in C: 5 Nov 85 ceased & 8 to half pay = 8 December 1885 Malabar (Indian Troop Ship): 16 Dec 85 Supd sick owing to sea sickness. 21 Dec 85 reported unfit for further service

23 Feb 76. Gazetted for services as A.D.C. to Capt Buller in operations of Naval Brigade against Malay pirates.

Placed on retired list unfit for service 21. Dec. 1885.

Retired Pay £109.10 per annum

9.7.89 Told if he has changed his name he should at once report the change

15. July 1889. Name changed to Mansfield George Smith-Cumming =

30 April 1898 To join Torpedo Course for retired Officers commencing 2 May 1898 = on board Vernon = withdrew from this course from 1 June '98 on a/c of private affairs =

1 August, 1898 – Appointed for 6 weeks for Boom defence at Southampton. (See G. Pl: Papers 26 July 98)

26 Nov. 1898 appointed to Australia addl for duty at Southampton

7 Feb. 03 — " — Venus addl for — " — on comm

13 Aug 03 — " — D of Welln addl for Southampton Boom Defence.
ceased 1.10.09

Application for step in rank. refused (N 15290/03)

25 Jan 1906. (A 256 (26-1-06)) Granted rank of Retd Commander

A.11082/09 Expression of Their cordial appreciation of his valuable services while in charge of Boom Defence conveyed 23 Nov 09

C.W. 5387 Recommended for a decoration by Adm of Fleet Sir Arthur Fanshawe on giving up his command as C in C Portsmouth 30/4/10 =

N.13821/12 Apptd Member of Committee on Motor Boat crews as Reserve –
5 Dec 1913 obtained French Aviators certificate
10 Nov 1913 – Royal Aero Club "

N.12832/7/14. Apptd. Member of Committee to draw up the scheme of training for Motor Boat Section of the R.N.V.R.

3.10.14 Injured in motor accident – France: both legs broken – left foot amputated: Telegram 7.10.14 condition serious =
Telegram 8.10.14 — " — satisfactory
2nd Nov report progress satisfactory

The Royal Navy personnel record of Mansfield Smith, noting his change of name to Mansfield Smith-Cumming.

Captain Mansfield Smith-Cumming, the sea-sick sailor who proved to be a brilliant spymaster.

The letter to Mansfield Smith-Cumming from Admiral Bethell inviting him to London to discuss his appointment as head of the Foreign Section of the new Secret Service Bureau.

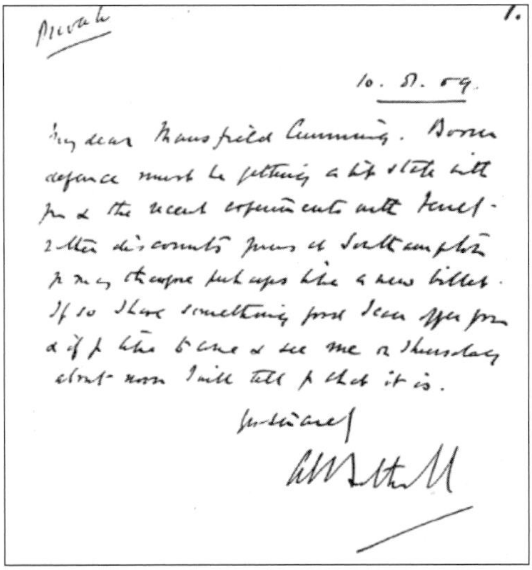
Private

1.

10. 8. 09.

My dear Mansfield Cumming. Boom defence must be getting a bit stale with you & the recent experiments with Thorneycroft's [illegible] at Southampton so you may therefore perhaps like a new billet. If so I have something good to offer you & if you like to come & see me on Thursday about noon I will tell you what it is.

Yours sincerely

A. Bethell

Admiral Hugh 'Quex' Sinclair, the Chief who saw his organisation decimated by the Treasury but saved by politicians who were misled about SIS's role in the publication of the Zinoviev Letter.

Sir Stewart Menzies, the Chief who saved SIS's tarnished reputation by retaining tight control over the secret wartime source codenamed ULTRA.

Sir John Sinclair, the much-respected Chief who was overwhelmed by the tumultuous events of 1956.

Sir Dick White, a reluctant SIS Chief with plenty of skeletons in his cupboard who transformed the organisation into a branch of Whitehall.

Sir Maurice Oldfield, pictured at Buckingham Palace in 1973 after he had been awarded a knighthood never previously given to any Chief.

Below left: Kim Philby in Beirut, pictured with his daughter Miranda, shortly before his confession, exchanged for an immunity from prosecution, and his sudden disappearance to the Soviet Union.

Below: George Blake, in the Korean internment camp in 1951 where he volunteered to help the Soviets. He continued to betray secrets until his arrest in April 1961.

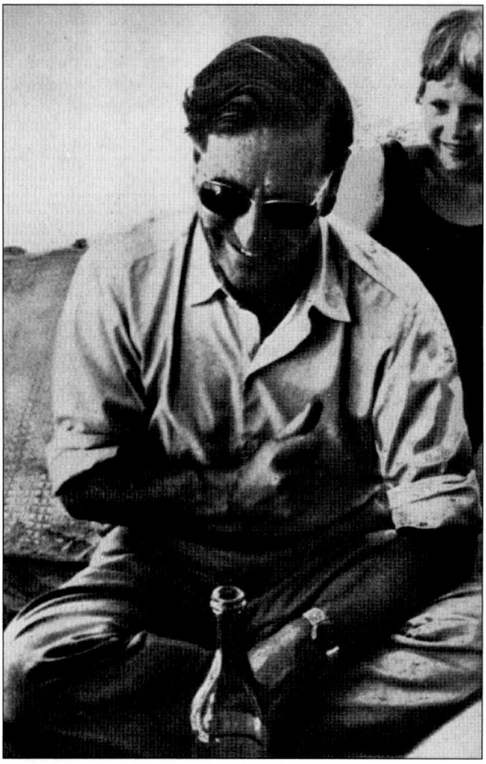

Ashley Gardens: The first C, Mansfield Smith-Cumming, rented a flat on this street using part of it as his office.

2 Whitehall Court: location of SIS headquarters 1916–24.

Broadway Buildings, 54 Broadway, which accommodated SIS's head-quarters, the Government Communications Bureau, and the Minimax Fire Extinguisher Company.

21 Queen Anne's Gate, the elegant town house bought by Sir Hugh Sinclair which backed onto SIS's headquarters in Broadway and provided him with a bachelor apartment.

Century House, 100 Westminster Bridge Road: SIS headquarters 1966–96.

The Chief's office, Vauxhall Cross, over-looking the Thames and Vauxhall Bridge.

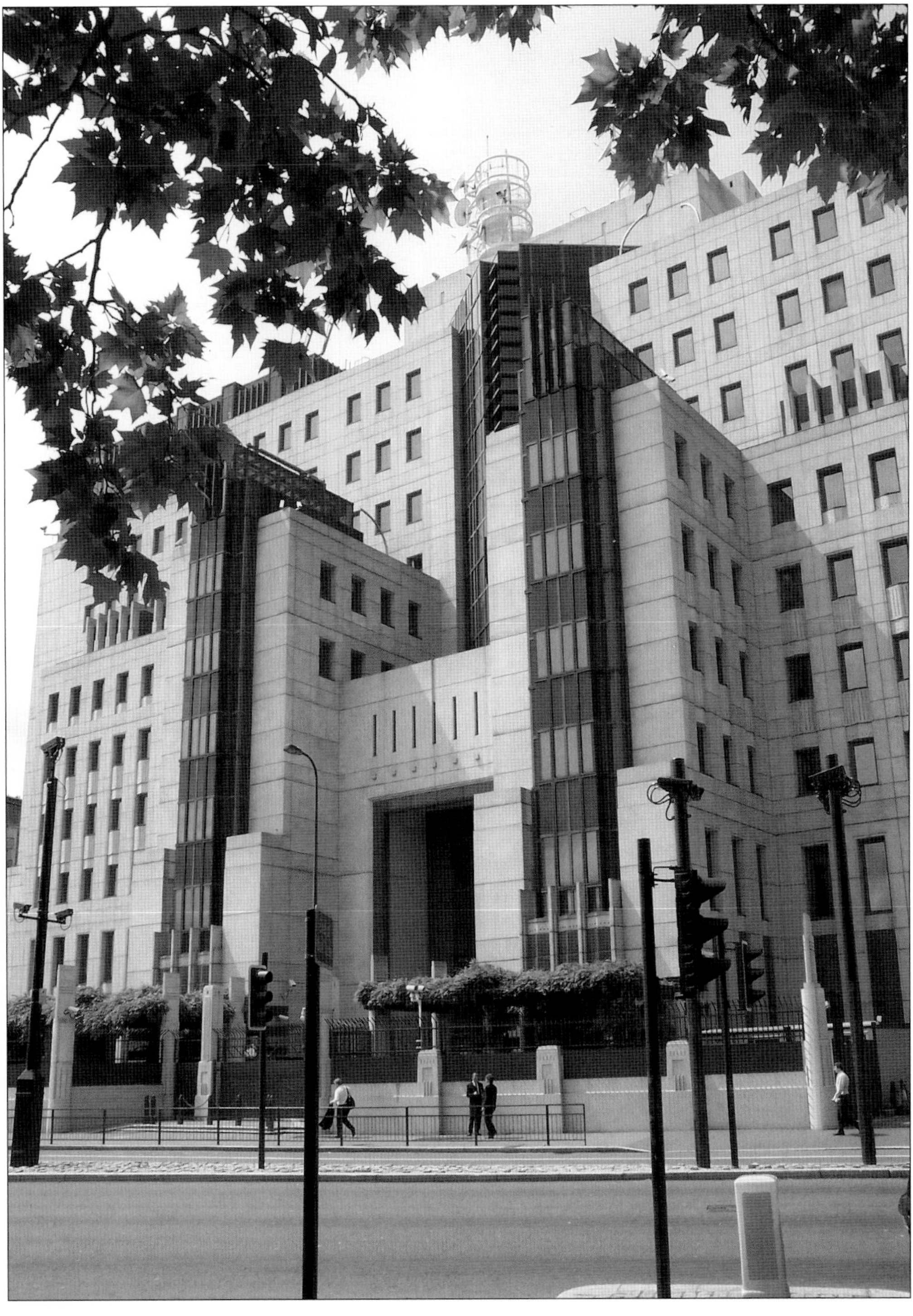

Vauxhall Cross, SIS's modernistic, flamboyant headquarters which was adapted for the organisation at short notice and huge cost when Century House was condemned as a health risk.

Sir David Spedding, the chain-smoking, golf-loving Arabist who was decorated by the Queen after he had helped foiled a bomb plot in Amman.

Above left: Sir Colin McColl, the Chief who negotiated the drafting and passage of the 1994 Intelligence Services Bill that placed the organisation on a statutory footing and put an end to the fiction that the service did not exist.

Above, centre: Sir John Scarlett, the only SIS chief to have been expelled from an overseas station during the earlier stages of his career. He subsequently bungled the publication of *The Mitrokhin Archives*, but was appointed Chairman of the JIC before his controversial return to Vauxhall Cross as Chief.

Above right: Sir Richard Dearlove, the Chief who gave evidence in public about Iraqi weapons of mass destruction to Lord Hutton's enquiry, and then in private to Lord Butler's committee and to the Parliamentary Intelligence and Security Committee.

Chapter VIII

Dickie Franks 1978–1981

'It is generally accepted by almost all intelligence officers whom I have questioned that, when Sir Arthur Franks was in charge of MI6, it was run with competence.'

Chapman Pincher in *The SpyCatcher Affair*[1]

A CAREER SIS officer, Arthur Temple Franks had joined the organisation in 1949, having been educated at Rugby and Queen's College, Oxford. He had served in the Army and then SOE between 1940 and 1946, and his first overseas SIS posting was to the station in Cyprus, operating under British Middle East Office cover, in 1952. The following year he was sent to Tehran, where he remained for three years, playing a key role in BOOT, the plan which overthrew Mossadeq and established the Shah. In 1956 he returned to Broadway as Controller Middle East. Later, as head of the London station, he laid the foundations of the operation to run Colonel Oleg Penkovsky, which was to prove so important.

Franks's recruitment of Greville Wynne as an agent and courier in the Soviet Union and Eastern Europe must have seemed fortuitous at the time, especially when his contact, Oleg Penkovsky, turned out to be a veritable goldmine of intelligence. This became clear at his first debrief in London, an event attended by two CIA officers, George Kisevalter and Joe Bulic, who acknowledged that Penkovsky was an authentic GRU officer, despite the suspicions briefly articulated at headquarters by the Counter-intelligence Chief, James J. Angleton, when Penkovsky had attempted to pitch the CIA. Although Penkovsky's was to be one of the most important cases of the Cold War, it was handicapped by his over-enthusiasm which led his case officers to believe that he had something approaching a death-wish. Equally dangerous was the behaviour of his British contact, Wynne, although these were matters that Dick White never alluded to when he had gathered SIS's headquarters staff together at the conclusion of the Cuban Missile Crisis to disclose SIS's covert role in resolving the confrontation.

Then a 43-year-old engineer and foreign trade negotiator, Greville M. Wynne had been approached by Penkovsky in Moscow to pass secrets to London, his previous attempts having been rebuffed by the Americans and Canadians the previous year. Different versions are given of how the two then met. At their trial Penkovsky and Wynne confirmed that Penkovsky's approach had occurred in a Moscow restaurant on 12 April 1961. However, Wynne was later to say that he had been deliberately but unsuccessfully 'dangled' in front of Penkovsky during two earlier trips to Moscow, in November and December 1960. However, the link forged in April 1961 was to remain firm until both men were arrested eighteen months later.

Wynne was the dyslexic son of a foreman in an engineering works from a poor mining village in South Wales who had been brought up with his three sisters in a small Victorian terraced house in Tredomen Villas, Ystrad Mynach. He had left school at the height of the depression in 1933, aged fourteen, to work as a labourer for an electrical contractor in Caerphilly, and later was to be apprenticed to a telephone company in Nottingham which, according to Wynne, was to lead him into the world of espionage.

The politically-convenient pretence that Wynne had been an innocent traveler who had been deliberately entrapped by the KGB came to an end in 1965 when Wynne learned that Penkovsky's story was to be published. Up until that moment the official British line was that Wynne had been an ordinary businessman and the victim of a tit-for-tat retaliation by the KGB. In fact Wynne's trading company in London, of which he and his wife were sole directors, had a sleeping partner: Dickie Franks of SIS. The company's main asset, at that time the longest articulated truck ever built in England, had been paid for in full by SIS so as to provide Wynne with suitable cover, that of a mobile trade fair demonstrating British goods in

Eastern Europe. However, all the elaborate deception came to an abrupt halt when the CIA authorised a Soviet defector, Piotr Deriabin, and a *Time* journalist, Frank Gibney, to reconstruct *The Penkovsky Papers*, which purported, somewhat improbably, to be the daily observations of Colonel Penkovsky of the GRU, written before his arrest, and smuggled out of his Moscow apartment before the KGB could act. Outraged that he had not been mentioned anywhere in the text, Wynne had insisted on writing a short foreword which, though brief, disclosed his true role as a conscious agent for the very first time, much to the embarrassment of Franks because of all the official ministerial denials that had been issued whenever anyone had questioned whether Wynne really had been the innocent businessman he had claimed to be. Successive ministers had ridiculed any link between Wynne and SIS, so Wynne's disclosures, contradicting the government's own public statements, were unwelcome and resented.

Wynne's own story, ghosted by his brother-in-law, John Gilbert, was released two years later as *The Man from Moscow*. Far from being innocent of the charges he was convicted of, Wynne revealed that he had been specifically recruited by SIS to contact Penkovsky and act as his courier, carrying microfilms of GRU secrets to London.

Wynne died on 27 February 1990 and during his lifetime had exercised what amounted to proprietorial rights over almost anything to do with Penkovsky; in some respects thus was quite understandable as his prison ordeal in the Soviet Union had been devastating, and upon his return to England he had experienced a nervous breakdown. He had divorced his wife Sheila, virtually disowned his only son Andrew, and had developed an acute alcohol problem which sometimes made him violent. The episode for which he became so well known dominated him entirely, and none of his subsequent business ventures ever amounted to the successes he claimed them to be. His second marriage in 1980 to a Dutch girl, Hermione Van Buren, ended 'because of his drunken rages' caused by his abuse of alcohol which, she claimed in a newspaper interview, had 'changed his personality'. He moved from the Canaries to Malta, Marbella and finally to Majorca, and became a well known figure in the bars frequented by the expatriate community in Palma. 'Wynne's drink problem started in Lanzarote where whisky was cheaper than a glass of mineral water' recalled Hermione.[2]

Wynne had been employed to sell villas at a development in the grounds of the San Antonio Hotel but his efforts ended in failure. Perhaps because of his inability to sustain relationships, Wynne became increasingly litigious and brought numerous legal actions against almost anyone who wrote about him.

In addition to *The Man from Moscow*, Wynne also released a sequel in 1981, *The Man from Odessa*, written with Bob Latona, in which he claimed he had first come into contact with British intelligence in 1938, just prior to the Second World War, when he had accidentally discovered a German spy using a clandestine transmitter in the Nottingham factory where they were both working. Having denounced the Nazi agent Wynne supposedly was selected for an undercover security role acting as an *agent provocateur*, identifying potentially disloyal Fascist sympathisers. Although posing as an ordinary soldier, Wynne alleged that he had ended the war with the rank of major and then had gone into business on his own, first as a property developer and club owner, and then as a representative abroad of several leading British engineering companies.

Wynne's first book had included an intriguing reference to Odessa, and a visit he had made there 'about five years' before his arrest (which would have placed him there in 1957)[3] and further details were to follow in *The Man from Odessa* in which Wynne revealed that, before his involvement with Penkovsky, he had undertaken an earlier mission for his SIS contact whom he only referred to as James. This dangerous operation had occurred in 1959 and had enabled a Soviet GRU officer, known to Wynne as Sergei Kuznov, to defect to the West with vital information. Wynne's second book was to also to make new disclosures about the celebrated Penkovsky case, claiming that he had accompanied Penkovsky on a secret visit to Washington DC where they had been received by President Kennedy. Like much of everything else Wynne said, this was sheer invention, and his tale about how he was originally recruited into British intelligence was a fiction His claim, that in November 1938 he had accidentally discovered a German spy operating an illicit wireless from within the factory at Beeston, Nottingham where they both worked, was untrue. At the time Wynne had been an engineering apprentice at the Ericsson Telephone Company and said that he had returned to a storehouse after hours to recover some tools he had forgotten, when he stumbled upon the Nazi agent. The spy was in an underground cellar, and Wynne had heard 'a series of staccato-like phrases in German'.[4] When he looked more closely, he could see a transmitter and an aerial, and this is what he reported to the authorities and what subsequently led to his recruitment.

SIS had been embarrassed by Wynne's bizarre stories, but was powerless to prevent him from spinning his yarns. In fact Wynne's Army service was a member of an anti-aircraft battery with the rank of private, and he had invented for himself an alternative undercover career as an *agent provocateur*, testing the loyalty of suspected Communists and Fascists. Although Wynne always insisted that he 'finished up at the end of World War II a major',[5] this was also false, although it was true that Wynne had manifested some distinctly leftist politics while still in the Army, as is demonstrated by his authorship of an undated four-page pamphlet calling for a postwar socialist administration. Entitled *After the War – What then Soldier?* it denounced capitalism and the government in strident terms and demanded a new order to replace the system that had been responsible for the slump after the Great War.

As for his SIS handler 'James', Wynne vouchsafed that he was 'a good ten years older than I', that he was a 'Sandhurst man', had been educated at Trinity College, Cambridge, had been 'parachuted into Yugoslavia to make contact with Tito's partisans' and, finally, is 'now approaching eighty, is retired and farming in Sussex'.[6] In reality, of course, Wynne had been run by Dickie Franks whose career coincided with none of the claims made for him. Franks was never in the Security Service, never jumped into Yugoslavia, and in 1981 (when *The Man from Odessa* was published), aged sixty, was still the Chief of SIS. He had been educated at Queen's College, Oxford, had not gone to Sandhurst, and his home was in Aldeburgh, Suffolk.

Wynne said that 'James' made contact with him again in 1959 in anticipation of a secret mission to Odessa where he was to assist in the exfiltration of an officer who 'held a high position in the GRU'.[7] Once at the port he had been introduced to the man he was to know as Major Sergei Kuznov and received an important package from him which he hid on the *Uzbekistan*, a Russian liner on which he was scheduled to travel to

Varna. However, the *Uzbekistan*, which Wynne described as 'a fairly new ship', was not launched until 1962 ... well after Wynne's imagined adventures.

Wynne's two contradictory accounts of his dealings with Penkovsky did not draw on the transcript of their four-day trial in Moscow in May 1963, nor an English-language booklet entitled *Penkovsky: Facts and Fancy*, published by Novosti and devoted to denigrating Penkovsky and ridiculing the idea that he might have been an ideologically-motivated spy. However, the transcript of Wynne's interrogation by Nikolai Chistiakov and Aleksandr Zagvozdin of the KGB on 22 November 1962 reveals that he made an offer to work for the KGB for a period of two years after his release, although this may have been a convenient ploy to facilitate an escape from his predicament.

In reality, and in contrast to Wynne's version, Dick White had been introduced to Penkovsky during the latter's second visit to London, and during his trial Penkovsky disclosed that White had been referred to simply as 'Raj'. The operation itself had been supervised by Oliver St John, a veteran SIS officer who had once run a network of agents in Cairo, leaving two case officers to deal with Penkovsky and Wynne separately. They were Harold Shergold, who never met Wynne, and Dickie Franks. In addition, there were two other senior officers indoctrinated into the case: Harry Stokes, then Oldfield's deputy in Washington DC, and John Collins, Shergold's Controller. The latter's London flat, at 52 Coleherne Court, had been used to entertain Penkovsky in London, and had been the venue for Dick White's meeting with him. While giving evidence at his trial Wynne could say very little about the involvement of the CIA as precautions had been taken to prevent him from learning the identities of Penkovsky's two American case officers, George Kisevalter and Joe Bulic. However Wynne had identified various SIS personnel, including Ruari Chisholm who had run SIS's Moscow station until July 1962 and his wife, Janet, who had held regular meetings with Penkovsky in December 1961 and January 1962. The clandestine role of this pair, of course, had already been disclosed to the KGB by Chisholm's former colleague in Berlin, George Blake. Indeed, Blake had admitted to his SIS interrogators in April 1961 that he had compromised Chisholm before he had even arrived in Moscow.

One of the reasons for SIS's defensiveness about Wynne was the problem that, when Penkovsky had been arrested, Wynne was still in the West, preparing for what would turn out to be his final mission, to Budapest. Penkovsky had been taken into custody in Gorky Street at 1.55 on the afternoon of Monday, 22 October 1962, yet Wynne crossed over from Vienna to Hungary on 31 October, only to be arrested there at 7.00 in the evening on Friday, 2 November. Thus, by the time Wynne was arrested in Budapest, Penkovsky had been in the hands of the KGB for at least ten days.

On the day that Wynne was arrested, the KGB had conducted an experiment in Moscow to test the information extracted from Penkovsky during his lengthy interrogation. Penkovsky had revealed his instructions on how to make contact with the CIA and had described the elaborate procedure they had adopted. It was tradecraft of the most classic variety. First, a signal had to be sent to two American diplomats at their homes. Shortly before nine in the morning the KGB had made a silent telephone call to Alexis Davison, an assistant air attaché who also happened to be the US Embassy's Russian-speaking doctor. Conforming to Penkovsky's arrangement. the KGB had hung up without a word and repeated the exercise on another number which had been answered by the CIA's Hugh Montgomery, who also lived in an apartment at 18 Kutuzovsky Prospekt. In addition, a black mark had been placed on lamp-post 35 on Kutuzovsky Prospekt. Having received the call, Davison drove along Kutuzovsky Prospekt and got out of his car to examine the appropriate lamp-post. He then was seen to drive to the US Embassy and at 3.15 p.m. the same day another American diplomat, Richard C. Jacob, was seized by the KGB while attempting to recover a small canister concealed behind a central heating radiator in the hallway of 5/6 Pushkin Street. Thus, having demonstrated that Penkovsky's confession was certainly true in so far as it referred to his means of communicating with the CIA via dead letter drops, the KGB had arranged for Wynne's arrest.

The CIA's Moscow station had been unaware that Penkovsky had been compromised until 2 November when Jacob was entrapped while attempting to service the drop in Pushkin Street, so no warning was given. Under these circumstances it would be understandable that there was insufficient time to tell Wynne in Budapest of the danger he was in. However, there is another bizarre side to the story, for it would seem that shortly before his arrest Penkovsky had sent a coded 'Doomsday message' to his new SIS case officer, Gervase Cowell, indicating that a Soviet nuclear strike on the West was imminent. At the time Penkovsky's behaviour had caused consternation among those indoctrinated into the case, but in retrospect it may have been his way of alerting SIS to the fact that he had either come under direct KGB control, or had merely detected hostile surveillance.

Penkovsky's last dealings with the CIA had been in September when he had spotted his principal contact, Rodney Carlson, at a reception given by the US Ambassador for a group of visiting executives from the American electrical industry. On 6 September he had attended a film show of *A Taste of Honey* at the British Embassy where he had been spotted by Cowell, who had taken over from Ruari Chisholm after the latter's return to London on 14 July 1962.

There are still many question marks hanging over the Wynne and Penkovsky case, and not a few of them have been placed there by Wynne himself. Some of those who worked with him on his overseas trips considered his consumption of alcohol to be a hazard to his regular business, quite apart from any espionage on the side, and he was a familiar figure to habitués of the British Club at the British Embassy who frequently saw him the worse for wear. Joe Bulic, for one, considered that SIS's inexplicable reluctance to cut Wynne lose was dangerously unprofessional, but his protests were ignored.

The KGB's opinion of Wynne was also pretty low. Viktor Kutuzov, speaking on behalf of the organisation, remarked:

> Wynne hated the British secret service agents who had ruined him, used him and discarded him like so much refuse. He wept and sobbed in front of the Interrogating Judge and in court, castigated himself, his rashness, his trust in those ruthless sharks from the Intelligence Service. Apparently this was why Wynne made to Soviet authorities some important revelation about certain high ranking person in the British secret service, which

> with time may be made public. Wynne did not stop there. He cynically offered the Soviet authorities to perform espionage assignments against the West.[8]

After their convictions in Moscow in May 1963, Wynne had been sentenced to eight years' imprisonment, five of which were to be spent in a labour camp, and Penkovsky had been executed by a firing squad. On a bleak windswept morning on 22 April 1964 a slightly bewildered Wynne was escorted by a group of KGB guards to the Heerstrasse checkpoint in the Berlin Wall where he was released. Simultaneously, a KGB illegal, Konon Molody, alias Gordon Lonsdale, walked in the opposite direction, having been freed from a twenty-five year prison sentence in Britain.

Certainly Wynne's experience in the Soviet Union changed his life. Thereafter he was regarded as a pest by SIS and, to a lesser extent, by the CIA which twice tried to assist him on visits to America. On neither occasion did Wynne take any interest in the business leads he was offered, but instead concentrated on drinking. He led a nomadic existence, working initially in Malta selling holiday apartments, a project that was abandoned in 1972, and then moving to the Canary Islands where a friend employed him to promote a villa development on Lanzarote. Finally he bought an apartment in Palma de Majorca where he became a well known member of the hard-drinking British expatriate community led by Lady Docker. Here he went into a rose growing partnership, and later contracted cancer of the throat. His continued alcohol-induced abuse of his second wife led to her estrangement, and she went to live in a windowless basement sauna at a property he had once owned in Lexham Gardens in west London. In March 1985, in an interview with Philippa Kennedy of the *Daily Express*, she complained that she had been deserted by Wynne and said that he had 'missed the secrecy and tension of his other life'.[9]

Wynne's decline into fantasy, as manifested by *The Man from Odessa*, which was full of bizarre claims, included the suggestion that the destruction of the Tupolev 144 supersonic jet which crashed so spectacularly at the Paris Air Show in June 1973 had been a consequence of a scheme to plant deliberately falsified Concorde data on the Tupolev's

Soviet designers. Such assertions were absurd, but there was always a danger that someone in the Kremlin or the KGB might believe them.

In the aftermath of the Penkovsky affair, Franks was posted in 1962 to Bonn. In November 1966 he returned to London, and twelve years later he was appointed Chief.

Franks had scarcely taken over from Oldfield, in a very smooth, uncontroversial succession, taking on Allan Rowley as his deputy, when he was confronted, fortuitously, with the opportunity to receive a defector, Vladimir Rezun, who was a GRU officer based in Geneva. At the time SIS had achieved the impossible by running Gordievsky without incident, but Major Rezun's offer to SIS's Gordon Barrass in June 1978 represented a significant breakthrough because a GRU defector was an exceptionally rare commodity. Apart from Grigori Tokaev, back in 1948, SIS had not come even close to attracting a line-crosser from the GRU which exercised a strict military discipline over its personnel and was generally considered virtually impenetrable. Quite apart from Rezun's symbolic value as further proof that SIS could accomplish one of its primary tasks, to attract valuable defectors, he possessed a deep knowledge of the history of the GRU which he capitalised on, during his resettlement in Britain, by releasing a series of books on the subject.

Thirty-one years old, and working under United Nations cover, Rezun was smuggled out of the country to England with his wife and two young children. A career soldier, he had participated in the invasion of Czechoslovakia in 1968 and later had supervised the training of the elite *Spetsnaz* special forces. He had also undertaken missions in Munich, Rome, Basel, Amsterdam, Vienna and Hamburg. Using the cheeky pseudonym 'Viktor Suvorov', the name of a respected Soviet military commander, Rezun wrote *Inside the Soviet Army* which discussed the relationship between the KGB and its military counterpart, the GRU. This was later followed by *Inside Soviet Military Intelligence*, and his autobiography, *Inside the Aquarium* and *Spetsnaz*. In 1993, still using the pseudonym Victor Suvorov, Rezun released *Icebreaker* in Russia, a controversial interpretation of the origins of the Second World War which concluded that Stalin had always intended to go to war against Germany in July 1941, a theory not entirely novel, but widely discredited in Western academic circles. Despite the criticism of aspects of his writings, Rezun had helped to expand the West's knowledge of the GRU, an organisation largely unknown in comparison to the KGB. Rezun's books gained very wide circulation, thereby enhancing SIS's status as an organisation that could compete with the CIA and 'punch above its weight'.

Rezun's example was followed in March 1980 by Ilya Dzhirkvelov, a KGB officer working under journalistic cover in Geneva, who contacted SIS following an incident which had threatened to jeopardise his career, and negotiated his defection. The result was the entirely successful receipt of an experienced, well-placed 'Line PR' officer with detailed knowledge of KGB operations in the Middle East, who was encouraged to release an account of his career in *Secret Servant* which was published in 1988.

Dzhirkvelov had spent his entire career in the organisation, having joined the NKVD in 1943 while working in the resistance to the German invasion of his native Georgia. Both his parents had been active Bolsheviks and he was also a committed member of the Party. By April 1944, when the Nazis retreated from Sevastapol, he had been appointed a cadet officer in a small commando unit assigned to clear up what was left of the Waffen-SS in the newly liberated areas. During the Yalta Conference in February 1945 he was one of the guard detachment which maintained security for the visitors, and later in the war he operated against nationalist guerrillas in Latvia. By the end of hostilities he was back in Tblisi, only to be selected in September 1945 for a course at the NKVD's training school in Moscow. After two years he and his wife were sent on a short assignment to Romania, which lasted six weeks, and then he was posted to the Iranian section of the FCD's Middle East department; in 1949, having learned Farsi, he was transferred to Tehran. On his return to Moscow Dzhirkvelov worked in the KGB's archives and attended the Higher Party School in the evenings. His career then took an unexpected turn following the disclosure that his father, whom he had never known, had not died at sea in the way described by his mother, but in fact had been executed in 1937, while serving a ten-year prison sentence for undefined political offences.

Nevertheless, in August 1952, despite this setback, Dzhirkvelov was rehabilitated and transferred to the FCD's American department. Later he moved to the newly-formed Second Chief Directorate, responsible for the surveillance of suspect foreigners in Moscow, specialising in diplomats from Iran, Egypt and Turkey. In 1955 he returned to the FCD's Tenth Department, monitoring the Turkish frontier and liaising with the Georgian KGB in Tblisi, and in August 1957 was back in Moscow with the Second Chief Directorate, ostensibly working for the Soviet Informburo (the predecessor of Novosti), but actually reporting to General Norman Borodin. His special responsibility was the Foreign Journalists' Development Department, the word 'development' in Russian, *razrabotka*, being a KGB euphemism for a combination of surveillance, influencing, misinforming and recruiting.

As part of his cover, Dzhirkvelov worked for *Soviet Sport* and became General Secretary of the Union of Journalists of the USSR, a post he held from 1957 until September 1965 when he joined TASS and was assigned as the agency's correspondent in Zanzibar, where he arrived with his wife in September 1967. There they remained until early 1970 when they moved to Dar-es-Salaam temporarily before taking up a permanent post in Khartoum in May. While in Tanzania Dzhirkvelov reported to the local *rezidentura* where Colonel Arkadi Boiko kept him supplied with:

> . . . well-written articles revealing scandalous connections between the Peace Corps and the CIA. Using my journalistic contacts and simply paying some local pressmen, I managed to plant several such articles in Tanzanian and Ugandan newspapers signed, of course, by popular native names.

The Dzhirkvelovs spent just over two years in the Sudan and in April 1974 he flew to Geneva as a press officer for the UN World Health Organisation. This attractive posting came as a surprise because in that year Dzhirkvelov had been listed in John Barron's *KGB: The Secret Work of Soviet Secret Agents* as a KGB asset who, Barron alleged, had been expelled from Turkey and in 1971 had been spotted in the Sudan.

Dzhirkvelov's mission to Geneva remained uneventful until New Year's Day 1980 when, after a minor traffic accident, he was accused of drink-driving. Dzhirkvelov denied the charge but when he declined to resign, insisting on completing his contract which was due to run until May 1981, he was recalled to Moscow in March. Within hours of landing he learned that his career was in ruins so, without waiting for the final interview at which he knew he would be confined to Moscow, he hastily flew to Vienna and took a train back to Geneva where he explained his predicament to his wife and daughter who agreed to join him and apply to the SIS station commander, Julian Wiseman, for political asylum in Britain. His 'meal-ticket' was his wide knowledge of KGB operations and his confirmation that a substantial proportion of TASS correspondents around the world were undercover KGB officers, including those in Dublin and London.

Franks's role as a Cold Warrior in the classic mould, and his ideological commitment to confronting the KGB may have been of some interest to Mrs Thatcher when she entered Downing Street in May 1979, but she mentioned neither him nor Oldfield in her memoirs *The Downing Street Years*. Given her views on the importance of secrecy this may not be entirely surprising, but there can be little doubt that she had been favourably impressed by Oldfield, who had been authorised to brief her while she was still in opposition before her election victory, and to whom she was to turn for help in Northern Ireland. Of course, her first security crisis had occurred in November 1979 when she had supervised the exposure of Anthony Blunt, but on that occasion her dealings had been with a new MI5 Director-General, Sir Howard Smith, and that entire episode was also omitted from her autobiography. However, Mrs Thatcher's first diplomatic challenge of her premiership, and indeed of her political career, was obtaining a settlement in Rhodesia. This was obtained at the constitutional conference called at Lancaster House in September 1979, chaired by Lord Carrington, having been negotiated by Tony Duff. The supreme skill required to bring the main three warring groups to the table, as demonstrated by Duff, was due in no small measure to the unseen contribution made by SIS, which remains classified.

When Franks retired as Chief in July 1981, his recommendation for the succession of his deputy, Colin Figures, was uncontroversial and unopposed by the four other members of the Permanent Secretaries' Committee on the Intelligence Services, chaired by Sir Robert Armstrong. Most importantly, during his three years in office, he had acquired and passed on SIS's most valuable source inside the KGB, Oleg Gordievsky, who continued to operate unsuspected, supplying the most significant information. However, although he did not realise it at the time, he had played a quiet, but ultimately disastrous role in what was to become known as the *SpyCatcher* affair, a debacle that would cause worldwide embarrassment for MI5, the Cabinet Secretary and the Prime Minister.

The involvement of Franks in the *SpyCatcher* affair began in December 1980, just eighteen months before his departure from Century House, when he was informed by a social acquaintance that the former *Daily Express* journalist Chapman Pincher intended to write a book, entitled *Their Trade Is Treachery*, about Soviet penetration of the British establishment, obviously based on information gleaned from inside the intelligence community. Franks acquired from his friend, acting as an intermediary with the knowledge of Pincher's publisher Sidgwick & Jackson, a two-page synopsis of the book, which was scheduled for publication in March the following year, and he circulated news of this impending event to his own senior staff and to MI5. However, it was not until February 1981 that he received, through his intermediary, a copy of the completed typescript, on the strict understanding that neither the publisher nor the author should be penalised for having given SIS an opportunity to read and comment on the project. In return, Franks had received an assurance from the publisher that the book would not be published if he expressed 'serious concerns'. The precise nature of this arrangement was to cause considerable problems for MI5 and the Cabinet Office as the Chief felt that he was under an obligation to protect the identity of his source, and accordingly he did not disclose it.

An analysis undertaken by Franks and his staff concluded that the material primarily concerned the Security Service but contained plenty of detail about classified SIS operations and disclosed that John Cairncross and Dick Ellis had confessed to having betrayed SIS's secrets. There was little doubt that Pincher's detail had come from an MI5 retiree, and when Dick White was shown a copy of the manuscript he exclaimed instantly that it had been the handiwork of Peter Wright, a molehunter who had begun his MI5 career as a technician in 1955. Wright had taken early retirement in January 1973 but had continued as an adviser, on a part-time basis, to the Director-General, Sir Michael Hanley until he emigrated to Tasmania three years later. As a counter-intelligence expert who had worked alongside Arthur Martin, and had taken the lead role in debriefing Anthony Blunt after his confession in April 1964, Wright knew practically all there was to know about MI5's most sensitive operations, and it was clear from Pincher's manuscript that much else had been omitted, apparently in an exercise of self-censorship or maybe on advice from lawyers anxious about the libel implications.

While the damage to MI5 was immense, SIS appeared to escape quite lightly, and this was the view expressed by Dick White and the former Cabinet Secretary, Lord Hunt of Tanworth, to Sir Robert Armstrong. Among those who were consulted on the content in March 1981 was Sir Michael Hanley, MI5's D-G who had been replaced in 1979 by a diplomat, Sir Howard Smith, and, although few doubted Peter Wright had been Pincher's source, there was at that stage no firm evidence to support the view. Only much later would MI5 trace Pincher's travel movements and demonstrate that he had visited Tasmania in October 1980. Within MI5, there was initial disbelief that, of all people, Wright could have broken MI5's code of *omerta* and haemorrhaged so much, including authentic operational codenames, to Pincher. At Century House, the view was rather different. Wright had made himself unpopular with SIS by dreaming up a bizarre theory that Oleg Penkovsky had been planted on SIS deliberately by the KGB as part of a complex *dezinformatsia* strategy. Not many insiders subscribed to this weird interpretation of a case generally regarded as one of the great coups of the Cold War, and not even the ever-suspicious Golitsyn had seriously questioned Penkovsky's bonafides, although he did once assert there was 'serious, unresolved evidence' that he had been controlled from the outset by the KGB. Wright had been indoctrinated into the case at an early stage to supervise the surveillance during Penkovsky's visit to London in July 1961 but when, years later, his paper on Penkovsky had been circulated it had been met with 'howls of outrage' and in a meeting soon afterwards one of Penkovsky's case officers, Harry Shergold, had to be physically restrained from attacking him. Oldfield had warned Wright that his unusual interpretation would be poorly received because there were so many knighthoods 'and gongs riding high on the back of Penkovsky'. The fact that Pincher had retailed Wright's version so faithfully gave a strong clue to his book's true authorship. Similarly, Pincher had given a very detailed account of the EMERTON investigation into Dick Ellis which had been conducted jointly by Wright and Pantcheff, and only a handful of officers in both organisations knew even a fraction of the account contained in *Their Trade Is Treachery*. In short, the pages screamed the identity of Pincher's collaborator.

Although *Their Trade Is Treachery* concentrated on MI5's failures, there were some passages which caused grave concern at Century House, among them the assertion that Gunter Guillaume, the East German spy found in Chancellor Willi Brandt's private office, had been arrested in April 1974 after a tip from the British. Under normal circumstances such a comment might have gone unnoticed or unremarked but, although the author did not realise it, this was the very first time anyone anywhere had disclosed a British role in unmasking Guillaume, who had worked successfully and undetected as a spy since his arrival in West Germany, posing as a refugee, in 1956. Hitherto all credit for tracking down Guillaume had gone to the BfV, the Federal German security service, but the authoritative statement that the British had supplied the clue potentially jeopardised the British source. The anxiety in Century House was that Oleg Gordievsky's safety had been compromised, and MI5 could not give a firm commitment that Peter Wright had not learned of SIS's coup before his final retirement in 1976. While the material in *Their Trade Is Treachery* was considered bad enough, SIS feared that far worse might follow if Wright was provoked. In those circumstances, Franks urged that no action should be taken that might prompt further revelations, advice that allowed the book to be published without interference, much to the author's relief and disbelief.

The first serialisation of *Their Trade Is Treachery* appeared in the *Daily Mail* on 23 March 1980, sensationally revealing that MI5's former D-G, Sir Roger Hollis, who had died in 1973, had been investigated as a Soviet spy suspect, and on that day Sir Robert Armstrong telephoned Sidgwick & Jackson and asked for a couple of advance copies of the book so the Prime Minister could be briefed for a statement to be given to the Commons. When asked for an assurance that this privilege would not result in any legal action to delay or prevent the book's release, Armstrong volunteered a personal, written undertaking, neglecting to mention that the original manuscript had been in his possession for some six weeks already, and that the matter had been discussed at a meeting held earlier in the month attended by the Home Secretary, Willie Whitelaw, the Prime Minister, Armstrong and Howard Smith. Very unusually, no minutes were taken of what was said.

The book was released on Thursday, 26 March, and that same afternoon Mrs Thatcher told the Commons that much of Pincher's information was either distorted or plain wrong, and announced that, despite Pincher's inaccuracies, she had instructed the Security Commission to prepare a review of the security procedures of the security and intelligence agencies to protect them against hostile penetration. This was Whitehall's conventional expedient, to kick an awkward issue into the long grass, and there it might have remained, except for two developments. One emerged when Pincher, who by chance had met Dickie Franks briefly at a lunch hosted by a mutual friend in April 1982, invited him to join him in a meal at a restaurant in Farnham, Surrey, on 16 September. Pincher's motive had been to question Franks, who had by then retired from SIS, about an allegation that Oldfield 'had been a practising homosexual and this had become known to the police and the security authorities'.[10] The story had reached Pincher through two authors working on a future book, but Franks had said only that he was aware that the claim had appeared in the Irish press, and could not comment on its accuracy. Pincher then dropped the subject, but in his book *Traitors: The Anatomy of Treason*, published in April 1987, he included the story that Oldfield had lost his security clearance because he had lied on his security questionnaires about his homosexuality.

This was the only occasion when Franks had met Pincher alone, and he had reported it to SIS, but the very limited extent of their relationship was to be misunderstood, to the point that when Sir Robert Armstrong was challenged during his evidence in the *SpyCatcher* trial in Sydney in November 1986, he said that he believed the two had met 'from time to time', thereby giving the mistaken impression that the two regularly exchanged information.

The second problem was Wright's disappointment with *Their Trade Is Treachery*, and his decision to embark on a further publishing project entitled *SpyCatcher*, assisted on this occasion by a Granada Television producer, Paul Greengrass. In March 1987, no sooner had Wright won the action brought against him in Australia to prevent the distribution of *SpyCatcher*, than it was released in the United States. Fortunately *SpyCatcher* omitted any reference to how Gunter Guillaume had been caught, but in any event Oleg Gordievsky by then had been exfiltrated to safety in England. Although *Spycatcher* covered much the same ground as *Their Trade Is Treachery*, the damage it inflicted on MI5 was considerably greater, mainly because Wright had declared himself to be the author, previously having taken elaborate steps to conceal his collaboration with Pincher. In operational terms, if *SpyCatcher* was to be an embarrassment for Christopher Curwen, it was a disaster for the Security Service and a catastrophe for Mrs Thatcher's administration, severely damaging the reputation of her Cabinet Secretary, who had acknowledged under oath in Sydney to having been 'economical with the truth'. Once again, the long-nurtured mystique of the Secret Intelligence Service had been undermined in yet another book about Britain's not-so-secret intelligence agencies.

Chapter IX

Colin Figures 1981–1985

EDUCATED at King Edward's School in Birmingham, and Pembroke College, Cambridge, Colin Figures served in the Worcestershire Regiment between 1943 and 1948. He joined SIS in 1951 and in June 1953 was posted to Germany, under Control Commission cover. In September 1956, in time to be a witness to the Suez debacle, he went to Amman, staying until April 1959, when he handed over to Michael Whittall, and then in December was posted to Warsaw for three years, working as an understudy to John Quine, a former wartime Navy officer, for the first four months. Here Figures was indoctrinated into three cases, all Polish UB intelligence service officers, who had been 'walk-ins', volunteering their services to the British. Naturally, SIS had capitalised on the deep affection felt by many Poles for Britain, appreciative of the sacrifices made by both countries during the Second World War. London remained the seat of the Polish government-in-exile and, apart from the WIN fiasco, when SIS and the CIA had been duped by the Soviets, there was a reservoir of goodwill towards the British, and that apparently extended into the UB. Of the three volunteers, NODDY, with the rank of colonel, was the most productive, and his information included material he had picked up during his frequent visits to Moscow. Initially, of course, there had been suspicion that NODDY was yet another KGB-orchestrated deception, but Robert Dawson, SIS's Director of Production for Eastern Europe, designated DP4, had authenticated him, and he had proved his worth time and again. Contact with him in a denied environment like Warsaw where there was ubiquitous hostile surveillance was dangerous, reliant on fleeting brush-past meetings and the familiar tradecraft of dead drops, but Figures and his agents had survived, and he had passed them on to his successor, Michael Pakenham.

Figures's last overseas posting was to Vienna, between October 1966, when he took over from Guy Bratt, and August 1969, handing over to Sandy Rosdol, and over the next ten years he held senior posts at Century House. In July 1981 he succeeded Dickie Franks as Chief, and took on Stephen Longrigg, a graduate of Magdalen College, Oxford, and former wartime Rifle Brigade officer with service in Baghdad, Berlin, Pretoria, Washington DC, Bahrain, Dakar and Hong Kong, as his deputy, although Longrigg was scheduled to retire the following year.

Within the month Figures was briefing the Foreign Secretary, Lord Carrington, on the advisability of expelling Viktor Lazin, a KGB officer under second secretary cover at the Soviet Embassy since 1977, who had been seen contacting PIRA suspects in Dublin. As there had not been any expulsions from London since FOOT, the decision to make Lazin *persona non grata* required the widest consultations but the evidence to incriminate him was available should the Soviets choose to challenge the Foreign Office. Lazin's removal went without incident, and the exercise was repeated early in February the following year when a GRU officer, Vadim Zadneporovsky, under Trade Delegation cover, was ordered out.

In April 1982 the new Chief was quickly plunged into the Falklands conflict, which was to define Mrs Thatcher's government. The war would be a moment of considerable triumph for SIS, as it responded to the crisis and made a considerable contribution to the snatching of victory from the jaws of what had promised to be a heavy, humiliating defeat and the collapse of Mrs Thatcher's unpopular administration.

The conflict with Argentina was a war for which SIS was completely unprepared, and in the first weeks of the campaign it sustained a series of body-blows. In terms of being a credible source of intelligence about Argentine intentions, SIS had not even been close to the starting grid. The SIS station in Buenos Aires, headed by Mark Heathcote, was declared to its hosts and there had been very little opportunity or support to develop local sources. There had been absolutely no advance reporting by SIS of any plan to seize the Falklands, and the Argentines had prepared their coup with commendable, uncharacteristic, secrecy that not even the CIA had penetrated. In the absence of a station in Chile, which had been closed under a directive from the previous Labour government in protest at General Augusto Pinochet's regime, or in any other country on the entire continent, SIS had been heavily reliant on the routine diplomatic telegrams from an embassy run by a lack-lustre ambassador and a staff that was at odds with itself, dominated by the Defence Attaché, Colonel Stephen Love, who had been viewed in London as someone prone to exaggerating the threat from General Galtieri's junta. Instead of relying on SIS, the JIC's Latin America Current Intelligence Group had been heavily dependent on GCHQ's monitoring of Argentine military traffic which had confirmed the continued presence on top of the Andes, overlooking the Chilean frontier, of the single unit identified as the most likely to participate in any amphibious landing on the Falklands. In the event, this well-trained group of special forces remained at their post throughout the conflict and was never deployed to the islands. Upon the outbreak of hostilities, Heathcote was expelled to Montevideo and then withdrawn to London where he ran a war room with the Western Hemisphere Controller, Alastair Rellie. In the absence of any station, SIS's few assets in Buenos Aires were entrusted to the local CIA station chief, Vinx Blocker.

Compounding the lack of advance warning, SIS had almost no knowledge of Argentine military capabilities and, fatally, accepted French assurances from Aerospatiale, relayed through Alexis Forter in Paris, that the avionics of the Super Etendard aircraft supplied to the Argentine Navy had not been married to the Exocet sea-skimming anti-ship missiles. Accordingly, the unexpected attack on the radar picket HMS *Sheffield* on 4 May transformed the prosecution of the war by the British Task Force. The Type 42 destroyer was consumed by a devastating fire after having been hit by an Exocet launched by a Super Etendard flying from Rio Grande. The Task Force had not anticipated any threat from Exocets, and had not believed that the Argentine fighter-bombers could be refuelled in the air to give them sufficient range to threaten the British ships. Both proved to be miscalculations and SIS was called upon to establish the precise numbers of Exocet missiles available to the enemy, and interdict any future resupplies, conscious that if either of the two carriers, HMS

Invincible or *Hermes*, was hit, the Task Force would have to withdraw. This was achieved by running a scam in Paris targeted against the Argentine naval procurement office which had been tasked to trawl the international arms black and grey markets for Exocet reloads. Tony Divall, a former SIS officer based in Hamburg, who had participated in the operation to sell arms to the Provisional IRA in March 1973, which resulted in the seizure off the Waterford coast of the *Claudia* and its cargo of Libyan weapons, was recruited to make a bogus sale to the Argentines, and this was accomplished twice. On the first occasion the naval attaché in Paris was persuaded to part with his money in return for a non-existent consignment of missiles, and on the second he was duped into participating in lengthy negotiations for a further sale which never materialised, thus denying the enemy their potentially war-winning weapon.

SIS also played a significant role in the interdiction in Spain of a three-man team of saboteurs sent from Buenos Aires to attack British naval targets in Gibraltar. Like their leader Maximo Nicolletti, the other two members of the team were former Montonero guerrillas, known as *El Pelado Diego* (Bald Diego), whose real name was Nelson Armando Latorre, and a diver simply known as *El Marciano* (The Martian). Nicolletti and his team had been provided with Italian-made wetsuits and Scuba gear, and on their arrival in Spain they had liaised with an Argentine naval intelligence officer whom they knew only as 'Lieutenant Hector', who had been sent to Spain to prepare the mission and provide three semi-spherical hanging Italian mines which had been smuggled into Spain in a diplomatic bag. On arrival in Madrid on 17 April the team had rented three cars and traveled to southern Spain using the back roads to avoid detection, and frequently changed hotels in the La Linea area. After carrying out a reconnaissance of the Gibraltar waterfront, noting the poor security and unmanned guard-posts, they decided that the easiest way was to enter the port by dinghy, and then dive and place the mines. Their escape was to be through Spain and then overland to Italy. A rubber dinghy with a small outboard engine was purchased at an El Corte Inglés store, and the team entered Gibraltar, unchallenged, from a beach on the Spanish side of the frontier.

The mission was unorthodox because they had both to undertake the reconnaissance and carry out the operation themselves. Furthermore, they were under orders from Buenos Aires, via Lieutenant Hector, not to go into action without prior clearance. According to Nicoletti, the group was refused authorisation to attack British ships entering Gibraltar on several occasions, including a frigate that presented a tempting target.

When finally, on 17 May, Nicoletti was given the green light to execute an attack on a BP oil tanker, the *British Tamar*, it was too late, for that was the day he was arrested by the Spanish police. The operation was to be carried out in the evening but early in the morning Hector and one of the group went to renew the rental agreements on the cars, and were detained by the Guardia Civil who apparently were searching for a gang of Argentine robbers thought to be in the neighbourhood. Hector immediately declared that he was an Argentine naval intelligence officer, and at midday the house where Nicoletti and the other divers were asleep was raided. After several hours detention they were put on a plane to Madrid, and then sent back to Argentina with no public statement.

Although Nicoletti was unaware of it, his mission had been monitored, from his arrival in Madrid, by GCHQ, which was routinely intercepting and decrypting the Argentine Embassy's cipher traffic. Once SIS learned of Lieutenant Hector's role a discussion took place in Whitehall to establish whether his activities were known, or even approved of by the Spanish authorities. The conclusion of the debate within the War Cabinet was that the Spanish government should be tipped off to Nicoletti's activities, on the basis that, whatever the circumstances, they would be forced to intervene. If the mission had an unofficial Spanish consent, the confirmation that it had been compromised would force Madrid to act. If, on the other hand, the Spanish had not collaborated, they would also be under an obligation to interdict the team. David Reddaway at the SIS station in Madrid was instructed to tip off the Spanish authorities and Nicoletti was arrested, but his silent expulsion strongly suggested a degree of Spanish diplomatic embarrassment, if not outright complicity.

SIS's role during the war was judged to have been of considerable value to the final outcome, not least because of the danger represented by the Exocet, but this was a political view, and not one taken into account by Lord (Oliver) Franks who was appointed to chair a committee of privy counsellors to investigate the reason for Britain's unpreparedness for the conflict. Franks took evidence from GCHQ, SIS and the JIC, and concluded that the warning from Argentine naval traffic, intercepted after the enemy's invasion force had put to sea, had been much too late to be acted upon with any hope of preventing the capture of the islands. Fortunately for Mrs Thatcher's government, in the version of the report made public, Franks was uncritical of the MoD's decision to scrap HMS *Endurance*, Britain's only Sigint platform in the region, to save its running costs of £3 million a year. The Argentines had interpreted John Nott's infamous Defence Estimates as an invitation to invade, as noted to the Defence Intelligence Staff by *Endurance*'s commander, Captain Nick Barker RN, following his call in to Ushuaia at the end of January 1982, but the Foreign Office had discounted his report, knowing his fondness for visiting his Argentine girlfriend and finding excuses to put in to port at every opportunity.

The key constitutional point that emerged from the Franks Report was the committee's inability to acknowledge the role played by SIS because of the increasingly anachronistic position that C's organisation should not be avowed. Accordingly, although Figures gave evidence to Franks, there is no reference to this in the report. To that extent, the resulting published report was virtually an irrelevance. Also omitted was Jim Callaghan's evidence regarding the 1977 deployment of HMS *Dreadnought*. Although he insisted, both in a speech to the House of Commons on 30 March 1982 and in his memoirs, published in 1987, that he had authorised Oldfield to leak news of JOURNEYMAN in Buenos Aires, his former Foreign Secretary, Dr David Owen, was equally emphatic that he had never done so:

> In fact the Head of MI6 would have read all the Cabinet Committee papers on this question. He would also have been aware from the Foreign Office that I had refused an MoD request to inform the US Navy about our deployment, for the very reason that I knew they had close links with the Argentine Navy and I did not want the Argentines to know. I do not believe that Maurice Oldfield, who was primarily answerable to me as Foreign Secretary, as well as to the Prime Minister, would have disclosed the naval deployment as a result of a discussion with the Prime

> Minister, at least not without talking to me first. Although in some delicate areas he would be entitled to respond only to the Prime Minister I do not believe that this was one of them.[1]

Thus there remains a fundamental conflict between the two Labour politicians on this vital issue:

> It was amazing [observed Owen] that the Franks Report never rebuffed or corroborated his statement that he had told the Head of MI6, Maurice Oldfield, to let his contacts in the Argentine government know that our submarines were in the vicinity of the Falklands and therefore able to act.[2]

Unwilling to address this potential embarrassment, Franks had simply overlooked it entirely, yet the point in question could hardly have been more germane. For example, Lord Carrington, who resigned as Foreign Secretary on 3 April 1982, the day after the Argentines invaded, disclosed that he had not been briefed on JOURNEYMAN until 5 March 1982, almost a week after Callaghan had mentioned it in the Commons. This was a colossal failure, yet Franks made no mention of the lapse which had been concealed behind the excuse of the Whitehall convention that incoming administrations should not see the papers of their predecessors.

The reality was that the entire conflict had been unnecessary and a monumental failure of intelligence, with the JIC having reported in early July 1981 that if Argentina failed to obtain a peaceful transfer of sovereignty, there would be a high risk of their resorting to more forcible measures against British interests, and that they might do so swiftly and without warning. In such circumstances military action against British shipping or a full-scale invasion of the Falkland Islands could not be discounted.[3]

Mrs Thatcher later claimed 'We had no intelligence until almost the last moment that Argentina was about to launch a full-scale invasion' and insisted it 'could not have been foreseen or prevented',[4] but in fact the unmistakable signs of increasing Argentine belligerency had been available since Colonel Love's prescient report of January, which had been shelved by the Defence Intelligence Staff. Mrs Thatcher had seen a telegram from the Ambassador in Buenos Aires, Anthony Williams, dated 3 March 1982 and warning of the deteriorating situation, and she had commented on it in manuscript, 'We must make contingency plans', but no action had been taken. As a reprise of the 1977 crisis, there were several options, but ministers were not told of JOURNEYMAN, so no nuclear submarine was diverted to the scene.

David Owen, who had played a key role in JOURNEYMAN, even insisting that the deployment not be reported to the Americans for fear of a leak, considered that despatching a maritime task force might have had the desired deterrent effect, and still believes that a simple bluff might have worked, perhaps with the Americans reporting to the Argentines that a British naval presence had been spotted in the South Atlantic. Instead the islands were occupied and the fateful July 1981 JIC assessment was never considered by the Oversea and Defence Committee. The reason? It did not convene between February 1981 and April 1982. Thus there were hideous intelligence, analytical and political reporting problems, all components in the final outcome.

Franks also made no comment on SIS's lack of representation in Latin America. This was bizarre because bitter experience had demonstrated that when SIS closes a station, such as in Tripoli, there is a natural and corresponding reduction in reporting from the region. In the Libyan example, SIS had failed to anticipate the coup that overthrew King Idris, an event that was to have lasting consequences for British and Western interests in that country and beyond the Maghreb. Even though Franks remained silent on the issue, SIS responded to the obvious need for increased Latin American reporting by reopening stations in Rio de Janeiro, Montevideo, Bogotá, and in the British Interests Section of the Swiss Embassy in Buenos Aires.

Franks reserved his main criticism for the assessment role of the JIC, recommending that future JIC chairmen after Sir Patrick Wright should not be drawn exclusively from the Foreign Office, and be appointed by the prime minister of the day, to whom they should have direct access. The result was the appointment of the Intelligence Coordinator, Tony Duff, to take on the additional joint role of Chairman of the JIC. Duff was to transform the JIC and make the Assessment Staff far more rigorous, but SIS escaped quite unscathed. When Duff left the JIC in 1985 to take over the Security Service he was replaced by Sir Percy Cradock who combined the post with his role as the Prime Minister's Foreign Policy Adviser, an innovative post initially held by Sir Anthony Parsons. Cradock, who was to hold both posts for eight and a half years until June 1992, had previously served as C's Foreign Office Adviser, and head of the JIC's Assessment Staff between 1971 and 1975, and therefore had an unrivalled knowledge of the intelligence community, making him a powerful ally for Figures and his two successors.

Figures was invited to the Prime Minister's celebration victory dinner at 10 Downing Street, where he was included in the group photograph, and the following year received his customary knighthood, adding to the perception that SIS had experienced 'a good war'. Successful clandestine operations had been mounted at short notice against the Argentines in Paris, Madrid and at the UN Mission in New York where Iain Mathewson tapped the enemy's telephones, and the principal objectives had been achieved. As for providing tactical intelligence to the Task Force, probably the single most significant item of intelligence was actually provided by GCHQ and consisted of an intercepted rations return for the Argentine occupation forces on the islands, proving the exact number of troops deployed.

It was in this atmosphere of great success that Figures was confronted with a hideous embarrassment. In anticipation of his return to London Forter's deputy at the Paris station had been asked to hand over his star agent, supposedly a senior, well-informed Communist in the French trade unions, to his successor Mike Reynolds, but each time a meeting was arranged the handler found an excuse to call it off. Finally challenged about the authenticity of his source, PAR/1, as he was designated with the station, confessed that he had invented the contact, fabricated his reports and pocketed the funds he had been given to finance his expensive lifestyle.

This admission came to Figures like a bombshell, and placed him in a considerable dilemma. PAR/1 was an experienced officer who had served in Jakarta and Dar-es-Salaam before being posted to Paris in October 1977 to join Forter who had taken over the station six months earlier from a veteran officer, Edward de Haan. Originally from Paignton, PAR/1 had joined SIS in 1969, had been educated at the University of Paris, and once had studied for the priesthood at St Mary's College in Devon. Yet, in spite of these apparently impeccable academic credentials, which included an MA from Hull University, he had perpetrated a classic scam, awkwardly reminiscent of Graham Greene's humorous spoof *Our Man in Havana*; inevitably word spread quickly of the scandal. At the time the Paris station had included Richard Dearlove, a future Chief, who had arrived in November 1980 on his third overseas posting. The unenviable choice presented to Figures was to prosecute the culprit, and thereby attract extremely damaging attention to the Service, or to dismiss him quietly, and buy his silence with a recommendation for a top job in the City. Swearing all those who knew of the episode to silence, Figures took the second option thereby preserving SIS's reputation and avoiding the scandal that would inevitably follow, not to mention the opprobrium of having been duped for such a long period.

Such an expedient had the advantage of saving the Service from having to wash its dirty linen in public, but there were no precedents for Figures to rely on, and no external authorities to consult, except his Secretary of State or the Permanent Under-Secretary at the Foreign Office. In a previous case, where the SIS station commander in Lisbon had fabricated his reports, he had remained in Portugal and achieved some commercial success with a tourist postcard business. In that instance the culprit had not returned to London to face the music, whereas in this example the fraudster had not only confessed, but had received a recommendation which gained him a highly-paid post in the banking sector. As a short-term remedy the Figures solution looked superficially attractive, but it was effectively a bomb waiting to explode under the Service, and under Dearlove. In the meantime, the Prime Minister became a convert to the importance of intelligence, previously having relied on others to advise her on that arcane world.

Her introduction had been effected by Airey Neave, a former wartime SIS officer who had run MI9, the escape and evasion service, and since 1953 the Member of Parliament for Abingdon. Neave knew his way around SIS, and was close to Charles Elwell, MI5's Director F Branch who was the country's leading authority on left-wing subversion. A complete intelligence neophyte as Leader of the Opposition, Mrs Thatcher had relied on Neave not just as her election campaign manager in the contest against Ted Heath, but had depended upon him for guidance on all security and intelligence issues. His loss, to an Irish National Liberation Army assassin's bomb on the ramp of the House of Commons carpark shortly before the 1979 General Election had robbed her of a potential Secretary of State for Northern Ireland, forcing her to appoint her Chief Whip, Humphrey Atkins. Without Neave, Mrs Thatcher had been bereft of good advice on this vital topic and in the vacuum had come to rely on her Parliamentary Private Secretary, Ian Gow, who had access to a network of well-connected retirees, but there was no single, knowledgeable mentor to guide her apart from Dame Guinevere Tilney, one of her closest confidantes, who had served in SIS during the war. Later SIS was to assign Lois Stewart-Black to No. 10 to act as an adviser and link to Century House.

In her first major security crisis, that of MI5's strong recommendation to protect the reputation of Professor Sir Anthony Blunt in November 1979, she had been guided by her Attorney-General, Sir Michael Havers, who had reminded her of her oath as a barrister, and her duty to the courts in the event that Blunt perjured himself in a libel action brought to defend his reputation. She had rejected Sir Howard Smith's view that by his immunity from prosecution, granted by Sir John Hobson in April 1964, Blunt was entitled to continuing confidentiality, and had not only denounced Blunt as a Soviet spy but arranged for Buckingham Palace to strip him of his knighthood. Thereafter the Prime Minister had been sceptical of MI5's perspective, but it had taken the Falklands War to demonstrate to her the vital role played, or neglected, by the intelligence services.

In the vital weeks before the Argentine invasion on Friday, 2 April 1982, SIS had supplied precious little advance warning, and the best intelligence had come from Cheltenham, but much too late. GCHQ's Director, Sir Brian Tovey, had given Whitehall a running commentary on the Argentine joint naval anti-submarine exercises being conducted in the South Atlantic off Puerto Belgrano with the Uruguayan fleet, but the alarm was only sounded on the afternoon of Wednesday, 31 March, when the intercepts showed that a diesel submarine, the *Santa Fé*, had been deployed to the area around Port Stanley, presumably to reconnoitre a landing beach, and that the Army commander, General Osvaldo Garcia, had embarked on the *Santisima Trinidad*, a Type 42 destroyer. Instructions had been given for the fleet to disperse into prearranged units, Task Force 20 and Task Force 40, and all classified papers were to be destroyed. Taken together, these four intercepts suggested an invasion scheduled for early Thursday morning, delayed for twenty-four hours by bad weather, but surprisingly this detailed knowledge was not shared with the rest of Mrs Thatcher's Cabinet when it held its regular meeting on Thursday morning, April Fool's Day. The Prime Minister, John Nott and the Foreign Office by then knew that an amphibious attack was inevitable, but the existence of the intercepts was kept secret because, as Nott later acknowledged, 'Signals intelligence of this kind ... was treated on a "need to know" basis.'[5] A week earlier, on Thursday, 25 March, an impending Falklands crisis had been discussed briefly at Cabinet, but Nott had been absent, attending a NATO conference at Colorado Springs.

In fact the signals intelligence throughout had been very detailed and had been gleaned from the traffic exchanged between the ships of the Argentine fleet, which comprised two destroyers; two frigates; a merchantman, the *Bahia Buen Suceso*; a polar ship the *Bahia Paraiso*; a supply transport, the *Isla de los Estados*; and an amphibious landing ship, the *Cabo San Antonio*. The troops, 904 in total, had embarked early on the morning of Sunday, 28 March, but the operation, codenamed AZUL, had been planned in earnest since mid-January. In addition, work on the *Guerrico*, in dry dock in Puerto Belgrano, was hastily completed, allowing the frigate to participate in the attack. All this activity had generated plenty of wireless traffic which had been monitored by *Endurance* and GCHQ's other listening posts, but the full impact had not been appreciated until some four days after the force had put to sea.

The Falklands conflict proved, against all the odds, and the advice of the Ministry of Defence, to be a great victory and more than any other single event served to establish Mrs Thatcher as a leader of global influence. It also transformed her into a voracious consumer of the product, as Percy Cradock witnessed at close quarters:

> [She] was aware from personal experience that we lived in a dangerous world. She was a realist and recognised that we were not likely to learn the true intentions of foreign governments, let alone terrorist groups, from the public prints or even the diplomatic telegrams. I suspect she also experienced, as many ministers do, a certain frisson at the receipt of those heavily classified pieces of paper, with their air of urgency and menace, and their flattering suggestion of superior and exclusive knowledge. She was aware that Britain had a powerful intelligence machine, was good at the game, and enjoyed in consequence valuable influence in Washington. That mattered. Certainly, I always found her receptive and supportive. This extended to funding, always a difficult issue, as technical intelligence grew ever more expensive.[6]

Although intelligence is always a concealed preoccupation for every prime minister, and every recipient of the JIC's so-called *Red Book* on Friday mornings, Mrs Thatcher's lonely education in the field had been bruising. After the Falklands War, now acutely aware of the shortcomings of the Foreign Office, she had seen the need to enhance her foreign policy advice and had selected a Middle East specialist, Sir Anthony Parsons, who had excelled in New York, heading Britain's mission to the UN throughout the conflict. Parsons had worked well, but only on a part-time basis, three days a week, with C and Duff as Chairman of the JIC, but two of the three were soon to move on, Duff to MI5 and Parsons into a semi-academic retirement near Exeter University at the end of 1984.

With unfortunate timing, MI5's D-G, Sir John Jones had disclaimed all responsibility before the Security Commission for having harboured a grotesque security risk, Michael Bettaney, who in April 1983 had passed some of the Security Service's most highly-valued secrets to the KGB *rezident* in London, Arkadi Gouk. Jones's complacent evidence to the four-man Security Commission, chaired by Lord Bridge, personified MI5's anachronistic management style and the organisation came in for sustained criticism and, when Jones retired early in 1985, he was replaced by Tony Duff with a mandate to modernise.

Although Duff had impressed the Prime Minister during the Rhodesia settlement talks, in Salisbury and Lancaster House, during which he had been heavily dependent on Sigint, Mrs Thatcher had not been keen for him to take over MI5. However, there was no obvious internal candidate, for Jones's deputy, Cecil Shipp, was also at retirement age, and the next candidate, David Ranson, at the age of fifty, had neither the seniority nor the support of the Cabinet Secretary, Sir Robert Armstrong. Instead, Ranson was appointed Duff's Deputy D-G, and Sir Percy Cradock took over Duff's role as Chairman of the JIC, and Parsons's position as the Prime Minister's Foreign Policy Adviser, an unorthodox arrangement opposed by Armstrong and Geoffrey Howe.

> They were briskly overruled by the Prime Minister [recalled Cradock]. Intelligence and policy are usually kept apart in separate rooms. The partition has to be thin, otherwise assessments, however interesting to their composers, fail to answer the questions uppermost in ministers' minds. But if there is no partition, there is a risk of intelligence being slanted to provide the answers the policy-makers want. This is a grave sin: the analyst must convey his message, usually unpalatable, without fear or favour.[7]

Thus the Prime Minister now came to depend on Figures and Cradock as her filters of intelligence. 'I felt no temptation to cook the books', said Cradock, 'and if I had, my JIC colleagues would not have tolerated it'.[8]

In terms of prestige within the international community, Britain's stock was never higher than in the aftermath of the Falklands victory, and this may have been a factor in the decision later the same month of Vladimir Kuzichkin to choose to be resettled in Britain. A 'Line N' illegals support officer at the *rezidentura* in Tehran, Kuzichkin had mislaid some documents and feared his likely punishment. Anticipating imminent discovery, Kuzichkin had opted to approach Ian McCredie at the local SIS station. McCredie had joined SIS in 1975 and had spent three years in Lusaka before his posting to Tehran in April 1981. He had been in the country for a year, and his wife was pregnant, but McCredie instantly knew Kuzichkin's value and arranged for him to flee to Turkey and accept resettlement in the UK, where he too was encouraged to write his memoir, *Inside the KGB*, which eventually was released in 1990.

A member of the KGB's elite Illegals Directorate, Kuzichkin had spent five years at Moscow University studying Iran, followed by the usual two years at the FCD's Red Banner Institute, before he was posted to the Soviet Consulate in Tehran in the summer of 1977 under diplomatic cover as a Line N officer specialising in the handling of illegals. Fluent in Farsi and English, he ran a small network of KGB illegals, but in September 1981 his two best agents, a husband and wife team operating on West German passports, were arrested in Switzerland. Not long afterwards, in May the following year, Kuzichkin realised that an undeveloped roll of film, on which secret documents were routinely stored in the *referentura*, had disappeared while in his care. Faced with the extreme penalties for the loss of classified documents, Kuzichkin made contact with SIS and was exfiltrated early in June 1982. His motives only seem to have become clear after he had been resettled in London for, as he admits:

> I had never been pro-Western. I always thought that the West had its own interests, and that it needed a strong Russia like a hole in the head, whether it was a communist Russia or a free Russia. I believed that we, the Russians, had to solve our own problems, and that changes in the Soviet structure were possible only from within, and absolutely not from outside. Interference from outside would always unite the people and only strengthen the regime.[9]

As well as identifying the complete KGB and GRU order-of-battle in Iran, and the identities of those illegals he had handled personally, he was to give SIS an authoritative account of the KGB's role in supporting the Tudeh party, then the subject of considerable repression by the Ayatollah's regime. Kuzichkin was resettled in London where he remarried and, like other defectors, was paraded before allied agencies to demonstrate SIS's skill at handling defectors, although he saw himself as a victim of circumstance and the FCD's rigidity, rather than as an ideological convert. Nevertheless, he understood the price to be paid for resettlement, and by chance he was able to shed light on a Canadian case, codenamed NIKON by the FCD, which concerned a spy inside the RCMP Security Service.

The RCMP had long suspected the existence of a mole, but Gilles Brunet, codenamed TANGO and the son of a respected RCMP Commissioner, had not come under investigation until SIS provided the confirmation. SIS's contribution greatly enhanced the Service's standing across the Atlantic, although Brunet himself died in 1984, before he could be arrested and interrogated.

Kuzichkin's resettlement package, complete with a British passport, was approved by Francis Pym during his very short period as Foreign Secretary between Carrington's resignation in April 1982 and his replacement by Geoffrey Howe after the general election of June 1983. The Chief's only other significant encounter with Pym during this period was over a series of Soviet expulsions. The first to go, in December 1982, had been the naval attaché, Captain Anatoli Zotov, of the GRU, and he had been followed a month later by Vladimir Chernev, ostensibly a translator at the International Wheat Council. Finally, in April 1983, three diplomats and the *New Times* correspondent, Igor Titov, had been expelled. All had been fingered by Gordievsky, who had given SIS a comprehensive analysis of the KGB's *rezidentura*, thus allowing MI5 to concentrate its limited resources on the best targets.

Gordievsky's knowledge extended far beyond the Third Department, and he revealed that his brother had trained as an illegal for deployment by Directorate S into West Germany. He also knew where his contemporaries had been posted, and his information was a significant general contributor to the West's efforts to curb the KGB. The positive identification of a Soviet diplomat as an intelligence professional can be of immense value to an over-stretched security apparatus unsure of which target to concentrate on, and the statistics of Soviet expulsions world-wide began to escalate markedly in 1983 when 111 officials were PNG'd from 16 countries during the first eight months of that year. Between 1978 and August 1983 a total of 316 espionage suspects were removed from 43 countries, a figure that might have indicated to a vigilant Soviet analyst that the KGB had sprung a leak. If the tips had been traced back to SIS, doubtless the KGB would have conducted a molehunt to trace the culprit.

Following these successes, Figures agreed to accept an SIS role in supporting the *mujahidin* in Afghanistan, although of necessity Britain's covert contribution would be dwarfed by the resources applied in the region by the CIA which, under the leadership of William Casey, obtained approval to arm the resistance fighters with the shoulder-launched Stinger missile, a weapon that would protect them from the ubiquitous and lethal Soviet helicopter gunships. SIS's support for the Afghans, and in particular Ahmed Shah Mahsoud, was channelled through the Islamabad station, headed initially by Anthony Hawkes, who was to be replaced in 1986 by Mark Heathcote. In London the operation was supervised by the Far East Controller, Michael Thompson, who had temporarily 'debadged' members of the Special Air Service to train Mahsoud's men in the guerrilla tactics that would eventually lead the Soviets to withdraw from Afghanistan in 1988.

Geoffrey Howe approved SIS's involvement in Afghanistan, although it was Mrs Thatcher who took the lead role in encouraging the risky initiative, having swept aside her Foreign Secretary's embarrassment over the US invasion of Grenada. This episode, in October 1983, had threatened to jeopardise the transatlantic 'special relationship' and had led Geoffrey Howe to give an assurance to the Commons that no military action was anticipated in Grenada just a few hours before American troops stormed the island. The left-wing government of this independent Caribbean island, still a member of the Commonwealth, had been overthrown by a Marxist revolutionary and the US administration had feared for the safety of a thousand American students staying there. A full-scale invasion was planned by the Pentagon, but Howe was not informed. In fact the SIS officer in Washington DC had been kept out of the loop, and the SIS station commander in Bridgetown, Barbados, had been preoccupied with countering money launderers, and not counting the number of Cuban troops guarding the newly-built runway on Grenada. The American intervention, so soon after Howe's hapless parliamentary performance, caused the British government acute embarrassment and, as Mrs Thatcher described it, humiliation. From SIS's viewpoint, it was an unforeseeable incident, but not one with any lasting consequences.

Upon his retirement in July 1985 Figures succeeded Sir Antony Duff as Intelligence Coordinator to the Cabinet, and passed on the Chief's baton to a 56-year-old Far East specialist, Christopher Curwen.

Chapter X

Christopher Curwen 1985–1988

THE son of a vicar, Curwen was educated at Sherborne School and after serving in the 4th (Queen's Own) Hussars, which he joined in 1948 at the age of nineteen, graduated from Sidney Sussex College, Cambridge. In July 1952 he joined SIS and two years later, in August 1954, was posted to Thailand to work for Robert Hemblys-Scales, where he became fluent in Thai. In July 1956 he was moved to Vientiane, to relieve John Pedlar who had opened the station. There he married his first wife, Vera Noom Tai, a physiotherapist by whom he was to have a son and two daughters, and in October 1958 returned to Broadway. In 1961 he was back in Bangkok, taking over from the redoubtable Michael Wrigley, followed by two years in Kuala Lumpur. In 1965 he was posted to London, and in May 1968 was appointed SIS's liaison officer in Washington DC for three years, taking over from John da Silva and Stephen de Mowbray, and returned to London in February 1971. In 1977, having divorced Noom and married his secretary, Helen Stirling, by whom he was to have a son and a daughter, he went to Geneva as head of station, and in May 1980 was back in London as C's Deputy.

Curwen succeeded Colin Figures in July 1985 with no publicity acompanying the appointment until the *Sunday Times* published his profile. The portrait, written by Barrie Penrose and Simon Freeman, was entirely flattering and based on a long telephone conversation with the new Chief who expressed his approval of the article, demurring only at the assertion that the new C could expect to receive the usual knighthood. Unfortunately for Curwen, who went out to celebrate near his home in

Lewisham the night before publication, he returned to discover that burglars had stolen his treasured coin collection.

Despite this personal setback, Curwen's appointment had been uncontroversial and he had the advantage of a burgeoning budget. The Prime Minister, now fully convinced of the value of intelligence, had authorised the new Foreign Secretary, Francis Pym, and the Chancellor of the Exchequer, Geoffrey Howe, to allow SIS to expand, and to find the money to fund the increase. Suddenly, after years of financial cuts, it had taken a conflict thousands of miles away in the South Atlantic to persuade politicians that intelligence was a worthwhile investment which could obviate the need for actual war.

The first crisis for Curwen to deal with was the exfiltration from Moscow of SIS's star source inside the KGB, Oleg Gordievsky, who, with help from the Danish PET security police, had been recruited in Copenhagen back in 1974 by Robert Browning. Since then he had supplied his SIS handlers with large quantities of information from the FCD, and also from the *rezidentura* in London, where he had been posted in June 1982, then headed by Arkadi Gouk.

While in Copenhagen Gordievsky had alerted SIS to two of the KGB's most important sources in Norway, Gunvar Haavik and Arne Treholt. Codenamed GRETA, Haavik was a secretary in the Norwegian Ministry of Foreign Affairs and had been spying since she had conducted a love affair in 1947 with a Soviet while she had been working at the Norwegian Embassy in Moscow. SIS had tipped off the Norwegian security police and Haavik had been arrested in January 1977 in the act of passing information to her KGB case officer in an Oslo suburb. Her contact, operating under Soviet diplomatic cover, was released, and six months later Haavik died of a heart-attack while in prison awaiting her trial, having confessed to having engaged in espionage for almost thirty years.

Arne Treholt was also employed by the Norwegian Foreign Ministry, but when Gordievsky identified him as a spy in 1978 he had moved to New York to work for Norway's mission to the United Nations. The FBI placed him under surveillance but it was not until he had returned to Oslo, and was about to catch a flight to Vienna in January 1984 that he was arrested at the airport in possession of sixty-six classified documents he had taken from the Foreign Ministry. At his trial, held the following year, Treholt was sentenced to twelve years' imprisonment. Both cases served to strengthen the traditionally very close ties that had existed since the Second World War between the British, principally SIS and GCHQ, and their Norwegian counterparts. Gordievsky also succeeded in hearing some corridor gossip about another spy, this time a Swede who had served in the Sakerhetspolisen security service and then had been transferred to military intelligence and seconded to the UN in Israel. When identified, Stig Bergling was arrested in Israel and flown back to Stockholm where he was convicted of espionage.

Undoubtedly the greatest of Gordievsky's many triumph was to occur in London, preventing a potentially massive breach of MI5's own security. Michael Bettaney had been recruited to join the Security Service in 1975 when he had left Oxford, where he had gained a second-class degree in English at Pembroke College. Once approved for employment by MI5 he had worked in F Branch until June 1976 when he had been posted to Belfast, where he was slightly injured in a car-bomb attack. Two years later he returned to London to work in the newly-created anti-terrorist branch, by which time he had developed a severe drinking problem. In December 1982 he was transferred to the Soviet counter-espionage section, and it was while he was serving in this highly compartmented unit that he made three anonymous approaches to the KGB *rezident* in London, Arkadi Gouk, and offered to supply him with MI5 secrets. Although Bettaney subsequently claimed to have been inspired by political motives, the reality is that he had received a final warning following a criminal conviction for fare-dodging and an arrest for being drunk in the street. A further offence of using an out-of-date railway season ticket followed and, although Bettaney had failed to declare it, as he was required to do, he knew it would be discovered during his next routine positive vetting security screening and would inevitably lead to his dismissal. SIS's tip from Gordievsky led to a discreet molehunt swiftly conducted inside MI5 by Eliza Manningham-Buller who identified the culprit without compromising the source of the original tip.

With Haavik, Treholt, Bergling and Bettaney as his scalps, Gordievsky was considered SIS's star source, and elaborate measures had been taken to protect him. After his recruitment by Robert Browning he had been handled by a Scot, John Davies, and then by Philip Astley, so when Gordievsky reached London he had only ever encountered three SIS officers, but none of these had been immediately available to greet him. Browning had been posted to Belfast in March 1975 but, disenchanted with the work, had resigned from SIS soon afterwards. Astley had been posted to East Berlin, so he was quickly flown home to introduce Gordievsky to his new handler, John Scarlett, contact having been established via a dedicated telephone number which Gordievsky had memorised four years earlier, in 1978. When the KGB officer called the number, Astley arranged to meet him in a hotel in Sloane Street. They ducked out the rear, into Pavilion Road, to drive to a safe-house in Bayswater where, at the next meeting, Astley had introduced Scarlett. The two men enjoyed an instant rapport, perhaps because Gordievsky had two daughters, and Scarlett had three, and their relationship was to continue until Scarlett was posted to Paris in 1985 to replace Richard Dearlove. As a measure of his value, Gordievsky was given the front-door key to a flat close to the Soviet Embassy to which he could disappear with his family should the need ever arise.

It was during this final segment of Gordievsky's highly productive period as an agent that he provided the most valuable political reporting of his career. He had returned to the West fully briefed, and had been ideally placed to give crucial help to NATO in interpreting the tumultuous events taking place in Mikhail Gorbachev's politburo. Gordievsky's guidance was considered so vital that Geoffrey Howe, who was one of the beneficiaries of the relevant CX, observed that he had been 'more than content to receive his invaluable (not least because it was so regular) commentary on thinking in the Kremlin. It played an important part in shaping our own strategy.'[1]

When Bettaney was arrested at his home in September 1983, as he was preparing to fly to Vienna with yet another sample of MI5's secrets to hand over to the Soviets, he was unaware that his offers to Gouk had been compromised by the *rezident*'s deputy, Gordievsky, who had simultaneously advised the cautious *rezident* to regard the material as an obvious provocation, and had tipped off his SIS handler to the potentially disastrous leak from the heart of MI5's Gower Street headquarters.

In April 1984 Bettaney was sentenced to twenty-three years' imprisonment; he served his sentence in isolation at Coldingley Prison, and was released in 1996. A Security Commission report into the case was severely critical of MI5's Director-General, Sir John Jones, who claimed that MI5 was handicapped because it had nowhere to send problem employees like Bettaney. Far better, he had argued, to keep a potential trouble-maker on board, than allow him to become a loose cannon. Somewhat disingenuously, in order to protect Gordievsky, the Commission claimed that the would-be spy had been exposed by the vigilance of his colleagues, omitting details of the real source, and giving no hint that the credit for the narrow escape lay with SIS's original hint to the future D-G, Liza Manningham-Buller.

On Friday, 17 May 1985, having been named the *rezident* designate, Gordievsky was unexpectedly summoned home to Moscow, supposedly for consultations, but he was very suspicious and only agreed when he had been assured by his SIS handler at an emergency meeting that there was no reason to believe he was in any danger. However, upon his arrival he realised his apartment had been searched, and when he reached Yasenevo he was accused of being a spy. He denied the accusation and resisted his interrogators who used drugs in an attempt to extract a confession. He concluded that, although the KGB must have been tipped off to his dual role, there was not sufficient evidence to justify an arrest.

Although under heavy surveillance, Gordievsky was able to shake off his watchers while jogging in a park at the end of July and make contact with SIS, sending an emergency signal requesting a rescue, which was promptly relayed to London. The ostensibly innocuous signal was nothing more elaborate than Gordievsky appearing on a prearranged street corner, at a particular time, carrying a shopping bag, but this apparently innocent act prompted Curwen to fly to Scotland immediately to brief Mrs Thatcher, who was then staying with the Queen at Balmoral, while Foreign Secretary Geoffrey Howe was visited at Chevening. When informed of the need for their permission to undertake the perilous act of removing Gordievsky from Moscow over the weekend under the noses of the KGB who were maintaining a watch on him, both approved the submission and arrangements were made for him to be exfiltrated by the Moscow station commander, Viscount Asquith, in his Saab to Finland. Asquith acted as a good Samaritan, escorting a pregnant member of the embassy staff for medical treatment in Helsinki, while Gordievsky climbed aboard at a rendezvous outside Leningrad and was driven over the frontier at Viborg. Once in Finland Gordievsky was greeted by the Helsinki commander, Margaret (later Baroness) Ramsay, and then driven to Trömso in Norway for a flight the next day from Oslo to London. He was then accommodated briefly at a country house in the Midlands, where he was visited by the Chief, and then put up at Fort Monckton for a lengthy debriefing, lasting eighty days, conducted by SIS's principal Kremlinologist, Gordon Barrass. Although he had never served behind the Iron Curtain – he had previous postings to Hong Kong, Peking and Geneva (where he had received Rezun) – Barrass spoke Mandarin and had served on the JIC's Assessment Staff before becoming SIS's expert on the Soviet collapse. Among Gordievsky's other visitors was the DCI, Bill Casey, who was flown down to the Fort for a lunch hosted by Curwen.

Although Gordievsky's safe exfiltration was a source of great pride and celebration, there remained considerable concern about precisely how he had been compromised. Why had he been recalled to Moscow in May? One possibility was that, after so many losses, the KGB had worked out for itself that a mole had been at work within the organisation. As well as tipping off SIS to Bettaney and the spies in Norway and Sweden, Gordievsky had been responsible for the arrest in Denmark of a journalist, Arne Herlov Petersen, who had been run for years as an agent of influence recruited in 1973 by Leonid Marakov, later the *rezident* in Oslo. Petersen, who had penetrated the Danish peace movement for the KGB, had been arrested in November 1981, but was released without charge. In contrast a Danish businessman, Bent Weibel, also in the pay of the KGB and responsible for smuggling high-tech equipment to Moscow, was convicted of espionage and sentenced to eight years' imprisonment. Quite apart from these two cases of espionage, the KGB had also suffered an unprecedented seven expulsions of diplomats from the embassy. Although none of these incidents had been overtly linked to SIS or a source inside the Copenhagen *rezidentura*, had word of Gordievsky's dual role leaked? What had made the KGB so suspicious of him?

The answers were important because such events can reveal the existence of a hitherto unknown mole. No answers were forthcoming until the arrest of the CIA's Aldrich Ames in February 1994 when he confessed to having identified Gordievsky to the Soviets as a source codenamed AE/TICKLE who had penetrated the KGB in Denmark and London. Ames admitted responsibility for betraying a dozen other assets in the Soviet Union, but it was how the KGB had latched on to Gordievsky that had so preoccupied SIS. When debriefed by SIS, Gordievsky was emphatic that his KGB interrogators had been sure of his guilt, but without the proof required to make an arrest, and that his recall had been a consequence of his identity becoming known in Moscow, but how had the leak happened? Between the successful exfiltration in August 1985, and the arrest of Ames eight and a half years later, SIS was tormented by the fear that its own ranks had been penetrated by a mole. The identification of Ames appeared to lay those fears to rest, even if Gordievsky had in the meantime struck up a professional relationship with the counter-intelligence expert, until the CIA expressed some doubt about whether the dates matched. Gordievsky had flown to Moscow on Sunday, 19 May, having been recalled two days earlier, but in his sworn testimony Ames insisted that he had not betrayed Gordievsky until he had a meeting with Viktor Cherkashin on 13 June. He admitted having passed over the names of two FBI assets inside the Soviet Embassy in Washington DC, Sergei Motorin and Valeri Martinov, as his initial offer on 16 April, but insisted that he had not included Gordievsky on that occasion. Nor had he mentioned him when he had picked up his payment from Cherkashin on 15 May, so how had the KGB discovered Gordievsky? Either Ames had lied, for no apparent reason, or made a mistake, or there was another spy at work, either in the CIA or SIS.

Resettled under a new identity near London, and eventually reunited in November 1991 with his wife Leila and two daughters Anna and Maria, Gordievsky was to be divorced, but subsequently lived with an English public school matron, and in 1994 wrote his memoirs, *Last Stop Execution*. As well as describing his role in compromising the KGB's spies in Norway and Sweden, Gordievsky revealed that the KGB *rezidentura* had run a *Guardian* journalist, Richard Gott, as a paid agent of influence, and had taken steps to cultivate several highly-placed trade union leaders, among them Richard Briginshaw, Ray Buckton and Alan Safer. Gordievsky also explained that the embassy was also in touch with what he termed 'confidential contacts',[2] influential individuals who could be relied upon to take the Kremlin's lead on political controversies; these included three left-wing Labour MPs, Joan Lester, Jo Richardson, and Joan Maynard. The constitutional implications of Gordievsky's disclosures were considered sufficiently important for Curwen to brief the Cabinet Secretary, Sir Robin Butler, who in turn called in Tony Blair, as Leader of the Opposition, to explain the situation to him.

Once his debrief had been completed, Gordievsky traveled the world, lecturing Allied security and intelligence agencies on the KGB's operations, and acting as a goodwill ambassador for SIS, eloquent testimony to how a really good case could be run for years and to the organisation's integrity, proof that there really had not been any penetration of SIS since George Blake. Unfortunately, while this view was entirely valid in respect of Century House, it did not extend to other British institutions, as the arrest of Geoffrey Prime at the end of April 1982 showed. Prime had been a Russian linguist at GCHQ for twelve years until his resignation in September 1978, and had spied since he had volunteered his services to the KGB in Berlin in January 1968. Although Gordievsky had been well briefed prior to his departure for the London *rezidentura*, he had not been indoctrinated into Prime's espionage, which had been supervised by an entirely separate, highly compartmented branch of the FCD, which had specialised in the recruitment of sources with access to ciphers and crypto-equipment, While Gordievsky learned plenty about the numerous agents of influence managed from the *rezidentura*, he knew nothing about these other KGB assets, and very little about the illegals run by Directorate S, although occasionally he had been assigned temporary duty as an illegals support officer in London, serving dead-drops for transiting agents.

Gordievsky's defection was a devastating blow for the KGB, and the expulsion of the London *rezidentura*, ordered on the basis of his information, had a colossal impact on the organisation that apparently still had not entirely recovered from Operation FOOT in September 1971. To avoid further damage the KGB even withdrew its illegals from Britain, among them Kurt Stengl, a mature student at the London School of Economics. Posing as an Austrian, Stengl had enrolled at the LSE and found himself in the same class as Elspeth Howe, the Foreign Secretary's wife, who had befriended him, completely oblivious to his clandestine role as a Soviet spy.

Successively codenamed FELIKS and OVATION by SIS, Gordievsky had provided valuable political reporting from inside the KGB at a critical time in the Cold War, a period when Kremlin paranoia had reached new heights, to the point that NATO's 1983 ABLE ARCHER exercise had been misinterpreted in Moscow as a possible cover for a surprise attack on the Soviet Bloc. As well as producing masses of documents from the London *rezidentura*, Gordievsky had identified all the FCD's Third Department personnel known to him and had shed light on dozens of past cases. Personally, he was a very engaging individual, always popular with his case officers, although he would never forget the assurances he had received, when recalled to Moscow in May 1985, that SIS believed he was in no danger. However, the fact that a Prime Minister's grandson, Raymond Asquith, had masterminded his subsequent escape, proved to be a considerable compensation for him.

Curwen was to remain in his post for just four years, a period when he only dealt with one Foreign Secretary, Geoffrey Howe, who was for much of the time preoccupied with European issues, content to leave relations with Mikhail Gorbachev to the Prime Minister. Although he showed no special interest in CX, apart from Gordievsky's commentaries, Howe took a robust view of Soviet espionage and was always supportive of the measures taken since 1971 to cap the number of diplomats allowed to work in London. He had authorised the expulsion in April 1985 of four diplomats from the Soviet Embassy and the Aeroflot charter manager, all identified by Gordievsky as intelligence officers. Immediately after the announcement of Gordievsky's defection, in September 1985, a further twenty-five diplomats and officials were declared *persona non grata*, together with a further six a week later when Moscow had retaliated with a tit-for-tat response. Previously, Howe had been responsible for the removal of Vasili Ionov in September 1983, who had been trapped in an MI5 sting, and of course Arkadi Gouk, Gordievsky's hapless *rezident* incriminated by

Michael Bettaney in 1983. While on the surface these events appear to be part of the rough and tumble of international diplomatic life, there remains *sub rosa* a complex web of meetings and negotiations between C and departmental officials to approve the candidates for expulsion, and to calculate the anticipated consequences.

On Curwen's departure from SIS in November 1988 he succeeded Colin Figures as the Cabinet Intelligence Coordinator, and finally retired in 1991 when he took on a part-time role as a member of the Security Commission, a body which became redundant when the ISC was created three years later. Curwen was replaced as Coordinator by the retiring Deputy Chief, (Sir) Gerald Warner.

Chapter XI

Colin McColl 1988–1994

'James Bond is the best recruiting sergeant in the world.'

Colin McColl[1]

THE son of a Shropshire GP, McColl attended Shrewsbury School, served in the Army for a year between 1951 and 1952 and graduated from Queen's College, Oxford. He joined SIS in September 1956 and was sent to the School of Oriental and African Studies at London University to learn Thai in October the following year.

His first posting, to Bangkok in September 1958, was to serve under Geoffrey Hinton, and take over as deputy station commander from Michael Wrigley. Hinton was also an Oxford man, having been to Worcester College before the war, and afterwards had spent four and a half years in Cairo. Wrigley, a Harrovian, had also gone to Worcester College and had two years at the Brussels station before being sent to Bangkok in March 1956.

McColl's posting to Bangkok, where he married Shirley Curtis, was followed by Vientiane in April 1960, to serve under A. G. Trevor Wilson, a former Lloyds Bank manager in Cannes, and head of station in wartime Algiers. Two years later McColl was back at Broadway, and in 1966 went to Warsaw to replace Alan Auger, returning to London in May 1968. In January 1973 he was posted to Geneva, and was back in London four years later, to spend the next ten years in senior posts at Century House, before being appointed Chief by Mrs Thatcher in November 1988. His team, with Gerry Warner as Director of Counter-Intelligence and Security, and

Alan Petty as his PA/CSS, was to prove highly effective, and he quickly established a reputation for flamboyant dress, colourful ties, unconventional idea and a no-nonsense attitude. A colourful, affable raconteur, he also had an interest in music and it was not unknown for him to whip out his flute to put visitors at their ease.

The unresolved issue McColl inherited from his predecessor was a long-running double-agent case in London. In January 1989, as MI5 and SIS were playing a double agent against a member of the KGB's *rezidentura*, Vasili Kuznetsov, Geoffrey Howe was keen to initiate a follow-up to FOOT and expel the KGB officer, along with ten of his colleagues, but the plan was delayed by Mrs Thatcher who was anxious not to jeopardise her talks with Mikhail Gorbachev who was due to visit London imminently. That much-delayed trip eventually took place in early April 1989, clearing the way for a repeat of FOOT, albeit on a somewhat reduced scale.

There had not been any expulsions from London since those of September 1985, prompted by Gordievsky's defection, but the pressure to intervene was increasing, especially when MI5's Director-General, Patrick Walker, reported in May that he had acquired evidence that the Czech StB had become active. Finally Mrs Thatcher agreed to a 'silent *persona non grata*' with no publicity, and on 19 May the Soviets were told to withdraw eleven diplomats, and informed that a further three would not be allowed to re-enter Britain. The Prime Minister also wrote a personal letter to Gorbachev explaining that she had 'hoped not to take' this decision but she had been forced to do so because the KGB had 'step by step reconstructed their staff in London'.[2] The strategy failed when, in retaliation, Moscow announced publicly that an identical number of British diplomats and journalists would be expelled.

Although his appointment was not announced in 1988, Prime Minister John Major did refer to McColl in a speech in the House of Commons on the Queen's Speech, on 6 May 1992, announcing the government's intention to place SIS on a statutory footing, the very first time that SIS's continuing existence had been admitted or the Chief's name had been mentioned in Parliament.

McColl's tenure as Chief would be dominated by the events of August 1990 when Saddam Hussein ordered Iraqi troops into Kuwait, but it was the sudden collapse of the Soviet Bloc that was the major historical event of the era. By chance McColl was in Paris on the night the Berlin Wall was breached, and was on hand to witness the beginning of the demise of Communism across Europe, and the French reaction to the prospect of a unified Germany. The speed of the implosion took everyone by surprise, but McColl seized the initiative to offer SIS's help to the emerging democracies in establishing and training new security and intelligence structures to replace the discredited and hated totalitarian systems in Czechoslovakia, Romania, Bulgaria and, to a lesser extent, Poland and Hungary. The options were either to maintain a distance and allow the new governments to build completely new agencies, thereby inevitably leaving them vulnerable to contamination or penetration from the outset, or to participate in the development of services supervised by parliamentary oversight. McColl's strategy was to cultivate the potential new allies and develop links in areas of mutual interest such as terrorism, weapons proliferation, drug smuggling and organised crime. The policy would pay dividends, at minimal cost to SIS's security, and allowed the Service to continue to concentrate on the remnants of the KGB, now rebranded as the SVR.

This latter interest was manifested by the defection, in May 1991 of Mikhail Butkov, a member of the KGB *rezidentura* in Norway operating under journalistic cover as a TASS correspondent, who had been run as a source by Oslo's SIS station commander. Butkov was to be the first of several useful defectors who opted to jump ship following the disintegration of the Soviet system. Butkov and his girlfriend were resettled in the UK, and what propaganda value he had was extracted by the publication in Oslo of his memoir *The KGB in Norway*.[3] Although Butkov was to assist SIS in an operation conducted the following year in Spain, directed against an Iranian criminal gang, his subsequent history was to prove awkward for SIS. Short of cash, Butkov masterminded a language school scam from his home in Berkshire, advertising tuition and visas in foreign language newspapers in the United States. However, instead of supplying the courses, Butkov simply pocketed the deposits and fees, and caused considerable embarrassment for SIS when he was charged with fraud and imprisoned for three years.

Butkov was to be the first of several defectors over the following eighteen months, the next being Colonel Viktor Oshchenko, an FCD Line X science and technology officer in Paris who had served in London between 1973 and 1979. His value lay in his knowledge of a spy he had run in England. Using his information MI5 ran a false-flag operation against Michael Smith, a former CPGB member who, until he had been made redundant in May 1992, had worked for the defence contractor Thorn-EMI and had access to classified designs, including the fuze for the We-177 nuclear bomb. Persuaded that the Russians wanted to re-establish contact, Smith had been entrapped on 8 August 1992 by an MI5 officer masquerading as his new SVR contact, and incriminated himself by offering to resume his espionage activities. A search of his home in Kingston-upon-Thames revealed some classified documents he had taken home years earlier, and he was sentenced to twenty-five years' imprisonment.

Oshchenko, who was spirited out of Paris by SIS in July 1992, was soon to be joined by Vasili Mitrokhin, a KGB retiree who had travelled to Riga in March 1992 to offer an extraordinary meal-ticket, a huge cache of documents he had painstakingly copied from the FCD archive during the twelve years prior to his retirement in 1984. While McColl authorised Mitrokhin's eventual exfiltration, accompanied by his family, the full impact of his astonishing industry would not be fully realised, as we shall see, for a further seven years.

McColl's decision to rename the Soviet Bloc Controllerate as the Eastern and Central Europe Controllerate marked a significant milestone for SIS, a moment when SIS's clandestine conflict with the Soviet Union was demonstrably over, and won, to the point that the Service agreed with the SVR to establish formal liaison links, and declare each other's *rezident* in London and station commander in Moscow. This extraordinary development was negotiated in the British Embassy in Oslo by the SVR's Director, Yevgeni Primakov, and the SIS head of station in Moscow, John Scarlett. According to Primakov's account, contained in his memoir *Au Cour de Pouvoir* ('At the Heart of Power'), published in France, Scarlett offered to cooperate on condition that the SVR and GRU reduced their presence in London, and this took two years to achieve.

While the mutual declaration of *rezident* and station commander may have been cosmetic, the symbolism was not to be under-estimated. McColl was also responsible for establishing a Directorate of Global Issues, to deal with the new challenges of terrorism, proliferation and organised crime, all growing preoccupations of the JIC whose focus, temporarily, was distracted from Iraq.

The invasion of Kuwait in August 1990 took place with almost no warning from the Baghdad station, which closed when the embassy was withdrawn, although SIS had developed a very comprehensive picture of Iraq's efforts to rebuild its army and infrastructure following the decade-long, debilitating war with Iran which had started in 1980. Although SIS had monitored the reconstruction, and in particular Saddam's covert military procurement programme, it had been unable to predict his intention to occupy Kuwait. At the moment his tanks had taken up positions in the centre of Kuwait City at 2.00 in the morning of 2 August the Prime Minister was in Aspen, Colorado, with President Bush, and the Foreign Secretary, Douglas Hurd, had begun his annual three-week summer holiday at his country home in Oxfordshire, having been assured by McColl and GCHQ's new Director, Sir John Adye, that reports of Saddam's tanks assembling near Basra were of no consequence. The House of Commons had risen on 26 July, the same day that the JIC's Middle East Current Intelligence Group had noted 100,000 Iraqi infantry massing close to the Kuwaiti border, but the prevailing view was that Saddam Hussein had been sabre-rattling in an effort to influence the negotiations being conducted by the Arab League in Jeddah. Right up until the frontier had been crossed, nobody had predicted the invasion, although the JIC thought an escalation to military action was possible, and on 27 July the JIC Chairman, Percy Cradock, had sent the Prime Minister a note accompanying the *Weekly Digest of Intelligence* suggesting Saddam Hussein's strategy was blackmail but 'we must expect at least limited military action before too long'.[4]

There followed, early the next year, a swift intervention by an international coalition to liberate the Kuwaitis, but the scale of DESERT STORM's victory was marred for SIS by bureaucratic bungling in Whitehall which led to an SIS asset, Paul Henderson, being charged by Customs with breaches of the UN embargo on the export of weapons to Iraq. SIS's prime interest had been in nuclear non-proliferation and Henderson had been one of a stable of British businessmen in contact with the regime who had volunteered information about Saddam's illicit procurement programme.

The fiasco had occurred soon after the abortive prosecution of a Midlands steel firm, Sheffield Forgemasters, for manufacturing high-tensile tubes, ostensibly for use in the oil industry but to an unusually demanding specification, for clients in Baghdad. The company had suspected the tubes were for a military application, and in fact they were components of a long-range 'supergun' with a barrel 500 feet long, designed by a visionary Canadian scientist, Gerald Bull. The huge weapon, with an estimated range of 600 kilometres and a projectile weighing two tons, was intended to be deployed against Israel, but the project collapsed after Bull was assassinated at his apartment in Brussels on 22 March 1990, and German, Swiss and Italian authorities seized various consignments of engineering equipment destined for what the Iraqis had called Project BABYLON. Bull was found outside his front door with five bullets in his back and as he was carrying $20,000 it seemed unlikely that his killer's motive was robbery.

Acting on similar tips, British Customs officers had raided two companies in the Midlands, Walter Somers and Sheffield Forgemasters, and seized eight crates containing smoothbore pipes marked for delivery to a petrochemical scheme in Baghdad. However, when it emerged that the directors of both companies had been in touch with SIS since 1988, when the original Iraqi contracts had been signed, and that they had expressed concern about the military application of the orders, all charges against them were dropped. SIS had been fully aware of the Iraqi plans, and had been monitoring Saddam Hussein's illicit procurement programme, using sources in both companies to supply information, although the precise date when SIS first heard of it remained a matter of considerable debate.

Having failed to prosecute the steel fabricators, four months later Customs raided Matrix Churchill, a company employing 600 and based in Coventry, which was also engaged in exporting to Iraq, and charged the directors with supplying Baghdad with dual-use machine tools. The equipment included several consignments of sophisticated computer-controlled lathes which could have a military application, and when one of the three directors, Paul Henderson, protested that all his activities had been supervised by SIS he was served with a Public Interest Immunity Certificate (PIIC), a legal manoeuvre to prevent him from disclosing his previous contacts, dating back over twenty years, with SIS and MI5. The PIIC, usually issued to prevent the identification of informants in criminal trials, had the effect of a trump card and banned the defendants from deploying their defence, which was that their relationship with the Iraqis had been developed at SIS's behest, and that all the exports had been approved by SIS which had gained useful knowledge of how Baghdad was re-equipping.

Henderson originally had been recruited by MI5 in 1970 when he had been travelling across Eastern Europe as an export sales manager and had acted as a source supplying information about Soviet Bloc personalities visiting Britain. However, in April 1989 he had been contacted by an SIS officer interested in the Middle East and, as the controlling interest in Matrix Churchill was owned by Iraqis, Henderson willingly co-operated. Known only to him under the alias John Balsom, Henderson's case officer held frequent meetings and debriefed him on his return from eight visits to Baghdad, but when Balsom learned that Customs had arrested his agent he broke the connection and avoided all further contact with him. When Henderson disclosed to his defence lawyers that for years he had been an agent for MI5 and SIS, and his evidence was supported by another colleague, the former Matrix Churchill export manager Mark Gutteridge, who had also been recruited by MI5 and then passed to 'Ian Eacott' of SIS, Balsom was offered to the prosecution as a witness. Balsom would declare that he had not known of Henderson's previous contacts with Baghdad, nor of the potential dual use of his exports. Usefully, Balsom testified to Henderson's great personal courage, and his willingness to risk his life by visiting Iraq a month after Saddam Hussein had executed an Iranian-born British journalist, Farzad Bazoft. 'He was a very, very brave man who, on top of all the other pressures on top of him, took these extra risks.' This dramatic evidence had an electric effect in court, to the degree that the prosecuting counsel, Alan Moses QC, wrote privately about 'the propriety of continuing the prosecution against a man who, on the evidence before the court, had rendered great service to the country' to Sir Brian Unwin, Chairman of the Customs Board. Obviously infuriated, Unwin protested to McColl about Balsom's testimony which had shown the defendant in the dock to be a hero, nor a scoundrel, but McColl responded robustly that his officer had spoken 'sincerely and impartially' in his evidence. Henderson, said McColl, had shown 'considerable bravery ... whilst knowing of the Iraqi ruthlessness in dealing with spies' and would accept no criticism of his subordinate.[5] Clearly Unwin had been irritated by Balsom's helpful evidence to Henderson, but when challenged on this point later he claimed that he had merely protested that SIS had failed to inform Customs of the full extent of its relationship with the defendant. In reality, SIS had told Customs of Henderson's role in October 1990, and given a very full picture to Customs a month later at a meeting called to discuss the issue.

Henderson's trial at the Old Bailey subsequently collapsed when the judge inspected the government documents covered by numerous PIICs, which proved Henderson's role with SIS, and ruled that they were highly relevant to the defence. A judicial enquiry was established under Lord Justice Scott to investigate the circumstances of the prosecution, and after hearings over two years concluded that, astonishingly, the Attorney-General, Sir Nicholas Lyell, had never been told that Henderson had worked for SIS. The Scott Inquiry Report, released in February 1996, strongly criticised ministers for having been so willing to sign PIICs, thereby denying the Matrix Churchill defendants their proper defence, leaving the public with the impression that innocent men might have been imprisoned to keep them silent about SIS's operations. Among those who gave evidence before Sir Richard Scott was the Prime Minister, John Major, who was required to describe his approval of certain SIS operations when he had been Mrs Thatcher's Foreign Secretary. He also explained that the Foreign Office received:

> ... around 40,000 intelligence reports a year ... Split down, two-thirds GCHQ and one-third SIS, they would be of varying grades. Some of that intelligence would be extremely valuable, others not so. Quite a strong filtering process is needed.[6]

The impact of the Matrix Churchill affair on SIS was to be long-term because, despite the favourable evidence given at the trial by Henderson's handler, the Service was perceived to have gladly encouraged its agent, but then abandoned him when Customs had moved in. The fact that Balsom had then praised his agent at the trial as a man of tremendous courage only served to compound the offence, both inside and outside Whitehall, but the true facts of what had happened would take years to emerge, and were not released until Lord Justice Scott's Report was produced two years after McColl's retirement. Although Customs & Excise were excoriated by Scott, and ministers escaped without any resignations, the impression was left that SIS had done little to protect Henderson from prosecution, or from the government's PIICs. As for the Chief, he was criticised by Scott for having learned the true nature of Operation BABYLON by October 1989, but not having passed the information on to Percy Cradock at the JIC. Thereafter, this lapse had been concealed by SIS.

While coping with the demands of the Scott Inquiry, McColl was also preoccupied with the drafting of the Intelligence Services Act which, for the first time, brought SIS onto a statutory footing and created an element of parliamentary oversight for all three intelligence and security services. The compromise achieved was to make the Parliamentary Intelligence and Security Committee (ISC) a hybrid, with an all-party membership appointed by the prime minister from both houses of parliament, avoiding the constitutional problems of making it a parliamentary select committee. Thus the ISC, chaired at the outset by Tom King, the former Secretary of State for Defence and for Northern Ireland, reported not to parliament but to the prime minister, and was commissioned to draw up annual reports on the three agencies under its supervision.

Probably McColl's most significant, lasting contribution to the Service was to have undertaken the negotiations for the drafting of the Intelligence Services Bill. MI5, of course, had already been put on to a statutory footing with the Security Service Act 1989, but there was widespread concern in the Service that, when the Labour Party inevitably won power, SIS would become one of its principal targets for reform, if not closure. While in opposition the shadow Foreign Secretary, Robin Cook, had been highly critical of SIS during the debate on the Scott Inquiry, and had presented a masterly forensic examination of the evidence and the report's conclusions. SIS had emerged from the affair badly damaged as few had understood why, in the words of one witness, McColl had not 'ambled down the Strand and told the Attorney-General that Henderson was his man', thereby terminating the entire enterprise at the very outset. Cook had long had an interest in intelligence issues and had been highly critical of all three agencies which feared the consequences of the inevitable Labour victory at the polls. The solution was to legitimise SIS, extend the role of the commissioner, tribunal and complaints procedure created by the 1989 Security Service Act, and introduce an element of oversight, and the compromise formula achieved by McColl and Douglas Hurd ensured SIS survived beyond John Major's administration. Hurd, who had been switched to the Foreign Office in October 1989, had guided the Security Service Bill through the Commons as Home Secretary and therefore was well-placed to repeat the exercise with SIS and GCHQ, even if Mrs Thatcher had been less than enthusiastic about the need to legislate at all. It had been Tony Duff as MI5's reforming Director-General who had talked Hurd into altering his service's status in January 1987, but whereas Hurd was able to persuade Robert Armstrong to agree by April, it would take more than a year before the Prime Minister reluctantly accepted the idea, having authorised a Bill to be drafted in July. By the time the Bill received the royal assent, in December 1989, Duff had been replaced as Director-General by his deputy, Patrick Walker. The Bill had been welcomed by MI5's management, long tired and apprehensive about their quasi-legal status resting on an ancient, untested 'royal prerogative', and McColl was confident that Hurd could pull off another parliamentary success for his agency, and for GCHQ.

The ISC would comprise nine members, drawn from both houses, and appointed by the prime minister, and would prepare an annual report which would then be released for debate, having had any sensitive passages excised. As far as the Chief was concerned, his duties, as set out in Section 2 of the Act, were to ensure the efficiency of SIS and 'to ensure that there are arrangements for securing that no information is obtained by the Intelligence Service except so far as is necessary for the proper discharge of its functions' and to prevent the disclosure of information 'except so far as is necessary' in the interests of national security, for the purpose of prevention or detection of serious crime, or for the purpose of any criminal proceedings. In addition, the Chief has an obligation to write an annual report for the Prime Minister and not to 'take any action to further the interests of any United Kingdom political party'. SIS's legitimate functions, spelt out for the first time, were described as:

> to obtain and provide information relating to the actions or intentions of persons outside the British Isles, and to perform other tasks relating to the actions or intentions of such persons.
>
> The functions of the Intelligence Service shall be exercisable only
>
> (a) in the interests of national security, with particular reference to the defence and foreign policies of Her Majesty's Government in the United Kingdom, or in the economic well-being of the United Kingdom, or in support of the prevention or detection of serious crime.

This carefully chosen language amounted to the first encapsulation of SIS's role and, thanks to McColl's drafting and lobbying skills, was so widely drawn as to encompass virtually every eventuality, and did not attempt to define any of the terms used, such as 'political party' or 'serious crime'. McColl later described this exercise as writing his own job description, and the inclusion of a responsibility to protect the 'economic well-being of the United Kingdom' went unchallenged, just as it had done when it was originally inserted in the Security Service Bill in 1989. SIS would be free to apply for telephone and mail intercept warrants in the UK, through MI5's well-established procedures, and was given immunity from any civil or criminal liability within the UK for acts committed outside the jurisdiction if the act had been authorised by the Secretary of State.

While the government braced itself for the skeletons that might emerge from SIS's cupboard while the legislative spotlight was on the organisation, McColl mobilised his small Information Operations team, designated I/Ops, to brief their media contacts on how SIS had moved from the era of Cold War dirty tricks to such tasks as combating money-laundering in the Caribbean. Since 1988 SIS had been filling the gaps between the police, Customs, the National Criminal Intelligence Service and the Serious Fraud Office, with an expert on the drug cartels based in Barbados, or so the discreet briefings claimed, as they emphasised the growing threat from the Russian mafia, and hinted at SIS's participation in a massive drugs seizure at Harwich in which former Czech StB officers were implicated.

The Bill was debated in both houses, with Daphne Park, now Baroness Park of Monmouth, taking an active role in the Lords on behalf of the Government, challenging various amendments proposed by Opposition peers, among them Lord Richard, formerly Britain's ambassador in Washington DC, and the fiery London University academic, Baroness Blackstone. However, in the Commons, Cranley Onslow and the future Liberal leader, Paddy Ashdown, who had both served in SIS, remained silent, but among those who did contribute was Ray Whitney, a former diplomat who had headed the Information Research Department until it had been closed by David Owen, and six MPs who in later years would serve on the ISC: Tom King, Dr John Gilbert, Allan Rogers, Archie Hamilton, Dale Campbell-Savours and Michael Mates.

Douglas Hurd, whose second son Tom was then a serving SIS officer, opened the debate for the Government, and Dr Jack Cunningham replied for the Opposition, complaining that the Bill was inadequate because it 'proposed that the Committee should not report to Parliament but to the Prime Minister'.

> I do not regard that as Parliamentary scrutiny or oversight because the Prime Minister has the right to veto sections of its report – I call it Prime Ministerial oversight and scrutiny. If we are to have an effective parliamentary watchdog to oversee such matters and to probe and scrutinise, it should report to Parliament. It cannot legitimately be called a parliamentary committee unless it does so. That is another major difference of opinion between the Opposition and the Government over the details of the legislation.[7]

Cunningham's attitude to the Bill had been shaped by an SIS retiree, Meta Ramsay, formerly the station commander in Helsinki, who had become a special adviser to Labour leader John Smith after her retirement. Ramsay and Smith had known each other since they had both been students at Glasgow University, and following his unexpected death she had advised Cunningham, then shadow Leader of the Commons. Meanwhile McColl watched the progress of the Bill with considerable interest because the Opposition's view of SIS was not only of some constitutional importance, but it was an opportunity to learn more about the attitude of the Labour Party towards SIS. The position of the Tories was easy to ascertain because, quite apart from the official channels, the wife of the Chief's Personal Assistant worked in the Commons for a Conservative MP. Hurd himself was also no stranger to SIS, and in 1951 after leaving Cambridge he had contemplated joining, and had even attended an interview before deciding against it. In his subsequent career, as a diplomat, he had served abroad in Peking and New York, and had worked closely with Edward de Haan in Rome. He had always given the impression that he was never over-impressed by the quality of CX reports, and was fond of remarking that a high security classification was a reflection of the source, not the authenticity of the intelligence. Nevertheless, despite his scepticism, he observed at a press conference to introduce a relaxed McColl and the discomforted Director of GCHQ, John Adye, 'No week goes by without having drawn to my attention examples where the work of one or other of these agencies . . . actually protects British interests and saves British lives.' Never one to miss an opportunity, McColl pressed his case for SIS's expansion:

> After the Falklands War, when we were quite clearly seen to be too thin – not just there but in other areas as well – we increased our numbers during the 1980s. We are now on a declining path, and I think over the next two or three years we will be back to where we were before the Falklands War. – that is, very roughly.

If McColl harboured any reservation about the wisdom of putting SIS onto a statutory footing, he gave no indication of it, although he was anxious to reassure staff, allies and agents, acknowledging them as 'our most important constituency is [those] abroad' who:

> . . . believe SIS is a secret service. I am very anxious that I should be able to send some kind of signal to those people that we are not going to open up everything; we are not going to open up our files; we are not going to allow ourselves to be undressed in public with their name as part of our baggage.

Careful attention was paid during the debate to the comments of Peter Mandelson, then an Opposition backbencher known to be very influential within the Party, although few at the time could have predicted that in the future he would hold several high offices of states, and resign from two of them. Significantly, he described the Bill as 'a worthwhile set of checks and balances' but concluded by remarking that:

> Throughout the Scott Inquiry we have witnessed the ability and inclination of some Ministers to overlook matters from time to time that would be expedient for them not to see, to react and act expediently when they so wish and when it would be politically embarrassing for them to do otherwise, and even to mislead Parliament when it suited them and then try to shuffle off responsibility when they were found out. The Bill should guard against that happening in relation to the security and intelligence services and prevent such sloppy and cavalier attitudes on the part of some Ministers. I believe that the Bill will be extremely important, once enacted, as a means of guarding against such behaviour and arresting it.

Despite the Opposition's reservations on the ISC's status, and its subordination to the prime minister, the Committee produced an interim report in April 1995, disclosing that it had met on a weekly basis since January, visited the three agencies and been briefed by the Chairman of the JIC, Paul Lever, and the Intelligence Coordinator, Gerry Warner. Tom King noted that the members had been 'encouraged by the openness of the intelligence "insiders" and in particular by the helpful approach of the Heads of the Agencies themselves'. This was the last McColl would see or hear of the ISC as Chief, for the Committee's first full report did not go to the Prime Minister until December 1995, and was not published until

March 1996, by which time McColl had left Vauxhall Cross. Indeed, no ISC report would even be debated in the Commons until November 1998.

Upon his retirement, which was delayed to allow the passage of the Intelligence Services Bill through the Commons, McColl was the first SIS Chief to refer to his position in his *Who's Who* entry as 'Head of MI6'. His successor was not his long-serving deputy, (Sir) Gerald Warner, who had moved to the Cabinet Office as Coordinator in 1991, being replaced not by Alastair Rellie, who retired to join British Aerospace, but a Middle East hand, David Spedding. McColl, with a new family and a young son, found work as a consultant to a financial group in Edinburgh, and now lives in Oxfordshire.

Chapter XII

David Spedding 1994–1999

'Intelligence can play a crucial role in defence decision making, which is literally a life or death affair.'

David Owen[1]

THE son of a colonel in the Border Regiment, David Spedding was head of his house at Sherborne, marched with CND to Aldermaston, and joined SIS in 1967 at the age of twenty-four while working as a post-graduate student at Oxford, having read medieval history at Hertford College. In his gap year Spedding had travelled to Chile and had found temporary work as an assistant in the press office of the British Embassy in Santiago; this had given him an entrée into SIS. When he was appointed Chief he became the very first never to have served in the forces.

Upon joining SIS Spedding underwent the usual year training in Britain and, already fluent in French and Spanish, was posted to the Middle East Centre for Arabic Studies at Shemlan in the Lebanon to learn Arabic for two years before joining the SIS station in Beirut in May 1970. However, the following year, when the British government expelled 105 Soviet diplomats from London, Spedding was named by Kim Philby in *Izvestya* as the SIS station commander in the Lebanon. His transfer to Santiago followed in 1972, together with his wife Gillian Kinnear who had been brought up in Chile, but the country was then in turmoil under President Salvador Allende's short-lived left-wing regime which came to an end with General Augusto Pinochet's military coup in September 1973.

Spedding returned to London in September 1974 and, in a protest against Pinochet's regime, the station was closed down, and remained shut until the Falklands War when relations with the Chileans belatedly became a priority. In 1977 Spedding was posted to Abu Dhabi where he remained until 1981.

Back in London, Spedding was appointed to the Middle East Directorate, and then went as head of station to Amman in 1983. During the Queen's four-day state visit to the kingdom the following year Spedding was credited with foiling a plot hatched by Palestinian extremists led by Abu Nidal to assassinate her. Forty-eight hours before her arrival a bomb was detonated in the Inter-Continental Hotel's car-park and a second device, with thirty-one sticks of gelignite, was found nearby. The local security situation was considered so grave, with the certainty that Abu Nidal's men were active in the capital, that the Prime Minister held an emergency meeting of the Cabinet at Chequers to decide whether the visit should be cancelled, but the Queen and Mrs Thatcher were determined it should proceed. Spedding's timely intervention, with the Jordanian security apparatus which arrested the bombers, prevented a disaster and he was made a Commander of the Royal Victorian Order during her visit. Abu Nidal, born Sabri Al-Banna and based in Damascus and Baghdad, was a well-known terrorist who had broken away from the Palestine Liberation Organisation and had been responsible for numerous atrocities, including the shooting of the Israeli ambassador in London in 1982. On that occasion the three potential assassins, one of who was related to Nidal, had been caught and imprisoned. Apparently frustrated at their failure in Amman, Nidal's gunmen tried to ambush the SIS station commander in Athens, but instead killed Ken Whitty, the cultural attaché, as he was walking in the street.

Against the odds, the Queen's visit to Jordan, complete with a Bedouin picnic on the shores of the Dead Sea, proved a great success, a credit to the security measures taken by Spedding and his Ambassador, Sir Alan Urwick, who happened to be a former SIS officer.

In 1986 Spedding was placed in charge of a joint MI5–SIS task force monitoring Middle East terrorists in Britain, and became Controller Middle East to run SIS's operations during DESERT STORM, the Gulf War.

His promotion to head the Middle East Controllerate had been fortuitous – when hostilities opened he had been acting as the deputy head, but his superior had been on leave at the crucial moment, leaving Spedding to impress McColl and others with his grasp of the conflict.

In 1993 the Director of Requirements and Production, Barrie Gane, took early retirement to go to Group 4 Securitas, and McColl appointed Spedding as his successor, effectively placing him in charge of SIS's sixty overseas stations, and named him his Assistant Chief, to take over from him as Chief in September 1994. Gane's departure to the burgeoning private sector was part of a trend. Christopher James and Mike Reynolds, who had moved to a consultancy business, the Hakluyt Foundation, which specialised in political risk advice, and Alastair Rellie who went to British Aerospace, represented a significant loss of talent from the top. A Cambridge graduate, Gane had served abroad at Vientiane, Borneo, Kuching, Warsaw, Kampala and Hong Kong at sensitive times, and had been expected to reach the top if McColl had not stayed on. James, his subordinate, on the other hand, had served in Nairobi, Lagos and New Delhi. Similarly Reynolds had worked at the Düsseldorf, Budapest and Paris stations, and had been Robert Browning's replacement in Northern Ireland in 1977. Rellie, Gane's almost exact contemporary, had worked in Geneva, Cairo, Kinshasa and New York. All were experienced senior officers, and their premature retirements altered the balance of SIS's senior management in favour of a new generation.

Spedding's appointment, at the age of fifty the youngest Chief in SIS's history, was announced to the public in March 1994, only the second time the government had ever openly acknowledged the identity of a new Chief. Thus for the second time in his career, Spedding's name attracted publicity, but he continued to live at his homes in Richborne Terrace, near Vauxhall Cross, and in Church Street, Henley, play a few rounds at the nearby Huntercombe Golf Club and lunch in London at the Athenaeum. Spedding was perfectly willing to make further structural changes beyond those made by McColl, with the six geographical controllerates reduced by merging Africa with the Middle East, and the Western Hemisphere with the Far East, and creating two new controllerates, Operational Support and Global Issues. The improvements in SIS's internal wiring diagram were intended to reflect the dramatic realities of the new world order. SIS's historical adversary, the Soviet Bloc, had fled the field, allowing more resources to be concentrated on the JIC's targets in organised crime and Middle East terrorism.

The transition, of course, had pitfalls, one of which was discovered by Spedding's station commander in Berlin, Rosemary Sharpe, who nearly fell for a common enough scam, a plausible intermediary purporting to peddle military secrets and classified equipment from disaffected Russian personnel abandoned in eastern Germany. All the Western intelligence agencies were in the same market, competing for Soviet technology and Sharpe, who had served previously in Delhi and Brussels, had unwittingly overlapped with a Federal German Intelligence Agency (BND) sting operation which resulted in a period of cool relations between the two services, but no lasting damage beyond some temporary embarrassment.

Like his predecessors, Spedding was confronted with a crisis almost as soon as he took up his post, but this time the cause was not external, but with a member of SIS's own staff who was dismissed in April 1995.

Born in New Zealand to English emigrant parents, Richard Tomlinson had joined SIS in September 1991 after graduating from Gonville & Caius College, Cambridge, with a first-class engineering degree, and serving with the Territorial 21st Special Air Service Regiment. He spoke fluent Spanish and Russian and performed well in the required new entry course (IONEC) which lasts for six months, during which candidates are trained at the Fort and assessed for their skills. Tomlinson had rated highly in the 89th IONEC and had been posted to Soviet operations at the Eastern Europe Controllerate at Century House. In June 1993 he had been sent to Belgrade under journalistic cover as a targets officer to recruit a source, followed by another similar assignment to Skopje, and then in September 1993 was posted to a new station recently opened in Sarajevo. Tomlinson stayed in Bosnia under UNPROFOR cover until June 1994 when a station was established at the new British Embassy, and then returned to London for a stint in the counter-proliferation section where he participated in a couple of operations and, in April 1995, flew to Rio de Janeiro to meet a source from Buenos Aires who had been reporting on the Argentine civil nuclear programme.

However, upon his return, Tomlinson was told by the Director of Personnel, Richard Dearlove, that as a probationer his staff performance assessments had been sub-standard, and there was no future for him in SIS. He was to be escorted out of the building, given three months' pay, and the promise of help to find a new job in the City. This news, coming soon after the death from cancer of his girlfriend, devastated Tomlinson who protested that he had received nothing but praise from his line managers but his appeal, direct to Spedding as was his right, was rejected. Frustrated, and constantly blocked by John Scarlett, he tried to bring an action for wrongful dismissal before an Employment Tribunal, but it was blocked by a Public Interest Immunity Certificate signed by the Foreign Secretary, Malcolm Rifkind. Instead Tomlinson applied for a review of his case by the Intelligence Services Tribunal, an independent body chaired by Lord Justice Brown created by the new Intelligence Services Act, but the finding in March 1996 went against him. An approach to his Member of Parliament, Kate Hoey, also failed, after she was invited to lunch with the Chief at Vauxhall Cross to discuss Tomlinson's case and given Spedding's assurance that he had been treated fairly.

Running low on funds and convinced he had been badly treated by SIS, Tomlinson left the country using the alias passport he had been issued for his travel to Brazil, and drove a motorcycle down to the south of Spain to write a book based on his experiences. This, of course, was a hideous breach of the Official Secrets Act, as were his calls to the *Sunday Times* which started publishing a series of stories about recent SIS operations intended to embarrass his former employers. The first, in May 1996, revealed that SIS had recruited a spy inside the French naval base at Brest, and a second disclosed the identity of a Conservative MP who had been run as a source on the activities of well-placed Bosnian Serb emigrés in London. These articles, including one suggesting SIS had run a source inside the German Bundesbank, prompted SIS's personnel department to contact Tomlinson who agreed to a meeting in Madrid in November. Over the next four months three further meetings were held which resulted in an agreement signed in the British Embassy in February 1997. In return for a guarantee that he would not be prosecuted for speaking to the *Sunday Times*, a loan of £60,000 and help in finding a job, Tomlinson would surrender the hard-drive of his laptop computer, erase his manuscript and assign the publication rights to it to the Crown. Reluctantly agreeing to these terms, which included his future silence, Tomlinson returned to the UK but was disappointed by the offer of a job with the Jackie Stewart Grand Prix racing team that had been arranged by SIS. Instead he flew to Australia, seemingly determined to find work on the strength of his New Zealand dual nationality. However, in May 1997 Tomlinson offered Transworld Publishers in Sydney a seven-page synopsis of his autobiography and returned to Britain, having decided to accept the job with the racing team. He also wrote to SIS seeking advice on how to apply for permission to write a book, an event that set off alarm bells at Vauxhall Cross.

SIS had not been troubled by disclosures in the form of unauthorised memoirs since Leslie Nicholson had published *British Agent* in 1966 in the United States under the pseudonym John Whitwell. Nicholson had joined SIS from the Army in 1929 and had served in Prague and Riga until the Soviet occupation of Latvia in 1940, when he had returned to Broadway. After the war he had been sent to open the SIS station in Bucharest, and it was at this sensitive point that he had concluded his memoirs – but he had broken SIS's code of silence. On that occasion Dick White had been powerless to act, partly because the book had been released initially in America, but mainly because Nicholson had been a popular officer who had many influential friends, as demonstrated by his book which included a foreword by Henry Kerby MP, formerly an SIS officer in Sweden, and an introduction by Malcolm Muggeridge, once the SIS station commander in wartime Lourenço Marques. Nicholson had been willing to defy White because his application for a loan, to cover the medical bills incurred by his dying wife, had been rejected by Menzies who effectively had forced his subordinate's resignation. Thereafter Nicholson had been embittered by his treatment and had written what amounted to the first insider account of SIS's immediate prewar and postwar activities. Although no operational information had been compromised, SIS had learned the lesson of how disgruntled former employees could inflict disproportionate damage.

In contrast, MI5 had endured a long and painful torture at the hands of Peter Wright in 1981 when a disaffected former officer had collaborated with a journalist, Chapman Pincher on his exposé, *Their Trade Is Treachery*, and then compounded the offence by taking a ghostwriter, Paul Greengrass, to produce *SpyCatcher* in 1986. The government's timid response to the first book, which was never the subject of any legal action against either the author or his source, encouraged Wright to take a second bite at the cherry, with catastrophic consequences for the Security Service which was obliged to travel to Sydney to seek an injunction enforcing the tort of breach of confidence in an Australian court against an Australian citizen, as Wright had taken up residence in Tasmania and acquired Australian nationality. Although the action failed in Australia, the House of Lords upheld the principle of 'a lifelong duty of confidentiality', but by then the genie was out of the bottle and *SpyCatcher* had become a worldwide best-seller, containing a wealth of highly classified information, including dozens of authentic codenames. SIS had been caught up in the debacle because, among the many SIS operations referred to, the existence of the international CAZAB counter-intelligence organisation was revealed, requiring it to be renamed and restructured. While the main damage of Wright's disclosures was sustained by MI5, there was inevitably a considerable adverse impact on SIS as a sister service and both organisations came belatedly to realise that disgruntled staff had the potential to wreak havoc, however compartmented the structure.

The *SpyCatcher* affair had demonstrated the problem of foreign publication, as SIS had learned from Nicholson, and SIS's Director of Security, John Gerson, understood the implications of further leaks from Tomlinson, especially with the opportunity for instant, international dissemination offered by the internet. A balance had to be struck between maintaining staff morale and discipline by cracking down hard on a breach of security, and undermining the authority and status of the Service by opting for a full-scale public humiliation. What then was probably not fully appreciated was the consequence of invoking criminal sanctions, and when Tomlinson was arrested by Special Branch detectives and charged with offences under the Official Secrets Act, SIS was virtually powerless to intervene to prevent a prosecution, short of persuading the Attorney-General that such an action would not be in the public interest. Tomlinson was arrested at his parents' home in Cumbria and in December 1997 pleaded guilty to breaches of the Official Secrets Act. He was sentenced to a year's imprisonment and served six months at Belmarsh top security prison before he was released on parole in April 1998, but broke the terms of his parole by driving to Paris shortly before the end of his sentence, which amounted to a further criminal offence.[2]

While in Paris Tomlinson met up with another former intelligence officer who was beginning to gain some notoriety, David Shayler, who had left MI5 in early 1997 after five years in the Service. Shayler had engaged a literary agency to circulate a book proposal to publishers, masquerading as a senior woman retiree who had served in Northern Ireland, but it had been turned down because of the legal implications. Instead he had sold a long article to the *Mail on Sunday* which had published it at the end of July 1997. Additional articles would have followed, except that the government obtained an injunction to prevent further unauthorised disclosures, and Princess Diana was killed the following weekend, seizing the newspaper headlines for weeks to follow. However, Tomlinson and Shayler, together in Paris, represented a potent threat to both organisations and the French security agency the DST was persuaded to detain both. Shayler was to remain in French custody at La Santé prison until November when the British extradition application, on an arrest warrant issued in London in July for two offences under the 1989 Official Secrets Act, was rejected, while Tomlinson, for whom no warrant had been issued, was released within twenty-four hours.

SIS's worries about Shayler rested on his experiences while serving as a desk officer for Libya in G Branch, MI5's counter-terrorism division, which liaised closely with its SIS counterpart in the Global Issues Controllerate. According to Shayler, SIS had failed in an attempt to recruit Khalifa Baazelya, the Libyan external intelligence service *rezident* in London, but had succeeded in pitching a source codenamed TUNWORTH who had been plotting to replace Colonel Ghadaffi. He also claimed that one of his SIS contacts, David Wilson designated PT16B, had told him that SIS had paid TUNWORTH more than £100,000 for information, and that he (Wilson) had acted as an intermediary with the Islamic group that had tried to kill Ghadaffi in Tripoli in February 1996. The substance of Shayler's allegation was that this assassination attempt had been sanctioned within SIS, and had never been approved by the then Secretary of State, Malcolm Rifkind. Perhaps worse, Tomlinson exacerbated the situation by claiming that he had been consulted on a scheme to blow up the Serbian leader Slobodan Milosevic in a Swiss road tunnel, a plot that he linked to the death of Princess Diana in a Paris underpass. The revelations were intended to create a political controversy, and they certainly succeeded in that objective, with the new Foreign Secretary Robin Cook being briefed by SIS Public Affairs Director, Ian Mathewson, so a public denial of any SIS assassination plot could be issued on behalf of the Foreign Office.

Although Shayler and Tomlinson had not known each other professionally, and only met briefly in Paris to give additional publicity to each other's cases, they represented a powerful, potentially destructive combination, and living proof that both organisations were extremely vulnerable to disclosures made by ex-employees. Both had been probationers who had received poor annual assessments at a time when their organisations had been contracting in size, and when there were no non-sensitive posts into which they could be shunted. Whereas MI5 had a ready answer for most of Shayler's criticisms, and his newspaper revelations amounted more to voyeurism than whistle-blowing, SIS could not afford to endure a constant, recurring spotlight of publicity. Tomlinson's capacity for mischief-making was considerable, as demonstrated by his assertion that Princess's Diana's driver on the night she died, Henri Paul, had been a long-term SIS asset as well as director of the Ritz Hotel's security. Tomlinson, testifying to the investigating judge in Paris, Hervé Stephan, claimed to have heard at Vauxhall Cross in 1992 from his immediate superior, Nick Fishwick, that Henri Paul had been on SIS's payroll. Furthermore, he claimed that Dearlove had been in Paris two weeks before the fatal accident, and had held meetings there with the two senior officers based at the Paris station, Richard Spearman, formerly Spedding's Chief of Staff, and Nicholas Langman. The proposition that SIS had conspired to assassinate the Princess of Wales was quite ludicrous, but it was taken sufficiently seriously to be retailed across the globe, to the point that MI5's D-G, Stella Rimington, felt an obligation to make an unprecedented public denial, and even include a formal statement rejecting the allegation in the official Security Service handbook produced by the Cabinet Office.

While Shayler languished in La Santé prison, Tomlinson was quickly on the move, flying between New Zealand, where he was served with an injunction, and Switzerland, which expelled him in May 1999 following the publication on the internet of a list of 115 serving or recently-retired SIS officers. Although Tomlinson denied being the source of the information, claiming that all the names had been made public before, or were retirees, Robin Cook denounced him in the strongest terms. Now Tomlinson had nothing to lose and, after a spell in Rimini, working in a bar, he settled in Cannes where he completed his book, *The Big Breach*, which was published in the English language in Moscow with an advance of £28,000 and gave a detailed account of his training and his assignments. Although Tomlinson had altered the true names of several of his former colleagues, giving them semi-transparent cover-names, further material surfaced on the internet, revealing their authentic identities. The Court of Appeal subsequently ruled that the book could be serialised in the *Sunday Times*.

According to SIS, Tomlinson's Russian publisher, Sergei Korovin, had no known previous experience in publishing, but had travelled to Switzerland and the United States using the alias Kirill V. Chashchin, and was sponsored by the SVR which was still smarting after the embarrassment of Vasili Mitrokhin's disclosures. SIS thought it detected the SVR's distinctive handiwork in the published version of *The Big Breach* particularly in the book's treatment of Platon Obukov, a junior Russian Foreign Ministry official who was arrested in April 1996 while meeting his SIS contact, Norman McSween, in Moscow. The son of a senior Russian diplomat, Obukov had been recruited while working as a consul in Sweden, and in his defence claimed that he had been collecting material for one of his spy novels. He was convicted of espionage, sentenced to eleven years' imprisonment, and transferred to a psychiatric hospital; McSween was expelled. However, Tomlinson had known nothing about Obukov, who had been recruited *after* Tomlinson's dismissal, and the author's original draft had not mentioned the case at all. The insertion of the damaging passages about Obukov suggested either that Tomlinson had lost control over his manuscript, and the SVR had taken the opportunity to insert the additional material, or that he had actually switched sides and had to be regarded as an SVR adherent.

To SIS's dismay, *The Big Breach* was reprinted in Scotland by Mainstream, giving wider circulation to the most comprehensive insider's view of the modern Service ever produced. As well as covering much of the ground published two years earlier by the *Sunday Times*, the book referred to numerous other operations and individuals, leaving the author vulnerable to arrest if he ever ventured back into the UK's jurisdiction.

During Spedding's tenure as Chief he supervised SIS's move in 1994 from Century House to its flashy new headquarters at 85 Albert Embankment, known to those who work there as 'Legoland' and designed by the avant-garde architect Terry Farrell. The transfer was required because of the discovery of concrete cancer in the grim old building which anyway was due for major renovation and was thought to be affecting the health of some staff. However, the new building, bought for £230 million, proved a considerable embarrassment because of the huge cost over-runs incurred while converting the palatial structure into one suitable for the Service's 1,500 headquarters staff, and its ostentatious design with terraces, marble-lined atriums, open-plan offices and even a gym and sports hall on the ground floor. The move attracted so much adverse publicity that, almost inevitably, on the evening of 21 September 2000 it became the target for a terrorist attack, with the Real IRA launching a rocket-propelled grenade, from a small park in Spring Gardens a hundred yards away, into the screen protecting the eighth floor personnel department. The Russian-made RPG-7 was fired by a motorcycyle pillion passenger who was driven away from the scene at speed, abandoning the weapon which was recovered moments later. The building suffered minimal damage and there were no injuries among the hundred of so staff still at work.

The Real IRA was a break-away faction of the Provisional IRA, a group of hardliners led by Michael McKevitt, a Dundalk shopkeeper who had rejected the peace process in October 1997. McKevitt had been PIRA's quartermaster and was believed to have supplied the explosives for another splinter group, the Continuity IRA, which had been responsible for detonating a massive car bomb in Omagh in August 1998. In March 2001 McKevitt was arrested at his home by the Gardai and charged in Dublin with the real IRA's leadership. His conviction and sentence of twenty years' imprisonment was secured largely on the evidence of an FBI mole, David Rupert, a truck-driver who had penetrated the organisation in 1999 posing as a wealthy republican sympathiser from Florida. Rupert had been co-handled by an MI5 case officer and provided compelling testimony of his numerous contacts with McKevitt's paramilitaries, and had been able to identify some of the venues used by the organisation for meetings so they could be bugged and the conversations recorded. Although the two men who had fired the RPG-7 at Vauxhall Cross were not named in court, the Security Service identified them just as the Real IRA effectively ceased to exist.

The collapse of the republican paramilitaries in Northern Ireland represented an important milestone in Britain's long struggle against domestic terrorism. Although it had taken thirty years, the successful formula combined political accommodation, compromise and containment, combined with aggressive counter-measures undertaken by the RUC Special Branch, MI5 and the Army's covert agent-running and surveillance units. The experience acquired throughout the long years of negotiation during the peace process, initiated by Mrs Thatcher and then pursued by John Major and Tony Blair with their successive counterparts in Dublin, was to prove useful in the period following the Al-Qaeda attack on the United States on 11 September 2001 when knowledge of combating terrorist organisations was to be at a premium.

During Spedding's tenure the Service's focus had shifted from Eastern Europe towards the Middle East, and this theme was central in the briefing he gave the ISC in May 1995 when he described the change as one of the most significant in SIS's history, involving considerable difficulties in effort and resources in moving two-thirds of its activities away from Russia to the Balkans and the Arab world. While explaining this unprecedented challenge, Spedding took the opportunity to express his anxieties about the arrest of the CIA officer Aldrich Ames, who was caught after a long molehunt that had concluded in February 1993. Ames had haemorrhaged secrets from his vantage point in Langley, and had confessed to having supplied the KGB with classified information since April 1985, but Spedding told the ISC that he still had not received a detailed damage assessment describing the impact on SIS. Ames had not admitted having compromised AE/TICKLE, who was Oleg Gordievsky, but nonetheless might have been responsible for his unexpected recall to Moscow in May 1985.

When briefing the new Foreign Secretary in 1997, Spedding shrewdly emphasised the service's contribution to drug interdiction in Colombia and south-east Asia, a role that appeared to coincide with Robin Cook's commitment to what he termed 'an ethical foreign policy'. If SIS had ever harboured any concerns about the incoming Labour administration, it certainly need not have been concerned about Cook who, despite his withering analysis of the Matrix Churchill debacle, and his hugely impressive performance during the Commons debate which John Major's shaky government only survived by a single vote, was more than ready to be seduced by the secret world that had intrigued him for so long. Cook proved to be a lazy secretary of state, preoccupied by his covert affair with his secretary Gaynor, whom he persuaded the Foreign Office to employ, and with no appetite to dismantle SIS. In April 1998, at a Mansion House dinner in the City, Cook praised SIS, saying they 'cannot speak for themselves' because 'the nature of what they do means that we cannot shout about their achievements if we want them to remain effective. But let me say I have been struck by the range and quality of the work.' Nevertheless, under Cook's supervision the Single Unified Vote was reduced to £693m, the lowest figure since the end of the Cold War.

Cook's irritating claim to have introduced ethics into British foreign policy foundered when he complained about the activities of a British company, Sandline International, run from offices in the King's Road, Chelsea, which was accused by Customs and Excise of breaching the United Nations ban on the export of arms to Sierra Leone, the former British colony in West Africa wracked by civil war. Much to Cook's embarrassment, Sandline's involvement in Sierra Leone had been authorised by the Foreign Office, and one of its directors, Rupert Bowen, was a former Parachute Regiment officer who had served in SIS at Windhoek and Tirana. Far from running a renegade, unapproved operation, Sandline's Colonel Tim Spicer, a decorated former Coldstream Guards officer, demonstrated that his organisation had kept the Foreign Office fully informed of its activities, leaving the impression that Cook, who had gained a reputation for being easily distracted, had simply failed to read his boxes.[3]

Spedding was widely regarded as a youthful modernist, and certainly promoted that image of himself. He allowed the riverside exterior of Vauxhall Cross to be filmed for the 1999 James Bond movie *The World Is Not Enough*, and even invited Dame Judi Dench, the actress who played M in the movie, to SIS's Christmas lunch in December 1998. She was not allowed to be driven in her own car, and the SIS driver had difficulty finding her house, with the result that she was forty-five minutes late. Nevertheless, she later declared herself to have 'found the experience very exciting' and was 'fascinated, but not surprised, at how many languages everyone spoke'. At the end of the lunch Spedding presented her with a miniature spy camera in a red leather case, but no film.

Another of Spedding's widely-publicised initiatives was his announcement, in February 1999, that SIS had posted its first gay couple to an overseas post. The officer concerned was Christopher Hurran, who was sent to Prague accompanied by his Venezuelan partner. Although this development prompted considerable mirth, the Chief's objective had been to make the point that declared homosexuality was no longer a barrier to a security clearance, and that SIS was experiencing considerable difficulty in persuading staff to take on overseas stations where their families might be exposed to risk. Indeed, most middle-ranking personnel with young children were reluctant to interrupt their education by going abroad at all.

Spedding retired from SIS at the end of August 1999, just two weeks before the publication of *The Mitrokhin Archive*, a book that was to plunge the Service into controversy. Always a heavy smoker, Spedding suffered from cancer throughout his short retirement and finally succumbed to it in June 2001, at the age of fifty-eight. His memorial service was attended, among others, by the Director of Central Intelligence, George Tenet, and King Abdullah of Jordan.

Chapter XIII

Richard Dearlove
1999–2003

'CX reports as produced by my Service are necessarily single source, and much high quality intelligence which is factual or proved to be factual is single source material.'

'C' to Lord Hutton, September 2003[1]

THE appointment of Richard Dearlove as Spedding's successor was announced by the Foreign Secretary, Robin Cook, in February 1999, six months ahead of the actual changeover date. Cook revealed that Dearlove had been Spedding's 'Director of Operations' for the past six years. According to the biographical details released, Dearlove had been born in Cornwall, was educated at Monkton Combe School, near Bath, and at Kent School, Connecticut, before reading history at Queens' College, Cambridge.

The official Foreign Office brief did not go into any detail, but Dearlove was a career SIS officer who had joined Century House in 1966 and his first posting had been to Nairobi in 1968 where he remained for three years understudying two senior SIS officers. During this period his wife Rosalind bore him a son and a daughter. In 1973 he was appointed station commander in Prague and returned to London in 1976. In June 1980 he went to Paris as deputy to Alexis Forter, for whom he had worked in Nairobi, and took over from him after the Falklands War, returning to London in 1985. By 1993 he was SIS's Director of Personnel, and supervised the dismissal of Richard Tomlinson.

The project Dearlove inherited from Spedding in August 1999, which was to prove both controversial and a major embarrassment, was the publication of *The Mitrokhin Archive*, the revelations of a KGB defector, Vasili Mitrokhin, who had been exfiltrated from Riga seven years earlier, in October 1992.

Mitrokhin had presented himself unexpectedly at the new British Embassy in the newly independent Latvia in March 1992 and had offered a sample of what he claimed was a massive collection of documents that he had copied from the KGB archives over the twelve years he had served as the FCD's archivist. He had supervised the transfer of the organisation's files when the FCD had moved from the KGB's old base in the Lubyanka to the new headquarters in Yasenevo, and had taken the opportunity to copy selected items which he had considered of historical importance. For eight years his vast accumulation of manuscripts and notes had been hidden in a pair of milk churns buried beneath one of his two *dachas*, and his condition for handing them over to SIS was that they should be published in the West as an authentic testament to the evils of the Soviet system. After his samples had been scrutinised, and his credentials verified, Mitrokhin had been escorted to the UK by a senior officer who had joined SIS in 1958 and subsequently had served in Jakarta, Guyana, Tehran, Islamabad and finally Lagos before returning to London in September 1979. Mitrokhin was resettled in England, together with his wife and son, who were soon to succumb to illness. While SIS supervised the transfer of his material onto a computer, and passed thousands of espionage leads on to allied agencies, a plan was prepared for the eventual publication of a book, *The Mitrokhin Archive*, edited by the Cambridge historian, Professor Christopher Andrew. Spedding deliberately kept the ISC's Chairman, Tom King, completely ignorant of the project. The publication arrangements began on 17 October 1995 when Professor Andrew was invited to Vauxhall Cross for a briefing, and he was shown some of the raw material a few weeks later. He was introduced to Mitrokhin himself towards the end of the year, and then invited him to lunch at Corpus Christi College in early 1996.

Originally codenamed JESSANT, Mitrokhin had always insisted, as a condition of his defection, that his material should be published, and a project had been approved by Malcolm Rifkind at the outset, who had set certain guidelines, one being that nobody should be named as a Soviet source, or a target for Soviet recruitment, unless they had been convicted of the crime. Secondly, the Foreign Secretary insisted that the judgment on who to include in the book, and what names to exclude, should not be left exclusively to the Security Service. Thus, with a lawyer's approach, Rifkind had spotted and dealt with the one area of controversy that could be anticipated with such a risky undertaking. Thereafter, the project was managed by an inter-departmental committee chaired initially by Gerry Warner's successor as Intelligence Coordinator, John Alpass. A former Deputy D-G of MI5, Alpass had completed a review for the Cabinet on the intelligence services and was responsible for liaising with all the different branches of government with an interest in Mitrokhin.

However, as the project neared completion attention began to focus on two Soviet agents, neither of whom had been prosecuted for espionage. Somehow the true names of both SCOT and HOLA, ex-Detective Sergeant John Symonds and Mrs Melita Norwood, leaked to the BBC which had gained SIS's support for *The Spying Game*, a documentary television series, and SIS faced a dilemma. As neither Symonds nor Norwood had been convicted of espionage, their names should have been excluded from *The Mitrokhin Archive* under the conditions imposed by Malcolm Rifkind, but the book's publishers, Penguin, recognised that much of the value of the book lay in exposing the pair, albeit at some risk of a defamation action. The solution was for the BBC to obtain admissions from both spies which would eliminate the legal risk, and although this enabled the book to be published and serialised in *The Times*, it also attracted considerable media attention to the fact that Mrs Norwood was not only free, but had never even been interviewed by MI5, which had discovered her identity from a VENONA text in 1966. According to the material copied by Mitrokhin in Moscow, Melita Norwood had begun her career in espionage in 1936, had betrayed atomic secrets during the war, and had been active as a recruiter into the 1970s when she had pitched a Ministry of Defence employee. Naturally, MI5's lapse was a considerable embarrassment for the Director-General, and the subject of great public clamour as 'the granny spy' held a press conference at her garden gate and insisted that she was an unrepentant Communist, and would spy again if she had the opportunity. Not surprisingly, there was widespread astonishment that she had avoided arrest for so long and the government, caught completely unprepared by the furore, ordered the ISC to conduct a full inquiry.

The SIS officer responsible for supervising the Mitrokhin project was John Scarlett, formerly the station commander in Moscow who had been expelled in January 1994, during his second tour in the Russian capital, when he had been caught meeting an agent, Vadim Sintsov, who was later sentenced to ten years' hard labour. Sintsov had been the export manager of a Russian weapons manufacturer and confessed that he had been recruited the previous year while attending an arms fair in London. Since then he had been paid £8,000 for details of Russian deliveries of weapons to the Middle East and had met his contacts in cities in third countries such as Budapest, Paris and Singapore.

Scarlett had joined SIS in 1971, after graduating from Cambridge, and had been posted to the Nairobi station in 1973 to serve as deputy to W. J. R. G. P. Dawson, an old hand who had spent five years in Tehran over the Suez period, but in September 1974 was withdrawn and sent on a language course to learn Russian, in anticipation of his posting to the Moscow station in January 1976. That tour lasted just sixteen months, until May 1977 when he returned to London. In 2001 the JIC's Chairman, Peter Ricketts, who had been in the post for less than a year, was sent to Brussels as the UK's representative at NATO, and Scartlett replaced him, the first time an SIS officer had been appointed.

If there was a single event, apart from the collapse of the Berlin Wall, which could be described as a defining moment for the era, for the international intelligence community it must be the terrorist attack on New York and Washington DC on 11 September 2001. Whereas Islamic extremism and fears of nuclear proliferation had been used to justify pleas for fewer cuts in budgets, the audacious and ingeniously executed atrocity proved a milestone for counter-terrorism organisations. Dearlove's instinctive reaction had been to fly to New York on the first Concorde allowed to land at JFK, to see for himself the remains of the World Trade Center in Manhattan, the second tower of which, incidentally, had housed the CIA's New York station, though this had been evacuated before the tower collapsed. Dearlove offered SIS's unconditional support to the DCI, George Tenet, and a new era dawned in which politicians would be unable to challenge intelligence budgets. Retirees were called back to the colours, new joint analytical and operational units were created, and an emphasis was placed on the recruitment of human sources, swinging the pendulum back from a reliance on technical intelligence. The Middle East became the focus of SIS's attention, with a renewed effort to cultivate sources with access to Kabul and Baghdad.

Dearlove's demands for additional funds were granted by a Labour government anxious to avoid accusations of starving the intelligence community of resources, and £4 million was immediately allocated to an Afghan Task Force to buy information and influence from the Taliban then controlling some of the Al-Qaeda training camps. Unfortunately SIS's principal asset in Afghanistan, Ahmed Shah Mahsoud, the charismatic leader of the Mujahidin in the Panjshir valley who had fought the Soviets with British equipment a decade earlier, was murdered by two suicide bombers posing as Moroccan television journalists, two days before Osama bin Laden's 11 September attack on the United States, requiring SIS's Paul Bergne to find new friends among the warlords of the Northern Alliance. Backed by SIS and the CIA, the Northern Alliance quickly swept the Taliban from their areas and enabled British and American special forces and airborne troops to liberate the country. The contribution made by SIS evidently impressed Prime Minister Tony Blair, who described its officers in Afghanistan as 'unsung heroes' who had made the intervention possible. Thereafter Dearlove developed a close relationship with the Prime Minister and frequently accompanied him on his overseas trips, including one to Camp David where the Chief almost participated in a press conference organised by the White House. His name was added to a list of senior officials accompanying President Bush and Tony Blair, but he hastily withdrew at the last moment, protesting that he did not wish to be photographed.

Dearlove's scramble to transform SIS into a counter-terrorist organisation directed against Osama bin Laden, matched by the CIA's determination to decapitate Al-Qaeda, would result in a series of setbacks and disappointments, among them the accusations directed at the British government following the bombing of the Bali resort of Kuta in October 2002. A suicide bomber had destroyed much of a nightclub, forcing revellers onto a street where a car bomb detonated soon afterwards, leaving more than 200 dead. By accepting the lead role in combating global terrorism SIS had left itself vulnerable to criticism of intelligence failure every time terrorists committed atrocities where there were British casualties. Although the intelligence community understood that such episodes could not be predicted without access to Al-Qaeda's leadership or its communications, expectations had been built up to such a degree that the Parliamentary Intelligence and Security Committee launched a futile inquiry to establish whether clues to the attack in Indonesia had been overlooked. They had not, but thereafter any future incident would be regarded as indicative of SIS's impotence.

The controversy that was to dominate Dearlove's tenure as Chief was SIS's involvement in the preparation of two documents intended to justify the Blair government's intention to go to war with Iraq to remove Saddam Hussein. The first document, drawn up in haste in September 2002, ostensibly by the JIC, and accompanied by a foreword written by Tony Blair, purported to detail the threat posed by Iraq's continued possession of weapons of mass destruction (WMD) in defiance of successive UN Security Council resolutions. In particular, the paper reported that Iraq had been detected in several efforts to purchase nuclear materials and components, and had been prevented from buying uranium yellowcake in Niger, the third largest producer of that precious commodity (after Canada and Australia). The evidence for the illicit procurement in Niger was a series of letters which, upon detailed examination by the International Atomic Energy Agency in Vienna, turned out to have been forged. So where had they come from? During the various investigations conducted into the provenance of the forgeries, they appeared to have been acquired from an employee of Niger's Embassy in Rome run by a French intelligence service (DGSE) contract agent, Rocco Martino. Codenamed GIACOMO, Martino was an Italian businessman who protested that he had passed on the documents in good faith, unaware that they had been fabricated.

Nevertheless, SIS insisted to the ISC that it had acquired other evidence of Iraq's attempt to buy yellowcake in two other African countries, implying that the origin of the information had been an allied intelligence agency which had demanded that its role remain confidential, and maybe inferring that the French DGSE had relayed the tip from assets in the former French colony's capital, or perhaps somewhere else. Either way, the suggestion was that the attempt had been made in Niger, where the two mines in Arlit, run by the Somair and Cominak enterprises, two joint European and Japanese consortia, had been directly supervised since 1977 by the IAEA. Furthermore, the quantities of ore required to refine the yellowcake would have been considerable, involving thousands of tons which would have been hard, if not impossible, to conceal.

The second problem for SIS was the reference in the paper to the claim, made by a single unverified source, that Iraq's weapons of mass destruction could be ready for deployment within forty-five minutes of the order being given in Baghdad. However, the text in the September dossier presented the reference to forty-five minutes as being the time in which British interests, the two sovereign bases in Cyprus, could come under attack once Saddam had taken the decision to launch.

The second paper, to become notorious as 'the dodgy dossier', was a document released by the government in February 2003 in an effort to justify the imminent coalition attack on Iraq. This publication was presented as an intelligence analysis, written and cleared by the JIC, setting out the current threat posed by Saddam Hussein's regime, but it was quickly exposed as having been constructed from some open sources, among them a ten year-old doctoral thesis written by a university student in the United States and apparently downloaded, without any attribution, from the internet. A line-by-line comparison with the original version showed that it had been deliberately edited at Downing Street to exaggerate the threat from Baghdad. Worse, the chairman of the JIC, John Scarlett, complained that the dossier contained some authentic intelligence which had not been cleared for publication by the originating agency, and this issue was the subject of criticism in the ISC's annual report, released in June 2003, after the successful occupation of Iraq by the coalition. Anticipating a ruckus, and taking personal responsibility for the 'dodgy dossier', Alastair Campbell, Downing Street's controversial Director of Communications, wrote a letter of apology to Scarlett, Dearlove, the Director of GCHQ and the Director-General of MI5.

The ISC, chaired since Tom King's retirement at the 2001 General Election by a former Labour Chief Whip, Ann Taylor MP, was coming to play a significant role in the Chief's life. Initially the ISC, assisted by a single clerk, with a request for additional staff refused, was really of no great significance. Although established in January 1995 under the terms of the 1994 Intelligence Services Act, the Committee had never included anyone with any knowledge of intelligence, although Tom King and Michael Mates had experienced some ministerial contact with the agencies at the MoD and the Northern Ireland Office. Apart from its annual reports, which invariably contained the repeated recommendation that the Ministerial Committee on the Intelligence Services really ought to meet, a suggestion consistently ignored by the government, the ISC had produced two separate, special reports. The first, in the spring of 1996, was never released to the public, but the second, on the Mitrokhin fiasco, had proved to be deeply flawed, and the ISC's inquiry had been sidestepped by Dearlove on the grounds that the entire Mitrokhin project had been undertaken by his predecessor, David Spedding, who had retired literally a fortnight before *The Mitrokhin Archive* had been published in September 1999.

The ISC's *Mitrokhin Inquiry Report*, sent to the Prime Minister at the end of April 2000, concentrated its fire on MI5, excoriating the Security Service for allowing Mrs Norwood's case to have 'slipped out of sight'[2] for five years, between 1993 when Mitrokhin confirmed her identity, and 1998 when the Alpass Committee realised she would become the centre of attention when *The Mitrokhin Archive* was finally released. MI5's defence was not helped by Dame Stella Rimington's evidence to the ISC, in which she admitted she had absolutely no recollection of ever having been briefed on Mrs Norwood's case. However, SIS only came under fire for not having informed Tom King about the Mitrokhin project until August 1999, when Dearlove introduced himself to the ISC Chairman as Spedding's successor. King clearly had been irritated by the delay of seven years in letting him know of such a major undertaking, and had spotted that both the Home

Secretary, Jack Straw, and the Foreign Secretary, Robin Cook, had been completely misled about *The Mitrokhin Archive* and, in particular, had never been told of the Rifkind conditions. Each, belatedly, had received a completely disingenuous individual briefing, implying that the other had approved the content of the book, whereas neither realised that Mrs Norwood's name was to be included in direct contravention of Rifkind's original sanction. Although the ISC did remark on these lapses, it failed to grasp a couple of the most significant problems, one of which had been alluded to in evidence by Mitrokhin himself. The author, for whom publication was a life's ambition, had made the preparation of a book a condition of his defection and collaboration, and was himself highly displeased by the treatment he had received. He had been especially outraged when he discovered that the American edition had been retitled *The Sword and the Shield*, with his name on the dustjacket below that of his editor, Christopher Andrew.

The reconstituted ISC, under the chairmanship of Mrs Taylor, although entirely devoid of any significant ministerial or other experience of intelligence, was called upon to consider the use made of intelligence prior to the Second Gulf War but its report, published in September 2003, only served to demonstrate the Committee's shortcomings. Surprisingly, soon afterwards the former Government Chief Whip announced she would be leaving Parliament and would not contest the next general election.

The issue of the validity of the claims made in the September dossier had only become critical when reluctant government backbenchers protested that its content had been used to apply pressure on them to support against their instincts a crucial division in the House of Commons on 18 March 2003. In the event the government won the vote handsomely, the first ever held by any British government to authorise hostilities, but afterwards the Prime Minister disclosed that if the motion had been lost he and most of his Cabinet would have resigned. Thus the suspicion emerged that government whips had relied upon faulty, misleading or demonstrably incorrect information to persuade recalcitrant MPs to support the Prime Minister in an unpopular war. The debate about the ethics and wisdom of supporting the American coalition in the Gulf, without the approval of the United Nations Security Council, led to several resignations from the government, including that of Tony Blair's long-serving former Foreign Secretary, Robin Cook, who had been reshuffled to the Cabinet post of Leader of the House. Disquiet about the precise circumstances in which Britain went to war increased when, in the months following the occupation of Iraq, absolutely no evidence was found of any WMD, one of the main reasons given for the war. Ironically, Cook's replacement as Foreign Secretary, Jack Straw, himself became increasingly opposed to going to war against Saddam Hussein and attempted, right up to the last minute, to dissuade the Prime Minister.

The reliability of the CX reporting on WMD was called into question by the CIA when the documents purporting to show Iraqi attempts to purchase uranium ore from Niger were checked by the UN International Atomic Energy Agency in Vienna and found to be forgeries. SIS had relied upon these letters as proof that the Iraqis had been engaged on a covert procurement programme, presumably to develop a nuclear weapon, and this information had been passed by the CIA to the White House for inclusion in President's Bush's State of the Union Address to Congress in January 2003. SIS had also reported on an Iraqi purchase of 60,000 aluminium tubes, perhaps to be used in a centrifuge to separate fissionable material, but the CIA had been less confident that there might not have been another explanation. However, the reference to the attempt to buy the Niger yellowcake did find its way into the President's speech, with appalling consequences.

Once the SIS documents were shown to have been fabricated the DCI, George Tenet, acknowledged the error and took responsibility for approving that section of the President's speech. There were, in total, just sixteen words which were clearly wrong: 'The British government has learned Saddam Hussein has recently sought significant quantities of uranium from Africa.'

Tenet made a humiliating public apology for the blunder. However, worse was to follow because a former US Ambassador to Iraq and Niger, Joseph Wilson, revealed that he had been commissioned by the CIA to check the authenticity of the British documents relating to the alleged uranium sales, and had concluded that they were bogus. He insisted that the CIA had known of his verdict *before* the President's speech on

28 January, thereby implying that false intelligence had been deliberately inserted into the text for political purposes. What greater crime could an intelligence officer be accused of than peddling information he knew to be wrong, or 'spinning' intelligence for the benefit of his political masters?

The discontent about the authenticity of the documents developed into crisis when a BBC radio correspondent reported on the *Today* programme in July that the forty-five minute figure had been inserted into the dossier at the last moment at the insistence of Downing Street, in the teeth of opposition from the intelligence community. Furthermore, the BBC reported that the figure had been included when 'the government probably knew it was wrong'. Although this allegation was broadcast only once, just after the morning six o'clock news, and was an opinion expressed by BBC Radio's Defence Correspondent Andrew Gilligan, and not a scripted item, the government reacted swiftly, with Richard Dearlove inviting the *Today* programme presenter, John Humphrys, and his editor, Kevin Marsh, to lunch at Vauxhall Cross where he defended SIS's position. This extraordinary event, which was also attended by the head of BBC News, Richard Sandbrook, was unprecedented for several reasons. Certainly individual Chiefs had entertained journalists before, and some of these had even referred to such convivial occasions, as John Simpson had in his memoirs when he recalled lunching with David Spedding, whom he had known when they had been up at Cambridge together. But the meal with the three BBC men was to prove momentous, not so much because of the disclosure that it had happened, which was anyway a breach of the terms under which it was held, but because somehow a version of what was said later emerged. An account of the meeting was later reported in *The Times*, including a long quotation attributed to Dearlove in which he appeared to concede that the CX was an insufficient justification for going to war with Iraq, which left readers with the strong impression that 'a verifiable record of the conversation' existed, which is journalese for tacitly acknowledging that someone had taped the entire meeting.

Not surprisingly, Dearlove was outraged that his hospitality should have been abused so egregiously, but the implications of the attributed comment were immense. Was the Chief admitting that there was no intelligence to support the government's policy, thereby contradicting the Prime Minister and laying the foundations for a first-class political row, if not a full-scale constitutional crisis, or was he merely saying that his own agency's product did not meet the criteria, leaving room for the defence that other material had been made available, perhaps from GCHQ or the Defence Intelligence Staff? Dearlove's reported remarks, though not fully appreciated at the time, were to acquire enormous significance when no WMD were discovered in Iraq.

Stung by the accusation of inappropriate interference in the drafting of the September dossier, Alastair Campbell launched a fierce counter-attack on the BBC and believed he had played a trump card when Dr David Kelly, an MoD expert on Iraqi WMD, revealed to his managers that he had spoken to the BBC about his disapproval of the way the first dossier had been drafted. Apparently in the confident belief that Kelly would undermine the BBC's allegations, his name was released to the media and he gave evidence to the Foreign Affairs Select Committee in a public session, and also appeared before the Intelligence and Security Committee, sitting in private. In his evidence Kelly denied that he could have been the BBC's source for the broadcast allegations, but it was only after he had been found dead, an apparent suicide, near his home in Oxfordshire two days later, that the BBC disclosed that Dr Kelly indeed had been its source, and that some of his conversations with its reporters had been tape-recorded.

The news that Dr Kelly had seemingly taken his own life and that his evidence to the Select Committee had not been entirely accurate transformed a media spat into a full-blown crisis, and a senior judge, Lord Hutton, was appointed to investigate the circumstances of the death. At the outset Lord Hutton made it clear that his inquiry would range as widely as he considered appropriate, and that it would include a detailed examination of the way in which the September dossier had been constructed in Whitehall.

The evidence presented to the inquiry included overwhelming proof that the September dossier had been substantially altered by Alastair Campbell, who had chaired two meetings at Downing Street to prepare the document for distribution, and had sent the JIC Chairman John Scarlett no fewer than fifteen recommended changes to the draft text, most of which were accepted. One result was that the 'forty-five minute claim', buried in the main text and hedged with caveats and qualifications, had been promoted to the 'executive summary', then highlighted in the Prime Minister's foreword, and was mentioned four times in all, having lost the usual cautions that the information had originated from a single, unverified source.

The inquiry hearings revealed that the September dossier had been influenced by Campbell, just as Dr Kelly had alleged, although curiously no minutes had been taken of Scarlett's meetings with Campbell. In his evidence Campbell insisted that Scarlett had 'ownership' of the dossier and his advice had been purely presentational, a view supported by the ISC in its report published in September 2003. Scarlett was also supported by Dearlove who gave evidence to the Inquiry over a voice link from Vauxhall Cross, and declared himself to be so pleased with the September dossier that he had proposed a vote of thanks for the JIC's Chairman. Under cross-examination Dearlove acknowledged that, with the benefit of hindsight, it had been inappropriate to have placed such emphasis on the controversial figure of forty-five minutes. Dearlove's testimony on this point was remarkable. He confirmed that the information had come from a single source, 'equated to an Iraqi military officer', and pointed out that much of SIS's intelligence came from single sources, which did not necessarily devalue it. However, he also acknowledged that the reference to forty-five minutes was in relation to battlefield artillery and mortar rounds, and not missile warheads, an admission that undermined the widely-circulated assertion that the weapons had posed a direct threat to British interests. The figure had been taken to mean that Saddam could launch an attack with enhanced Scud missiles on the British sovereign bases in Cyprus within that short time period, but Dearlove blithely demolished that proposition. When asked why the Ministry of Defence had not attempted to correct this misleading impression, the Secretary of State, Geoff Hoon, feigned ignorance, claiming not to have seen the relevant newspaper headlines, and that anyway he was not in the business of attempting to correct journalists' inaccuracies.

The Hutton Inquiry placed SIS and the JIC under a spotlight of a kind that had not been experienced since Lord Franks had picked over the entrails of the Falklands War, but on that occasion the evidence had not been made public, and his Committee of Privy Counsellors had sat entirely in private. In contrast, Lord Hutton published significant quantities of evidence on the internet and cross-examined the witnesses in public session. The result was the most detailed forensic scrutiny of how the JIC Assessment Staff had compiled the September dossier, and how two senior members of the Defence Intelligence Staff had declared their unease, in writing, with the process that had been adopted, and the content of the final draft. When he was brought back to give evidence for a second time, Scarlett admitted under close cross-examination that he had been prompted by Blair's Chief of Staff, Jonathan Powell, to alter the final agreed text *after* the JIC and the Assessment Staff had completed their deliberations.

Throughout the proceedings Dearlove stood by his decision to allow the reference to forty-five minutes to be included in the dossier, and Scarlett insisted that it had been his decision, and not Powell's, to make the last-moment alteration to the final draft. Nevertheless, these unconvincing propositions served to undermine the integrity of the JIC and cast doubt on the extent to which Dearlove and Scarlett had succumbed to political pressure.

One of the most compelling contributions to the swirling controversy was made by Robin Cook, Blair's former Foreign Secretary, and the man who had appointed Dearlove. He defended SIS, and said that he had grown:

> . . . to respect the caution of the Secret Intelligence Service and I would regard it as monstrously unfair to the men and women who serve in the agency if they were now made the fall guys because of the way their work was abused to produce the September dossier. The dossier did violence to their craft in two ways. First, it painted a one-sided picture, whereas every JIC assessment I saw would honestly present any contrary evidence that might be inconsistent with the final conclusion. Second, it definitely proclaimed a certitude for its claims that was at odds with the nuanced tone of every JIC assessment I read. Personally I have never doubted that No. 10 believed in the threads of intelligence which were woven into the dossier. But that does not alter the

> awkward fact that the intelligence was wrong and ministers who had applied a sceptical mind could have seen that it was too thin to be a reliable basis for war. No. 10 believed in the intelligence because they desperately wanted it to be true. Their sin was not one of bad faith but of evangelical certainty. They selected for inclusion only the scraps of intelligence that fitted the government's case and gave them an edge that was justifiable. The result was a gross distortion.[3]

Cook's observations on the Iraqi WMD were characteristically scathing, but also important for he had broken a long-standing convention which prevented former Foreign Secretaries from discussing secret intelligence or SIS's Chief. Neither Geoffrey Howe nor Douglas Hurd had referred to the Chiefs of their periods in office in their memoirs, yet Cook had plenty to say on the subject, complaining that 'Intelligence is supposed to be the evidence on which ministers reach decisions on foreign and defence policy. It is not meant to be the propaganda by which ministers sell a policy to a sceptical public. Nor are intelligence reports suited for the purpose.' As for Iraqi WMD, Cook confided to his diary that he had been briefed by John Scarlett on Thursday, 20 February 2003:

> The presentation was impressive in its integrity and shorn of the political slant with which No 10 encumbers any intelligence assessment. My conclusion at the end of an hour is that Saddam probably does not have weapons of mass destruction in the sense of weapons that could be used against large-scale civilian targets.[4]

Cook's criticism of the government's mismanagement of intelligence in the period before the Gulf War was trenchant, though blunted somewhat by the disclosure that the Cabinet Secretary, Sir Andrew Turnbull, had made only one change to Cook's manuscript when it had been submitted to the Cabinet Office for the required prepublication clearance. Apparently Cook had been under the mistaken impression that Scarlett had been SIS's Chief, not Dearlove, a strange error for him to have made.

When the coalition's Iraq Survey Group reported in the beginning of October 2003 that no weapons of mass destruction had been found, the debate about the war's legitimacy intensified. Had Saddam's threats of WMD been a hoax, intended to deter the coalition from attacking, or had he simply succeeded in concealing his WMD development programmes? Either way, SIS and the JIC came in for unprecedented criticism with a former diplomat, Sir Peter Heap, pouring scorn on CX. Remarking in an article in the *Guardian*, 'A report dressed up in a CX jacket and bearing a high-security classification can easily take on an importance and a gravitas that it does not deserve.' He recalled that, as the deputy head of mission in Lagos, he had challenged Peter Norris, the SIS station commander, over the content of one of his reports which obviously had been culled from the previous day's newspaper. The High Commissioner had confronted Norris and, dismissing his initial denials, demanded that he explain why he had 'claimed a different source and given it a high security classification? "Because" came the reply "if it were sent unclassified, other people would know what we are interested in."'[5]

Heap's breach of the long-respected convention that diplomats do not comment on SIS personnel or operations was in effect a scathing attack on SIS's ability to recruit reliable sources, and on the JIC's proficiency in testing intelligence's authenticity. He suggested that SIS routinely enhanced the status of dubious informants who had a monetary interest in embellishing their reports:

> As a diplomat who worked in nine overseas posts over 36 years, I saw quite a lot of MI6 at work. They were represented in nearly all of those diplomatic missions ... It was common to see MI6 reports on their channel that amounted to little more than gossip and tittle-tattle that the political and economic sides of the embassy would not have thought worth reporting. These 'intelligence facts' were frequently so at variance with known facts that we knew them to have little or no credibility.

Heap also asserted that,

> Among the wheat there is a lot of chaff, and the working methods of the intelligence agencies make it very difficult to know one from the other.[6]

For such a senior diplomat to speak out so vociferously was quite extraordinary, and Heap was not alone in his criticism. Sir Paul Lever, formerly Britain's Ambassador in Bonn and a past JIC Chairman, joined Sir Percy Cradock, Dame Pauline Neville-Jones and Sir Roderic Braithwaite in publicly expressing their concern about the way John Scarlett appeared to have succumbed to pressure from Downing Street, and in particular from the Prime Minister's Chief of Staff, Jonathan Powell, and had redrafted the September dossier to conform to what the politicians wanted to hear. As the former British Ambassador to Iraq, Sir Harold Walker, put it, 'The integrity of our intelligence system has been battered by the demands of Number Ten.' Braithwaite went further, insisting that:

> The system for providing objective intelligence for the Government was sadly abused.
>
> The JIC is there to provide an analytical service to policymakers. It is emphatically not there to contribute to the making of policy by its public justification. Once it starts down that slippery slope it's chances of producing an unbiased analysis diminish with increasing rapidity. To publish the JIC's analysis of the threat from Iraq in support of government policy was surely unprecedented. So was the process of fiddling with the text to make it more convincing to the public. The Chairman of the JIC gallantly took responsibility for the final wording. But every Tom, Dick and Harry in the Prime Minister's press office felt free to make suggestions. The end product, as Jonathan Powell said at the time – too generously, was capable of convincing only the converted.[7]

Lord Hutton finally published his report on 28 January 2004, making it clear as he did so that he had decided against pursuing any of the political issues arising out of the two government dossiers. Instead he interpreted his remit as being narrowly focused on the circumstances of Dr Kelly's suicide and declared that no blame could be attached to anyone for what had happened, although he made trenchant criticism of the BBC, highlighting the inaccuracies of the news reports originally broadcast, thus prompting the resignations of the BBC Chairman, the BBC Director-

General and the offending reporter, Andrew Gilligan. The Hutton Report exonerated the government and suggested only that Scarlett might have come under 'subconscious pressure' to acquiesce with Downing Street's demands to improve the language and content of the September dossier.

Although Hutton left unresolved the substantive issue of the accuracy of the CX from Iraq and the way the material had been handled, one answer emerged when Dr David Kay, the CIA's head of the Iraq Survey Group, unexpectedly resigned and acknowledged that there were probably no more WMD to be found in Iraq, and that there was no evidence there had been any build-up following DESERT STORM eleven years earlier, and Saddam Hussein's abandonment of his embryonic nuclear programme. So, although Lord Hutton had neatly avoided deliberating over the key question of Iraqi WMD and the quality of the CX, Dr Kay's observations went a long way to confirm that something had gone terribly wrong. The whole basis of Britain's participation in the pre-emptive strike against Iraq had been predicated on Parliamentary approval granted after the government had revealed the country was under direct and imminent threat from Baghdad. The threat assessment had been supplied by SIS and endorsed by the JIC, yet none of the WMD ever materialised. Who had been at fault, the case officers who had handled the sources, or the analysts who had exaggerated or misrepresented the true position? This thorny issue was to be the subject of further scrutiny by a committee chaired by the former Cabinet Secretary Lord Butler, convened in February 2004 to examine the intelligence available prior to Operation IRAQI FREEDOM. Unlike the Hutton Inquiry, which took its evidence in public and published it on the internet, Lord Butler heard his witnesses in private. Furthermore, he would not be sitting in judgment alone, but would be assisted by a panel of Privy Counsellors, being Ann Taylor and Michael Mates from the ISC, Field Marshal Lord Inge and Sir John Chilcot.

While Hutton's conclusions were rejected overwhelmingly by public opinion, the common assumption being that an establishment whitewash had taken place, Robin Butler's committee looked far more formidable, and if he himself was viewed as somewhat tainted, especially by some of his evidence during the Scott Inquiry referring to the widespread Whitehall practice of supplying incomplete answers to potentially embarrassing parliamentary questions, the inclusion of Peter Inge and John Chilcot was intended to prevent the kind of opprobrium endured by Hutton. Inge had been Chief of the Defence Staff until April 1997 and, as an Army professional whose career had spanned Malaya, Hong Kong, Libya and the British Army of the Rhine, had a no-nonsense, sharp mind which would focus on the intelligence issues whatever the political shading. The other member who could be described as a political outsider was Chilcot, formerly the PUS at the Northern Ireland Office, and more recently the Staff Counsellor for the intelligence agencies in succession to Sir Phillip Woodfield, who had also served in the same position in the NIO. Whereas 'the amateurs', Taylor and Mates, had already visited the scene of the crime, through their membership of the ISC, Inge and Chilcot were both experienced consumers of intelligence and there was justifiable confidence that they would find the explanation for what was widely perceived as an immense failure of intelligence.

Put simply, Britain, if not the United States, had gone to war in the belief that Saddam's regime posed a certain, and possibly imminent threat to his region, and to British interests. The two published government dossiers had purported to document the true scale of the threat, whereas their equivalent in Washington DC, the National Intelligence Estimate, had never been made public. Parliament had voted for combat on the assumption that Iraq had built up an arsenal of WMD, and in its absence there were three questions to answered. Was the intelligence collected by the individual agencies authentic and accurate? Was the analysis of the intelligence undertaken with the appropriate intellectual discipline and rigour? And then, the key issue, was the interpretation of the final product justifiable? Clearly much attention would focus on the alleged nuclear threat, as implied by the assertion of an illicit Iraqi uranium procurement programme, and on the crucial WMD lacuna. Did Iraq ever really have the stockpiles of chemical and biological weapons that Baghdad had openly boasted of (including 10,000 litres of anthrax declared to UN inspectors), or was that simply a bluff intended to prevent the country from being overrun by unlimited numbers of Iranian fanatics?

One possible explanation for the source of the infamous 'forty-five minute' danger was the information supplied to SIS by Colonel al-Dabbagh, until early 2003 the commander of one of four Iraqi air defence units in the desert west of Baghdad. He acknowledged publicly in December 2003 that he had passed SIS the critical intelligence relating to WMD during 2002, using as intermediaries contacts in the London-based Iraq National Accord, a group of exiled opponents of Saddam Hussein's regime. Colonel al-Dabbagh insisted that he had witnessed the delivery at night of a 'secret weapon', warheads containing toxic chemicals for hand-held rocket-propelled grenades to be used on the battlefield by Fedayeen and the Special Republican Guard. His role as an SIS source, over seven years, was confirmed by his brother-in-law, retired General A. J. M. Muhie who helped smuggle the information out of Iraq, which included details of the four factories, at Habbaniyah, al-Nahrawan, Nabbai and al-Latifia, that had manufactured the warheads. Al-Dabbagh remained in Baghdad after the coalition invasion and played a leading role in the Governing Council created as a temporary administration.

The extent to which SIS had relied upon Colonel al-Dabbagh was to be hinted at in the Butler Committee's *Review of Intelligence on Weapons of Mass Destruction* which contained a very detailed analysis of the intelligence relating Saddam Hussein's stockpiles of chemical weapons, and his plans to use them. Despite having worked on the Iraqi target for more than two decades, SIS had only acquired three sources in Baghdad. Of the three, one had never enjoyed any direct access to WMD information but had merely relayed gossip he had picked up, leaving SIS dependent on two 'dominant sources', who together were responsible for a full two-thirds of the CX on the subject circulated in Whitehall in 2002. In addition, both these two dominant sources passed on material from a sub-source each, and one of these two sub-sources appeared to be so reliable that his information was distributed under a separate codename, a very risky practice that could have led the uninitiated to think that in fact SIS had acquired a new, third source who was corroborating one of the 'dominants'. In the event, both sub-sources turned out to be unreliable, and their reports not only compromised them, but also served to undermine the credibility of the main agents. Astonishingly, the fact that these agents had been rejected as doubtful was not conveyed to the Prime Minister until the Butler Committee began to gather its evidence and, although both Dearlove and possessed WMD before the invasion of Iraq. Once Baghdad had been occupied the coalition forces had established an international Iraq Survey Group (ISG), drawn mainly from the intelligence community and from the teams of UN weapons inspectors, to search for the elusive Iraqi WMD. Initially led by Dr David Kay, a pugnacious Texan and former CIA officer, the ISG consisted of over a thousand specialists who fanned out across the country to conduct a detailed trawl for evidence of either the weapons themselves, or Saddam's research programmes. However, by January 2004 no WMD had been found, and Kay resigned with a damning personal statement that he did not expect any ever would be found because none had ever existed. His replacement was Charles Duelfer, and when he came to draft the ISG's interim report in March 2004 he and his staff found themselves under pressure, initially in January from the Deputy Chief of Defence Intelligence, Martin Howard, and then from John Scarlett, to slim down the report from 200 to twenty anodyne pages, and to insert some 'golden nuggets' that could not be supported by the evidence found by the ISG. Allegedly Howard had said that with the departure of David Kay there was no need for *any* report to be published, but when the ISG rejected this strategy the British position changed, with Scarlett's personal intervention.

Quite why John Scarlett, as the JIC Chairman, should have been pressing for the inclusion of these ten nuggets has never been explained, but among the items he wanted mentioned was confirmation that Saddam had developed a smallpox programme, a claim first made in the September dossier, had built a 'rail-gun' as part of Iraq's research into nuclear weapons, and had possessed mobile chemical weapons laboratories. In fact, all three assertions were without foundation.[1] The ISG had not found anything to support the charge that smallpox had been developed as a weapon, believed that there was a relatively innocent explanation for the 'rail-gun', and after careful examination of a pair of captured chemical laboratory trailers, had found they had been used to fill artillery observation balloons with nothing more harmful than hydrogen. Naturally the ISG resisted the pressure to distort the report which was finally released at the end of March 2004, prompting the immediate resignation of Duelfer's Australian special adviser, Rod Barton.

Scarlett had been aware at the time they had given their evidence that the principal WMD intelligence had been 'withdrawn', neither had mentioned this to Lord Hutton.

Thus, upon close examination, SIS had relied upon a total of five human sources. One, as we have noted, simply had conveyed gossip that 'he had heard within his circle'. The reporting from a sub-source of one 'dominant' was considered 'open to doubt'. The third main source was 'unreliable' and his intelligence was withdrawn. An additional principal source, reporting through the BND, and codenamed Red River by SIS (and Curve Ball by the CIA) was 'seriously flawed', leaving just two other agents whose reports on chemical and biological weapon capabilities were 'less worrying'. Thus, in short, SIS and the JIC had given emphasis to sources who turned out to be inaccurate in preference to agents, still considered reliable, who had given a less bleak picture. How could this have happened?

In his evidence to the Butler Committee, Dearlove acknowledged that, as a cost-saving exercise, SIS had scrapped the conventional division between the requirements and production sections, and had combined the two disciplines into teams of case and desk officers who had been urged to achieve results. In consequence, inexperienced requirements officers had been ill-equipped to undertake the verification process that the orthodox system had previously built in. Upon becoming members of the production team, the requirements personnel found themselves incentivised to accept information that almost certainly would have been screened out by the traditional method of validation.

Incredibly, the BND's sub-source, when interviewed after the conflict, flatly denied the reports previously attributed to him. Astonishingly, this individual had been responsible for the two key reports which had been used by the JIC to bolster its position in the September dossier. This extraordinary state of affairs went almost unremarked by the Butler Report, yet Richard Dearlove's previous testimony to Lord Hutton had emphasised his confidence in his valued source in Iraq who had supplied the notorious and now-discredited forty-five minute claim. Few commentators seemed to notice the chronology, which suggested that when Dearlove had given his evidence to Hutton, he had known that his source had been deemed unreliable, and that his intelligence reports had been 'withdrawn'.

Whatever SIS's original sources, their reliability, and the true nature of the Iraqi threat, Dearlove's tenure as Chief would be over before Lord Butler's report had been published. He had taken on the post to be instantly engulfed by the political storm caused largely by John Scarlett's handling of the Mitrokhin episode, and he was to leave in not dissimilar circumstances, with Scarlett having enveloped the entire intelligence community in a wholly avoidable maelstrom. Whereas the Mitrokhin fiasco had not threatened to undermine anything more than a few reputations, Scarlett's involvement in the notorious September dossier had played a significant part in taking the country into a major war.

When Dearlove announced, in August 2003, before the end of the Hutton Inquiry's proceedings, that he had been offered the mastership of Pembroke College, Cambridge, there was immediate speculation that his Oxford-educated deputy, Nigel Inkster, would be his successor. A contemporary at Oxford of the Prime Minister, Inkster had joined SIS in 1975 and had been posted to Kuala Lumpur the following year where he married Leong Chui Fun. In 1979 he was sent to Bangkok, returning to London in 1982, and in March the following year he went to Peking, and also served in Hong Kong. The issue of the succession was to become intensely political, with Downing Street letting it be known that John Scarlett, having emerged from the Hutton Inquiry free of criticism, was the Prime Minister's choice. That such a public contest should have occurred is itself quite remarkable, and an indication of the extent to which the post of C had become politicised. Even more remarkable was the fact that in February 2004, when the matter came to be decided, Scarlett was the older candidate, approaching his fifty-sixth birthday. Inkster, on the other hand, would not reach his fifty-second birthday until that April.

Chapter XIV

John Scarlett
2004–

THE speculation surrounding the succession to Dear
unprecedented, as was the succession of political leaks s
that John Scarlett was Downing Street's preferred can
Chief. When the announcement was made, in May 2004,
independent committee had selected Scarlett over Nigel Inkster, t
and media reaction was universally negative. Critics objected tha
had been so tainted by his participation in the discredited Iraqi do
his judgment was obviously flawed, and that the appointment w
inspire confidence with his foreign liaison counterparts.
remarkable was the speed with which the appointment became a
issue, with the Leader of the Opposition, Michael Howard, vowi
Scarlett if he became prime minister. These events we
extraordinary, with so many opponents making their views known
that sparked a debate that had never occurred before in the entir
of the post. So why was Scarlett's promotion so controversial?

No previous appointment of any Chief had ever been the subj
much public comment. Nor had any previous candidate been such
figure, nor one who had been expelled from an operational post
shrugged off the Mitrokhin fiasco, Scarlett had shouldered the b
the September dossier, and his loyalty to Downing Street h
rewarded.

However, no sooner had Scarlett moved back into Vauxhall C
the first week of August 2004, than it emerged that he had inter
recently as March 2004 to perpetuate the myth that Saddam Hus

The fact that Scarlett had sent the ISG an email on 8 March 2004, urging the inclusion of the 'golden nuggets', was only revealed after his appointment as Dearlove's successor had been announced, so it made minimal impact on him and none on his career prospects, but because the Butler report had by then been published it was possible to demonstrate conclusively the absolute falsity of three of the topics Scarlett had wanted the ISG to endorse. Butler found nothing to support the idea of a smallpox plot, and no physical evidence to show any continued research into the development of a nuclear weapon. As for the mobile biological laboratories, Butler was very specific, and dismissed the intelligence as flawed. Naturally, when Scarlett had made his bid to influence the ISG, he could not have anticipated that either Lord Butler, or anyone else, would conduct a detailed investigation into the evidence, or lack of it, supporting the ISG report on Iraqi WMD.

Not coincidentally, the resignations began from a senior level within SIS, starting with Mark Allen, a Downside-educated Arabist who had served in Abu Dhabi and Cairo. The unexpected departure of the Controller Africa and Middle East, to join British Petroleum, was widely interpreted to be a manifestation of the dismay in Vauxhall Cross at Scarlett's appointment, and his involvement with the government's misrepresentation of the threat from Iraqi WMD. Allen had joined SIS after graduating from Oxford and had perfected his Arabic at Shemlan before his first posting, to the Emirates in succession to Norman Cameron. Slightly older than Inkster, Allen too had been a candidate for Chief but, unlike his rival, chose not to serve with Scarlett. His resignation came immediately after capping a successful career with lengthy negotiations with Libya which resulted in an astonishing admission of responsibility for the Lockerbie bombing, a repudiation of support for the Provisional IRA, and Colonel Ghadaffi's decision to grant access to international inspectors to his secret nuclear development programme. The covert diplomacy conducted in Switzerland by Allen, doubtless aided by the American intervention in Iraq, represented an astonishing reversal in policy from a country labelled as a rogue state and a sponsor of terrorism, and was considered by the CIA, among others, as a very impressive triumph, bringing Tripoli back into the international community and providing a fascinating windfall of intelligence about the Provisional IRA. Soon after Allen's departure with a knighthood, Ian McCredie, who had engineered Vladimir Kuzichkin's defection from Tehran, also opted for the private sector, as did the Kabul veteran, Nigel Backhouse, who joined Hakluyt.

Scarlett's survival of this extraordinary episode was in marked contrast to the treatment of John Morrison, the former Deputy Chief of the Defence Intelligence Staff who remarked on BBC TV's *Panorama* in July 2004 that he 'could almost hear the collective raspberry going up around Whitehall' when Tony Blair had announced in the House of Commons in September 2002 that Saddam Hussein had posed 'a current and serious threat to the UK national interest' and 'has made progress on WMD'. At the time of his interview Morrison had served nearly five years as the ISC's lone investigator, and although the ISC's Chairman, Mrs Ann Taylor, had given her consent to his appearance in the programme, and he had deliberately avoided having identified his current role, he was dismissed instantly.[2] Thus Morrison, who had criticised the government's patently false assertion that Iraqi WMD posed a threat to Britain, had been sacked, John Scarlett, who had consistently attempted to fabricate the evidence, had received a promotion, and, having taken over from Dearlove, proceeded to restructure SIS's top level.

The Butler committee's report was a unique example of a detailed, independent analysis of all the intelligence available on a very specific topic in a particular time frame, and was assisted by evidence given by no fewer than six former JIC chairmen. Sir Percy Cradock, Sir Roderic Braithwaite, Sir Paul Lever and Pauline Neville-Jones had already expressed their opinions publicly, but Sir Michael Pakenham and Sir Colin Budd gave their views in private. Had they been equally sceptical of Scarlett's behaviour? Had they known of his attempt to skew the ISG report? Whatever the nature of their evidence, it had not prompted Lord Butler's committee to reprimand Scarlett. Indeed, on the contrary, and apparently at Mrs Taylor's insistence, it was recommended that John Scarlett should not withdraw from his appointment at Chief, noting a 'high regard for his abilities and his record'.[3] This statement, of course, begs the question of precisely what Lord Butler's committee thought was Scarlett's record. Did they know about the Mitrokhin deception? Were they aware of Sintsov's

Scarlett had been aware at the time they had given their evidence that the principal WMD intelligence had been 'withdrawn', neither had mentioned this to Lord Hutton.

Thus, upon close examination, SIS had relied upon a total of five human sources. One, as we have noted, simply had conveyed gossip that 'he had heard within his circle'. The reporting from a sub-source of one 'dominant' was considered 'open to doubt'. The third main source was 'unreliable' and his intelligence was withdrawn. An additional principal source, reporting through the BND, and codenamed RED RIVER by SIS (and CURVE BALL by the CIA) was 'seriously flawed', leaving just two other agents whose reports on chemical and biological weapon capabilities were 'less worrying'. Thus, in short, SIS and the JIC had given emphasis to sources who turned out to be inaccurate in preference to agents, still considered reliable, who had given a less bleak picture. How could this have happened?

In his evidence to the Butler Committee, Dearlove acknowledged that, as a cost-saving exercise, SIS had scrapped the conventional division between the requirements and production sections, and had combined the two disciplines into teams of case and desk officers who had been urged to achieve results. In consequence, inexperienced requirements officers had been ill-equipped to undertake the verification process that the orthodox system had previously built in. Upon becoming members of the production team, the requirements personnel found themselves incentivised to accept information that almost certainly would have been screened out by the traditional method of validation.

Incredibly, the BND's sub-source, when interviewed after the conflict, flatly denied the reports previously attributed to him. Astonishingly, this individual had been responsible for the two key reports which had been used by the JIC to bolster its position in the September dossier. This extraordinary state of affairs went almost unremarked by the Butler Report, yet Richard Dearlove's previous testimony to Lord Hutton had emphasised his confidence in his valued source in Iraq who had supplied the notorious and now-discredited forty-five minute claim. Few commentators seemed to notice the chronology, which suggested that when Dearlove had given his evidence to Hutton, he had known that his source had been deemed unreliable, and that his intelligence reports had been 'withdrawn'.

Whatever SIS's original sources, their reliability, and the true nature of the Iraqi threat, Dearlove's tenure as Chief would be over before Lord Butler's report had been published. He had taken on the post to be instantly engulfed by the political storm caused largely by John Scarlett's handling of the Mitrokhin episode, and he was to leave in not dissimilar circumstances, with Scarlett having enveloped the entire intelligence community in a wholly avoidable maelstrom. Whereas the Mitrokhin fiasco had not threatened to undermine anything more than a few reputations, Scarlett's involvement in the notorious September dossier had played a significant part in taking the country into a major war.

When Dearlove announced, in August 2003, before the end of the Hutton Inquiry's proceedings, that he had been offered the mastership of Pembroke College, Cambridge, there was immediate speculation that his Oxford-educated deputy, Nigel Inkster, would be his successor. A contemporary at Oxford of the Prime Minister, Inkster had joined SIS in 1975 and had been posted to Kuala Lumpur the following year where he married Leong Chui Fun. In 1979 he was sent to Bangkok, returning to London in 1982, and in March the following year he went to Peking, and also served in Hong Kong. The issue of the succession was to become intensely political, with Downing Street letting it be known that John Scarlett, having emerged from the Hutton Inquiry free of criticism, was the Prime Minister's choice. That such a public contest should have occurred is itself quite remarkable, and an indication of the extent to which the post of C had become politicised. Even more remarkable was the fact that in February 2004, when the matter came to be decided, Scarlett was the older candidate, approaching his fifty-sixth birthday. Inkster, on the other hand, would not reach his fifty-second birthday until that April.

Chapter XIV

John Scarlett
2004–

THE speculation surrounding the succession to Dearlove was unprecedented, as was the succession of political leaks suggesting that John Scarlett was Downing Street's preferred candidate for Chief. When the announcement was made, in May 2004, that an independent committee had selected Scarlett over Nigel Inkster, the public and media reaction was universally negative. Critics objected that Scarlett had been so tainted by his participation in the discredited Iraqi dossiers that his judgment was obviously flawed, and that the appointment would not inspire confidence with his foreign liaison counterparts. Equally remarkable was the speed with which the appointment became a political issue, with the Leader of the Opposition, Michael Howard, vowing to fire Scarlett if he became prime minister. These events were quite extraordinary, with so many opponents making their views known in a way that sparked a debate that had never occurred before in the entire history of the post. So why was Scarlett's promotion so controversial?

No previous appointment of any Chief had ever been the subject of so much public comment. Nor had any previous candidate been such a public figure, nor one who had been expelled from an operational post. Having shrugged off the Mitrokhin fiasco, Scarlett had shouldered the blame for the September dossier, and his loyalty to Downing Street had been rewarded.

However, no sooner had Scarlett moved back into Vauxhall Cross, in the first week of August 2004, than it emerged that he had intervened as recently as March 2004 to perpetuate the myth that Saddam Hussein had possessed WMD before the invasion of Iraq. Once Baghdad had been occupied the coalition forces had established an international Iraq Survey Group (ISG), drawn mainly from the intelligence community and from the teams of UN weapons inspectors, to search for the elusive Iraqi WMD. Initially led by Dr David Kay, a pugnacious Texan and former CIA officer, the ISG consisted of over a thousand specialists who fanned out across the country to conduct a detailed trawl for evidence of either the weapons themselves, or Saddam's research programmes. However, by January 2004 no WMD had been found, and Kay resigned with a damning personal statement that he did not expect any ever would be found because none had ever existed. His replacement was Charles Duelfer, and when he came to draft the ISG's interim report in March 2004 he and his staff found themselves under pressure, initially in January from the Deputy Chief of Defence Intelligence, Martin Howard, and then from John Scarlett, to slim down the report from 200 to twenty anodyne pages, and to insert some 'golden nuggets' that could not be supported by the evidence found by the ISG. Allegedly Howard had said that with the departure of David Kay there was no need for *any* report to be published, but when the ISG rejected this strategy the British position changed, with Scarlett's personal intervention.

Quite why John Scarlett, as the JIC Chairman, should have been pressing for the inclusion of these ten nuggets has never been explained, but among the items he wanted mentioned was confirmation that Saddam had developed a smallpox programme, a claim first made in the September dossier, had built a 'rail-gun' as part of Iraq's research into nuclear weapons, and had possessed mobile chemical weapons laboratories. In fact, all three assertions were without foundation.[1] The ISG had not found anything to support the charge that smallpox had been developed as a weapon, believed that there was a relatively innocent explanation for the 'rail-gun', and after careful examination of a pair of captured chemical laboratory trailers, had found they had been used to fill artillery observation balloons with nothing more harmful than hydrogen. Naturally the ISG resisted the pressure to distort the report which was finally released at the end of March 2004, prompting the immediate resignation of Duelfer's Australian special adviser, Rod Barton.

imprisonment? Did they look into the problems that had arisen in Nairobi and Paris while Scarlett had been stationed in those capitals? Did they look into the rumours of a debacle in South Africa where a source had been accidentally compromised by a blunder while Scarlett was at Vauxhall Cross? Had his insistence on a 'security-style interrogation' of Dr David Kelly been a factor in the scientist's decision to take his own life? By any measure, Scarlett's return to SIS was yet a further bizarre twist in the history of an office which, in a few short months, as a consequence of poor, lacklustre leadership and political interference, had lost the prestige and mystique built up over nearly a century.

The extent to which Dearlove was about to pass Scarlett a poisoned chalice became evident when, on 7 March 2004, an SAS Regiment retiree, Simon Mann, was arrested at Harare International Airport and charged with immigration offences and an attempt to procure weapons from Zimbabwe Defence Industries. Accompanying him were sixty-three mercenaries and the crew of a Boeing 727 which was to take them to the tiny West African state of Equatorial Guinea. Oil-rich and run by a despotic dictator, Teodoro Obiang, the former Spanish colony had been the target of several coup attempts, each of which had been ruthlessly suppressed. Evidently Mann, a member of a prominent English brewing family, had intended to seize the country, the airport at Malobo having been taken over by an advance party of thirteen men led by one of his associates, a former South African Special Forces officer, Nick du Toit. The plan collapsed when the aircraft was impounded in Harare and Mann's team was imprisoned at the notorious Chikurubi prison, charged with breaches of local immigration and aviation regulations. Their cover story, of providing security to the mining industry in the Democratic Republic of the Congo quickly unravelled when du Toit was interrogated at Malobo's notorious Black Beach prison and was forced to reveal the ambitious scale of the scheme.

Equatorial Guinea had been granted independence in 1968 and had been ruled by Obiang since 1979 when he had deposed his uncle in a bloody coup, but in 1999 the poverty-stricken nation of half a million inhabitants had been found to possess huge offshore mineral deposits, and Obiang had agreed lucrative licenses with three Texas-based oil companies, which had netted his family a vast income. However, his regime was constantly criticised for human rights abuses and a lack of democratic accountability. Despite having become sub-Saharan Africa's third largest oil producer, Equatorial Guinea was really nothing more than a banana republic run as Obiang's personal fiefdom, with much of his wealth deposited with the Riggs Bank in Washington DC.

At the end of August 2004 Simon Mann pleaded guilty to two charges while two of his companions were acquitted and deported, only to face new charges in South Africa where the Regulation of Foreign Military Assistance Act had been passed to prevent mercenaries from operating without the government's approval. Mann was sentenced to seven years' imprisonment while the rest of his team received eighteen months. Evidently Mann's recruitment activities in Cape Town in November 2003 had attracted the attention of the National Intelligence Agency which had monitored the coup plot and tipped off SIS and Robert Mugabe's Central Intelligence Agency. The problem for SIS was that Mann, an Old Etonian who was a former fellow director of Executive Outcomes with Tim Spicer and Rupert Bowen and had made several fortunes, had largely financed his venture through his company, Logo Logistics, with support from a group of wealthy investors, among them Mark Thatcher and Jeffrey Archer. The details of precisely who had backed Mann only emerged when the Scorpions, the elite South African anti-corruption police unit, raided Thatcher's home in Cape Town, and charged him with having paid for the helicopter which had been intended to fly in Obiang's political opponent, Severe Moto, to take charge of the new administration in Equatorial Guinea. Mann had dual British and South African nationality, and had raised money in London for his project, leaving his backers exposed as more details of the failed coup attempt leaked from the police investigation. Particularly embarrassing for the Foreign Secretary, Jack Straw, was Thatcher's arrest on the very day he arrived in South Africa on an official visit. Of course, for the ailing former prime minister's son to be arrested in such circumstances would have been politically awkward at any time, but for SIS to have played any role in scuppering the removal of a tyrant, and jeopardising several prominent London businessmen, was to prove more than unfortunate.

The fall-out from Mann's arrest served to highlight the sensitivities of the relationship between the private military companies, which burgeoned in response to the demand for security in post-occupation Baghdad, and SIS. Tim Spicer had long maintained good relations with SIS, and had been on friendly terms with Dearlove, whose nephew Justin Longley worked for Logo Logistics as a 'senior project manager'. The fact that the son of Dearlove's sister had worked with Mann for years suggested to some that the Chief, if not his subordinates, had been well-informed about what was intended for Equatorial Guinea. Expressing relief from having withdrawn to Cambridge from his hot seat in Vauxhall Cross, Dearlove had apparently escaped relatively unscathed from the two major crises to have dogged his last couple of years in office. But would Scarlett be able to achieve the same balancing act, acquiring useful information from the private sector without appearing to be in league with mercenaries who inevitably would, from time to time, prove a source of embarrassment for the government? In the case of the Obiang plot, SIS had exercised a passive neutrality, being unwilling to alert the participants to the fate awaiting Mann in Harare, and thus embroiling the Blair administration in a wholly avoidable *imbroglio*.

Postscript

THE transformation of SIS from a secret, one-man operation in 1909 to an expensive, internationally-acknowledged bureaucracy almost a century later has been matched only by MI5's metamorphosis into a publicly accountable, statutory body. Both organisations have been directed by fourteen heads, and have developed in similar, overlapping areas of interest, encompassing organised crime, weapon proliferation and international terrorism. It is there that the similarities end, for SIS remains the senior service, with its budget expanding from £112,000 in 1923 to a substantial proportion of the Single Unified Vote, also covering MI5 and GCHQ, which in 2003 amounted to £1,000 million.

One significant change to SIS in recent years is the organisation's acceptance of a public image. Probably more books, fiction and non-fiction, have been published about the work of SIS than any other intelligence agency on the planet, but whereas the prewar books tended to be quite flattering, and the appearance of James Bond in 1953 made the genre more popular than ever, the publication of *The Spy Who Came in from the Cold* offered an alternative view of the intelligence business. Whereas Ian Fleming had never worked for SIS, Cornwell had served in both MI5 and SIS, and had operated abroad under diplomatic cover in Bonn and Hamburg, experiences that made his jaundiced perspective more plausible.

Certainly the most authentic portrayal of SIS was to be found in *The Sandbaggers*, a low-budget television series made by Yorkshire Television in 1978 starring Roy Marsden, using scripts written by Donald Lancaster, the author of *The Emancipation of French Indo-China*, a region he knew well, having served in SIS for many years in the Far East. The series came to an end when the main scriptwriter, Ian MacKintosh, died in a plane accident in July 1979 in Alaska, leaving the producer, Michael Ferguson, without an alternative source. MacKintosh had gone to Dartmouth Royal Naval College in 1958, and had retired from the Royal Navy in 1976 after a posting to the Defence Intelligence Staff. Whereas Bond had created the myth of a glamorous espionage environment, and Cornwell had undermined it with a more sinister image, the reality lay somewhere in between, captured by the relative verisimilitude of *The Sandbaggers*.

That SIS has become an integral part of the Whitehall bureaucracy, instead of a semi-independent organisation, became clear when in 2003 Alastair Crooke was despatched to Gaza to assist in the negotiations between the newly-established Palestinian Authority and the European Union. Born in Ireland and brought up on a tobacco farm in Rhodesia, Crooke had joined SIS in 1974 and had been posted to Dublin. His brother Ian had commanded an SAS sabre squadron during the Falklands War, while Alastair was to serve in Islamabad, where he developed contacts with the Mujahidin, and finally Bogotá before acting as an intermediary in Gaza with the Palestinians.

In September 2003 Alastair Crooke was withdrawn, his position having become too dangerous when Palestinian extremists began to target foreign diplomatic personnel. Of course, the contrast between SIS's public image and its true existence has been known and recognised by *cognoscenti* for years, but probably not by outsiders until the publication of the reports prepared by Lords Justice Scott and Hutton, and Lord Butler's Committee, all with the benefit of those two great advantages, not always available to any intelligence agency, access and hindsight. Another milestone was achieved in January 2006 when the Queen made a visit to Vauxhall Cross, where she was received by C. Whereas on her previous visit no public announcement had been made, her second tour of the building was included in the Court Circular, a very public acknowledgement of Her Majesty's Secret Service.

Appendix

Secret Intelligence Service Stations

SIS Stations 1923

BALTIC GROUP	Estonia	Meiklejohn
	Finland	Boyce
	Lithuania & Latvia	Meiklejohn
SCANDINAVIAN GROUP	Denmark	Hudson
	Sweden	Hitching
	Norway	Lawrence
	Poland	Marshall
NEW YORK		Jeffes
GERMAN GROUP	Germany	Breen
	Holland	Wood
	Belgium	Westmacott
SWISS GROUP	Switzerland	Langley
	France	Langton
	Italy	McKenzie
	Spain	Hollocombe
	Portugal	Chancellor
CENTRAL EUROPEAN GROUP	Austria	Forbes Dennis
	Czechoslovakia	Norman
	Hungary	Kensington
	Bulgaria	Elder
	Romania	Boxshall
NEAR EASTERN GROUP	Turkey	Dunderdale
	Egypt & Palestine	
	South Russia	
	Greece	Welch

Far Eastern Group	Vladivostock	Kirby
	Hong Kong	
	Singapore	
	Canton	
	Shanghai	
	Harbin	
	Tokyo	Gunn
	Vancouver	

SIS Stations 1936

Athens	Crawford	Paris	Dunderdale
Berlin	Foley	Prague	Gibson
Brussels	Calthrop	Riga	Nicholson
Budapest	Hindle	Rome	Dansey
Copenhagen	O'Leary	Sofia	Smith-Ross
The Hague	Dalton	Stockholm	Martin
Helsinki	Carr	Tallinn	Giffey
Istanbul	Lefontaine	Vienna	Kendrick
New York	Taylor	Warsaw	Handscombe
Oslo	Newell		

SIS Stations 1943

Algiers	Trevor Wilson	Mexico City	Bell
Baghdad	Giffey	Moscow	Barclay
Berne	Vanden Heuvel	New Delhi	Pile
Buenos Aires	Millar	New York	Stephenson
Cairo	Bowlby	Pretoria	Lenton
Freetown	Greene	Reykjavik	Blyth
Gibraltar	Codrington	Rio de Janeiro	Oliver
Istanbul	Gibson	Stockholm	Martin
Lisbon	Johns	Tangiers	Ellis
Lourenço Marques	Muggeridge	Tehran	Spencer
Madrid	Hamilton-Stokes		

SIS Stations 1956

Amman	Howard
Athens	Phillpotts
Baghdad	McGlashan
Bangkok	Curwen
Basra	Whittal
Beirut	Prater
Belgrade	McKibbin
Berlin	Longrigg
Berne	Milne
Bonn	Mitchell
Brussels	Bratt
Budapest	Silverwood-
Cope	
Buenos Aires	Stockwell
Cairo	Critchett
Caracas	Woodfield
Copenhagen	Carr
Cairo	Gove
Damascus	Pidgeon
Djakarta	Ritchie
Düsseldorf	Walker
Geneva	Darbyshire
Haiphong	Rendall
Hamburg	da Silva
Helsinki	Wood
Hong Kong	Mackenzie
Istanbul	Martin-Smith
Jeddah	Carr
Kuala Lumpur	Ault
Lourenço Marques	Whittal
Madrid	Benton
Maymyo (Burma)	Onslow
Montevideo	Astlee
Moscow	Park
New Delhi	
Nicosia	Collins
Oslo	Sneddon
Paris	Dennys
Prague	Taylor
Rangoon	Badderley
Rio de Janeiro	Edge
Rome	Gibson
Saigon	Dempster
Seoul	Gardner
Singapore	Fulton
Stockholm	Boughey
Surabaya	Aiken-Sneath
Tel Aviv	Elliott
Tehran	de Haan
The Hague	Whinney
Tokyo	Hart
Tripoli	McNaught
Vienna	Barr
Vientiane	Pedlar
Warsaw	Gurrey
Washington DC	Mitchell
Zurich	Lecky

SIS Stations 1982

Accra	Stafford
Amman	Black
Ankara	Kelly
Athens	Orwin
Baghdad	
Bangkok	Inkster
Barbados	Williams
Beijing	
Belgrade	Terry
Berlin	Fulton
Bonn	Stuart
Brasilia	Ramscar
Brunei	
Brussels	
Bucharest	
Budapest	
Buenos Aires	Heathcote
Cairo	Cowper-Coles
Canberra	Collecot
Copenhagen	
Dacca	McMillan
Delhi	Partridge
Djakarta	
Geneva	Wiseman
Havana	Pagett
Helsinki	Ramsay
Hong Kong	Perry
Islamabad	
Jeddah	Shipman
Kabul	Newell
Khartoum	Collecot
Kuala Lumpur	
Lagos	Prosser
Lisbon	
Lusaka	Pagett
Madrid	
Maputo	Evetts
Moscow	Brooks
Nairobi	
New York	Mathewson
Nicosia	Venning
Oslo	
Paris	Forter
Prague	
Pretoria	Fall
Rio de Janeiro	Gibbs
Rome	
Sanaa	
Stockholm	
Tehran	McCredie
Tel Aviv	Cowell
The Hague	
Tokyo	Hamilton
Vienna	Gosling
Warsaw	
Washington DC	de Vere

Notes

Introduction

1. David Owen, *Time To Declare* (Michael Joseph, 2001), p. 171
2. Valentine Williams, *The World of Action* (Hamish Hamilton, 1938), p. 103
3. Colin McColl, Washington DC, 6 December 2002
4. Compton Mackenzie, *My Life and Times* (Chatto & Windus, 1968), p. 97
5. Compton Mackenzie, *Greek Memories* (Cassell, 1932), p. 396
6. *Ibid.*
7. Samuel Hoare, *The Fourth Seal*, (Heinemann, 1930), p. 28. Macdonough and Hall were the WWI Directors of Military and Naval Intelligence.
8. Paul Dukes, *The Story of ST-25*, (Cassell, 1938), frontispiece.

Chapter I: Mansfield Smith-Cumming

1. Alan Judd, *The Quest for C* (HarperCollins, 1999), p. 151
2. National Archive, ADM 196/39
3. Alan Judd, p. 180
4. *Ibid.* p. 192
5. *Ibid.*
6. *Ibid.*
7. *Ibid.*
8. Compton Mackenzie, *Greek Memories*, p. 324
9. Sam Hoare, *The Fourth Seal*, p. 33
10. George Hill, *Go Spy the Land* (Cassell, 1932), p. 262
11. Alan Judd, p. 354.
12. Ibid. 319
13. Ibid. 467
14. Valentine Williams, *op. cit.*, p. 338

Chapter II: Hugh Sinclair

1. George Hill, *Dreaded Hour* (Cassell, 1936), p. 11
2. National Archives. ADM 196/39
3. Gill Bennett, History Notes, *A Most Extraordinary and Mysterious Business: The Zinoviev Letter of 1924* (FCO, No. 14, February 1999)

4. Lewis Chester, Stephen Fay and Hugo Young, *The Zinoviev Letter* (Heinemann, 1967)
5. Bennett, p. 89
6. *Ibid.* p. 70
7. *Ibid.* p. 74
8. *Ibid.*
9. Henry Landau, *Secrets of the White Lady* (Putnam, 1935), p. ix
10. *Ibid.*
11. Frederick Winterbotham, *The Ultra Spy* (Macmillan, 1989), p. 153
12. Nicholas Elliott, *Never Judge A Man By His Umbrella* (Michael Russell, 1991), p. 100
13. Frederick Winterbotham, *op. cit.*, p. 115

CHAPTER III: STEWART MENZIES

1. Cavendish-Bentinck quoted by Patrick Howarth, *Intelligence Chief Extraordinary* (Bodley Head, 1986), p. 115
2. David Dilks (ed.), *The Diaries of Sir Alexander Cadogan* (Cassell, 1971), p. 234
3. R. V. Jones, *Most Secret War* (Hamish Hamilton, 1978), p. 67
4. Patrick Howarth, p. 115
5. *Origins and Establishment of the Foreign Office Information Research Department 1946–48* (History Notes, FCO, No. 9, August 1995), p. 10

CHAPTER IV: JOHN SINCLAIR

1. Kim Philby, *My Silent War* (McGibbon & Kee, 1968), p. 84
2. Lord Alanbrooke, *War Diaries 1939–1945*. London: Weidenfeld, 2001. p. 311
3. George Blake, *No Other Choice* (Jonathan Cape, 1990), p. 157
4. Kim Philby, p. 85
5. Wilbur Cleveland, *Ropes of Sand* (W. W. Norton, 1980), p. 170

CHAPTER V: DICK WHITE

1. Philby, p. 51
2. Peter Wright in *SpyCatcher* (Heinemann, 1985), p. 115
3. Chester Cooper, *The Lion's Last Roar, Suez 1956* (Harper & Row, 1978). p. 238
4. George Young, *Subversion and the British Riposte* (Ossian Publishers, 1984), p. 114
5. Geoffrey McDermott, *The Eden Legacy* (Leslie Frewin, 1969), p. 133
6. *Ibid.*
7. Rebecca West, *The New Meaning of Treason* (Viking, 1964), p. 303
8. E.H. Cookridge, *Shadow of a Spy* (Leslie Frewin, 1967), p. 55
9. George Blake, p. 94
10. *Ibid.*
11. *Ibid.*
12. George Blake, p. 173
13. Kim Philby, p. 97

14. George Blake, p. 173
15. H. Montgomery Hyde, *George Blake Superspy* (Constable, 1987), p. 63
16. Blake, p. 160
17. Hyde, *op. cit.*, p. 63
18. George Blake, p. 265
19. Desmond Bristow, *A Game of Moles* (Little Brown, 1993), p. 185
20. R.V. Jones, *Most Secret War*, p. 520
21. Brian Crozier, *Free Agent* (HarperCollins, 1993), p. 58

CHAPTER VI: JOHN RENNIE

1. Robert Cecil, 'The Assesment and Acceptance of Intelligence: A Case Study; British and American Approaches to Intelligence', *RUSI Journal*, 1987, p. 167
2. Peter Wright, *op. cit.*, p. 330
3. William Whitelaw, *The Whitelaw Memoirs* (Aurum Press, 1989), p. 100
4. *Documents on British Overseas Policy*, Series III, Vol. I (HMSO, 1991), p. 339
5. *Ibid.*
6. Anthony Verrier, *Through The Looking-Glass* (Jonathan Cape, 1983), p. 265

CHAPTER VII: MAURICE OLDFIELD

1. Richard Deacon, *'C': The Biography of Sir Maurice Oldfield* (Macdonald, 1985), p. 71
2. Kim Philby, p. 98
3. Nigel Clive
4. Wilson quoted in Barrie Penrose and Roger Courtiour, *The Pencourt File* (Harper & Row, 1978), p. 10
5. David Owen, p. 131
6. *Ibid.*
7. *Ibid.*
8. Nigel Clive, 21 February 1992
9. David Owen, p. 133

CHAPTER VIII: DICKIE FRANKS

1. Chapman Pincher, *The SpyCatcher Affair* (St Martin's Press, 1987), p. 48
2. *Daily Express*, 27 March 1985
3. Greville Wynne, *The Man from Moscow* (Hutchinson, 1967), p. 83
4. *Ibid.*
5. *Ibid.*
6. *Ibid.*
7. *Ibid.*
8. Viktor Kutuzov, *Penkovsky, Fact and Fancy* (Novosti, 1966)
9. *Daily Express*, 15 July 1985
10. Chapman Pincher, *op. cit.*, p. 117

CHAPTER IX: COLIN FIGURES

1. David Owen, p. 209
2. *Ibid.*
3. Franks Committee Report *Falkland Islands Review*, p. 22
4. Margaret Thatcher, *The Downing Street Years* (HarperCollins, 1993), p. 176
5. John Nott, *Here Today, Gone Tomorrow* (Politico's, 2002), p. 257
6. Percy Cradock, *In Pursuit of British Interests.* (John Murray, 1997), p. 44
7. *Ibid.*
8. *Ibid.*
9. Vladimir Kuzichkin, *Inside the KGB* (André Deutsch, 1990).

CHAPTER X: CHRISTOPHER CURWEN

1. Geoffrey Howe, *Conflict of Loyalty* (Macmillan, 1994), p. 349
2. Oleg Gordievsky, *Last Stop Execution* (Macmillan, 1995) p. 287

CHAPTER XI: COLIN MCCOLL

1. Colin McColl, Washington DC, 4 December 2002
2. Margaret Thatcher, p. 778
3. Mikhail Butkov, *KGB I Norge* (Tiden Norsk Forlag, 1992)
4. Percy Cradock, *op. cit.*, p. 172
5. Sir Richard Scott, *Scott Inquiry Report* (HMSO, 1996), p. 1020
6. *Ibid.*, p. 1020
7. *Hansard*, Vol. 238, No. 53, 22 February 1994, Col. 178

CHAPTER XII: DAVID SPEDDING

1. David Owen, p. 201
2. Richard Tomlinson, *The Big Breach* (Mainstream, 2001), p. 285
3. Tim Spicer, *An Unorthodox Soldier: The Sandline Affair* (Mainstream, 2000)

CHAPTER XIII: RICHARD DEARLOVE

1. Evidence to Lord Hutton, 23 August 2003
2. Parliamentary Intelligence and Security Committee Report, *The Mitrokhin Inquiry* CM 4764, June 2000.
3. Robin Cook, *The Point of Departure* (Pocket Books, 2004)
4. *Ibid.*
5. Sir Peter Heap, 'The Truth behind the MI6 Façade', *Guardian,* 2 October 2003
6. *Ibid.*
7. Sir Roderic Braithwaite, *The Times*, 5 December 2003

CHAPTER XIV: JOHN SCARLETT

1. Tom Mangold, *Mail on Sunday*, 1 August 2004
2. *Daily Mail*, 26 July 2004
3. Lord Butler, *Review of Intelligence on Weapons of Mass Destruction*, HC 898, 14 July 2004, para. 469, p. 115

Bibliography

Adams, James, *The New Spies*. London: Hutchinson, 1994.
Agar, Augustus, *Baltic Episode*. London: Hodder and Stoughton, 1963.
——— *Footprints in the Sea*. London: Evans Brothers, 1959.
——— *Showing the Flag*. London: Evans Brothers, 1962.
Alanbrooke, Field Marshal Lord, *War Diaries 1939–1945*. London: Weidenfeld, 2001.
Aldrich, Richard, 'GCHQ and Sigint in the Early Cold War 1945–70'. *Intelligence and National Security*. Vol. 16, No. 1.
——— *The Hidden Hand*. London: John Murray, 2001.
Allen, W. E. D., *David Allens: The History of a Family Firm 1857–1957*. London: John Murray, 1957.
Andrew, Christopher, *Secret Service*. London: Heinemann, 1985.
Aston, Sir George, *Secret Service*. London: Faber & Faber, 1930.
Barker, Ralph, *Aviator Extraordinary*. London: Chatto & Windus, 1969
Barron, John, *KGB: The Secret Work of Soviet Secret Agents*. London: Hodder & Stoughton, 1974
Beesley, Patrick, *Very Special Admiral*. London: Hamish Hamilton, 1980.
——— *Very Special Intelligence*. London: Hamish Hamilton, 1977.
Bennett, Gill (ed.), *Documents on British Policy Overseas*, Series III, Vol. 1. London: HMSO, 1997.
Bennett, Ralph, *Ultra and Mediterranean Strategy*. London: Hamish Hamilton, 1989.
——— *Ultra in the West*. London: Hutchinson, 1979.
Best, Sigismund Payne, *The Venlo Incident*. London: Hutchinson, 1950.
Blake, George, *No Other Choice*. London: Jonathan Cape, 1990.
Bloch, Jonathan, and Patrick Fitzgerald, *British Intelligence and Covert Action*. London: Junction Books, 1983.
Bourke, Sean, *The Springing of George Blake*. London: Cassell, 1970
Bower, Tom, *The Perfect English Spy*. London: Heinemann, 1995.
——— *Red Web*. London: Aurum Press, 1989.
Boyd, Carl, *Hitler's Japanese Confidant*. Lawrence: University Press of Kansas, 1993
Boyle, Andrew, *Climate of Treason*. London: Hutchinson, 1979
Bristow, Desmond, *A Game of Moles*. London: Little, Brown, 1993.
Brook-Shepherd, Gordon, *Iron Maze: The Western Secret Services and the Bolsheviks*. London: Macmillan, 1998

Brown, John, *In Durance Vile*. London: Robert Hale, 1981.
Bryant, Arthur, *The Turn of the Tide*. London: Gollancz, 1959.
Buckton, Henry, *Politicians At War*. London: Leo Cooper, 2003.
Butkov, Mikhail, *KGB I Norge*, Oslo: Tiden Norsk Forlag, 1992
Butler, Lord, *Review of Intelligence on Weapons of Mass Destruction*. London: The Stationery Office, HC 898, 14 July 2004
Bywater, Hector, *Strange Intelligence*. London: Constable, 1931.
Calvocoressi, Peter, *Top Secret Ultra*. London: Cassell, 1980.
Carré, John Le, *A Murder of Quality*. London: Victor Gollancz, 1962.
——— *A Perfect Spy*. London: Hodder & Stoughton, 1986.
Cave Brown, Anthony, *'C': The Biography of Sir Stewart Menzies*. London: Macmillan, 1987.
Cavendish, Anthony, *Inside Intelligence*. London: Collins, 1990.
Cecil, Robert, 'C's War'. *Intelligence and National Security*. Vol. 1, No. 2.
——— *A Divided Life*. London: Bodley Head, 1988.
——— *Five of Six at War*. Vol. 9, No. 2.
Chester, Lewis, Stephen Fay and Hugo Young, *The Zinoviev Letter*. London: Heinemann, 1967.
Childers, Erskine, *Riddle of the Sands*. London: Blackie, 1961.
Chisholm, Roderick, *Ladysmith*. London: Osprey, 1979.
Clive, Nigel, 'From War to Peace in SIS'. *Intelligence and National Security*. Vol. 10, No. 3.
——— *A Greek Experience 1943–48*. Winchester: Michael Russell, 1985.
Colvin, John, *Twice Around The World*. London: Leo Cooper, 1991.
Cook, Andrew, *On His Majesty's Secret Service: Sidney Reilly Codename ST1*. Stroud, Gloucestershire: Tempus Publishing, 2002.
Cook, Robin, *The Point of Departure* (Pocket Books, 2004)
Cookridge, E. H., *Secrets of the British Secret Service*. London: Sampson, Low, 1947.
——— *Shadow of a Spy*. London: Leslie Frewin, 1967.
——— *The Third Man*. London: Arthur Barker, 1968.
Cooper, Chester, *The Lion's Last Roar, Suez 1956*. New York: Harper & Row, 1978.
Costello, John, *Mask of Treachery*, New York: William Morrow, 1988.
Cradock, Percy, *In Pursuit of British Interests*. London: John Murray, 1997.
——— *Know Your Enemy*. London: John Murray, 2001.
Cross, John, *Red Jungle*. London: Robert Hale, 1957.
Crozier, Brian, *Free Agent*. London: HarperCollins, 1993.
Darling, Donald, *Secret Sunday*. London: William Kimber, 1975.
——— *Sunday at Large*. London: William Kimber, 1977.
Davies, Philip, *MI6 and the Machinery of Spying*. Frank Cass, 2004.
——— 'The SIS Singapore Station and the SIS Far Eastern Controller'. *Intelligence and National Security*. Vol. 14, No. 4.
——— 'From Special Operations to Special Political Action: The 'Rump SOE' and SIS Post-War Covert Action Capability 1945–77'. *Intelligence & National Security*. Vol. 15, No. 3.

Deacon, Richard, *'C': The Biography of Maurice Oldfield*. London: Macdonald, 1985.
——— *A History of the British Secret Service*. London: Frederick Muller, 1969.
Denniston, A. G., 'The Government Code and Cypher School Between the Wars'. *Intelligence and National Security*. Vol. 1, No. 1.
Dilks, David (ed.), *The Diaries of Sir Alexander Cadogan*, London: Cassell, 1971.
Dorril, Stephen, *MI6*. London: Fourth Estate, 2000.
Dukes, Sir Paul, *Come Hammer Come Sickle*. London: Cassell, 1947.
——— *Epic of the Gestapo*. London: Cassell, 1940.
——— *Red Dusk and the Morrow*. New York: Doubleday, 1922.
——— *The Story of ST-25*. London: Cassell, 1938.
Dzhirkvelov, Ilya, *Secret Servant*. London: Collins, 1987.
Elliott, Nicholas, *Never Judge a Man by His Umbrella*. Stroud, Gloucestershire: Michael Russell, 1991.
Ellis, C. H., *Transcaspian Episode*. London: Hutchinson, 1963.
Erskine, Ralph, 'Churchill and the Start of the Ultra–Magic Deals'. *International Journal of Intelligence and Counterintelligence*. Vol. 10, no.1.
Eveland, Wilbur Crane, *Ropes of Sand*. New York: W. W. Norton, 1980
Everitt, Nicholas, *British Secret Service during the Great War*. London: Hutchinson, 1920.
Fisher, John, *Gentleman Spies: Intelligence Agents in the British Empire and Beyond*. Stroud, Gloucestershire: Sutton, 2002.
Fielding, Xan, *Hide and Seek*. London: Secker & Warburg, 1954.
——— *One Man in His Time*. London: Macmillan, 1990.
Fleming, Ian, *Casino Royale*. London: Signet, 1953.
Fletcher, Reginald, *The Air Defence of Britain*. London: Harmondsworth Press, 1938.
Foot, M. R. D., *SOE in France*. London: HMSO, 1966.
Footman, David, *Civil War in Russia*. London: Faber & Faber, 1961.
——— *Dead Yesterday*. London: White Lion, 1974.
——— *In Memoriam Archie*, 1904–64. London: Privately published, 1967.
——— *Red Prelude*. London: The Cresset Press, 1944.
Fourcade, Marie-Madeleine, *Noah's Ark: Story of the Alliance Intelligence Service in Occupied France*. London: Allen & Unwin, 1973.
Freedman, Sir Lawrence, *The Falklands War*. London: Frank Cass, 2005
Gallegos, Adrian, *From Capri to Oblivion*. London: Hodder & Stoughton, 1959.
Garnett, David, *The Secret History of the Political Warfare Executive*. London: St Ermin's Press, 2002.
Gibson, William, *Wild Career*. London: Harrap, 1935.
Golitsyn, Anatoli, *New Lies for Old*. London: Bodley Head, 1984.
Gordievsky, Oleg, *Last Stop Execution*. London: Macmillan, 1995.
Graaff, Bob de, 'The Stranded Baron and the Upstart at the Crossroad; Wolfgang zu Putlitz and Otto John'. *Intelligence and National Security*. Vol. 5, No. 4
Greene, Graham, *The Heart of the Matter*. London: Bodley Head, 1948.
——— *The Human Factor*. London: Bodley Head, 1978.

——— *Our Man in Havana*. London: Bodley Head, 1958.
——— *The Tenth Man*. London: Bodley Head, 1985.
Gulbenkian, Nubar, *Pantaraxia*. London: Hutchinson, 1965.
Halsalle, Henry de, *Who Goes There?*. London: Hutchinson, 1927.
Hastings, Stephen, *The Drums of Memory*. London: Leo Cooper, 1994.
Haswell, Jock, *British Military Intelligence*. London: Weidenfeld & Nicolson, 1973.
Henderson, Paul, *An Unlikely Spy*. London: Bloomsbury, 1993.
Hennessy, Peter, *The Secret State*. London: Penguin, 2002.
Hesketh, Roger, *FORTITUDE: The D-Day Deception Campaign*. London: St Ermin's Press, 1999.
Hill, George, *Dreaded Hour*. London: Cassell, 1936.
——— *Go Spy the Land*. London: Cassell, 1932.
Hinsley, F. H., with E. E. Thomas, C. F. G. Ransom and R. C. Knight, *British Intelligence in the Second World War*. Vol. 1. London: HMSO, 1979.
Hinsley, F. H., and Anthony Simkins, *British Intelligence in the Second World War: Security and Counter-Intelligence*. Vol. 4. London: HMSO, 1990.
Hoare, Sir Samuel, *The Fourth Seal*. London: Heinemann, 1930
Hollingsworth, Mark, and Nick Fielding, *Defending the Realm*. London: André Deutsch, 1999
Holt, Thadeus, *The Deceivers*. London: Simon & Schuster, 2004.
Hopkirk, Peter, *The Great Game*. London: John Murray, 1990.
Horne, Alastair, *Macmillan*. London: Macmillan, 1991.
Household, Geoffrey, *Against The Wind*. London: Michael Joseph, 1958.
Howarth, Patrick, *Intelligence Chief Extraordinary*. London: Bodley Head, 1986.
Howe, Geoffrey, *Conflict of Loyalty*. London: Macmillan, 1994.
Hurd, Douglas, *Memoirs*. London: Little, Brown, 2003.
Hyde, Harford Montgomery, *George Blake: Superspy*. London: Constable, 1987.
——— *Secret Intelligence Agent*. London: Constable, 1982.
Jenssen, Baroness Carla, *I Spy!*. London: Jarrolds, 1930.
John, Otto, *Twice through The Lines*. Harper & Row, 1972.
Johns, Philip, *Within Two Cloaks*. London: William Kimber, 1979.
Jones, Aubrey, *The Pendulum of Politics*. Faber & Faber, 1946.
Jones, R. V., *Most Secret War*. London: Hamish Hamilton, 1978.
——— *Reflections on Intelligence*. London: Heinemann, 1989.
Judd, Alan, *The Quest for C*. London: HarperCollins, 1999.
Knightley, Philip, *The Second Oldest Profession*. London: André Deutsch, 1986.
Knoblock, Edward, *Round the Room*. London: Chapman & Hall, 1939.
Kutuzov, Viktor, *Penkovsky, Fact and Fancy*. Moscow: Novosti, 1966
Kuzichkin, Vladimir, *Inside the KGB*. London: André Deutsch, 1990.
Kyle, Keith, *Suez*. London: Weidenfeld & Nicolson, 1991.
Lancaster, Donald, *The Emancipation of French Indochina*. Oxford: Oxford University Press, 1961.
Landau, Henry, *All's Fair*. New York: Putnam's, 1934.
——— *The Enemy Within*. New York: Putnam, 1937.

——— *Secrets of the White Lady*. New York: Putnam, 1935.
——— *Spreading the Spy Net*. London: Jarrolds, 1938.
Langley, J. M., *Fight Another Day*. London: Collins, 1974.
Langley, J. M. and M. R. D. Foot, *MI9: Escape and Evasion 1939–1945*. London: Bodley Head, 1979.
Lawson, J. C., *Tales of Aegean Intrigue*. London: Chatto & Windus, 1920.
Leigh, David, *Betrayed*. London: Bloomsbury, 1993.
Liddell, Guy, *The Guy Liddell Diaries*. London: Routledge, 2005.
Lincoln, Trebitsch, *The Autobiography of an Adventurer*. New York: Henry Holt, 1932.
——— *Revelations of an International* Spy. New York: Robert McBride, 1916.
Lyall, Archie, *The Balkan Road*. London: Metheun, 1930.
——— *Russian Roundabout*. London: Douglas Harmsworth, 1933.
Lycett, Andrew, *Ian Fleming*. London: Weidenfeld & Nicolson, 1995.
McCall, Gibb, *Flight Most Secret*. London: William Kimber, 1981.
McDermott, Geoffrey, *The Eden Legacy*. London: Leslie Frewin, 1969.
Macdonald, Bill, *The True Intrepid*. Surrey, BC: Timberholme Books, 1998.
McKay, C. G., 'Our Man in Reval'. *Intelligence and National Security*. Vol. 4, No. 1.
McKenna, Marthe, *I Was a Spy!* London: Jarrolds, 1923.
Mackenzie, Compton, *Greek Memories*. London: Cassell, 1932.
——— *My Life and Times: Octave Seven* (Chatto & Windus, 1968)
——— *Water on the Brain*. London: Chatto & Windus, 1933.
Madeira, Victor, '"Wishful Thinking Allowed": Secret Service Committee and Intelligence Reform in Great Britain, 1919–23'. *Intelligence and National Security*. Vol. 18, No. 1.
Magan, William, *Middle Eastern Approaches*. Michael Russell, 2001.
Mahl, Thomas, E., *Desperate Deception*. London: Brassey's, 1998.
Marck, David de Young de la, 'De Gaulle, Colonel Passy and British Intelligence 1940–42'. *Intelligence and National Security*. Vol. 18, No. 1.
Marshall-Cornwall, Sir James, *Wars and Rumours of War*. London: Leo Cooper, 1984.
Maschwitz, Eric, *No Chip on my Shoulder*. London: Herbert Jenkins, 1957.
Mason, A. E. W., *The Four Corners of the World*. London: Hodder & Stoughton, 1925.
Masterman, J. C., *The Double Cross System of the War of 1939–45*. Boston, MA: Yale University Press, 1972.
——— *On the Chariot Wheel*. Oxford: Oxford University Press, 1975.
Masters, Anthony, *Literary Agents*. Oxford: Basil Blackwell, 1987.
Maugham, W. Somerset, *Ashenden*. London: Heinemann, 1928.
Merrick, K. A., *Flights of the Forgotten*. London: Arms & Armour, 1989.
Miller, Russell, *Dusko Popov*. London: Orion, 2004
Mills, Cyril, *Bertram Mills Circus: Its Story*. London: Hutchinson, 1967.
Mitrokhin, Vasili, and Christopher Andrew, *The Mitrokhin Archive*. London: Penguin, 1999.

Monkhouse, Allan, *Moscow 1911–33*. London: Victor Gollancz, 1933.
Montgomery, Brian, *A Field Marshal in the Family*. London: Constable, 1973.
Morrell, Gordon, 'Redefining Intelligence and Intelligence-gathering: The Industrial Intelligence Centre and the Metro-Vickers Affair, Moscow, 1933'. *Intelligence and National Security*. Vol. 9, No. 3.
Moss, Robert, *Carnival of Spies*. New York: Villard, 1987.
Mowbray, Stephen de, *Key Facts in Soviet History*, London: Pinter, 1990
Muggeridge, Malcolm, *Chronicles of Wasted Time*. New York: William Morrow, 1974.
Neave, Airey, *Saturday at MI9*. London: Hodder & Stoughton, 1969.
——— *They Have Their Exits*. London: Hodder & Stoughton, 1953.
Nelson, Michael, *War of the Black Heavens*. London: Brassey's, 1997.
Nott, John, *Here Today, Gone Tomorrow*. London: Politico's, 2002.
O'Brien, Terence, *The Moonlight War*. London: Collins, 1987.
O'Brien-ffrench, Conrad, *Delicate Mission*. Toronto: Skilton & Shaw, 1979.
Owen, David, *Time To Declare*. London: Michael Joseph, 2001.
Paine, Lauran, *Britain's Intelligence Service*. London: Robert Hale, 1979.
Pantcheff, Theodore, *Fortress Island*. London: Phillimore, 1981.
Penkovsky, Oleg, *The Penkovsky Papers*. New York: Doubleday, 1965
Penrose, Barrie, and Roger Courtiour, *The Pencourt File*. New York: Harper & Row, 1978.
Philby, H. A. R. Kim, *My Silent War*. London: MacGibbon & Kee, 1968.
Philby, Rufina, and Hayden Peake, *The Private Life of Kim Philby*. London: St Ermin's Press, 1999.
Pincher, Chapman, *The SpyCatcher Affair*. New York: St Martin's Press, 1987.
——— *Their Trade is Treachery*. London: Sidgwick & Jackson, 1981.
——— *Traitors: The Labyrinths of Treason*. Sidgwick and Jackson, London, 1987.
Popov, Dusko, *SpyCounterSpy*. London: Weidenfeld & Nicolson, 1973.
Prater, Donald, *A Ringing Glass*. Oxford: Clarendon Press, 1986.
Pujol, Juan, *GARBO*. London: Weidenfeld & Nicolson, 1985.
Putlitz, Wolfgang zu, *The Zu Putlitz Dossier*. London: Allan Wingate, 1957.
Randle, Michael, and Pat Pottle, *The Blake Escape*. London: Harrap. 1989.
Read, Anthony, and David Fisher, *Colonel Z*. London: Hodder & Stoughton, 1984.
Rees, Goronwy, *A Chapter of Accidents*. London: Chatto & Windus, 1972.
Reilly, Sidney, *Sidney Reilly: Britain's Master Spy*. London: Dorset Press, 1985.
Richards, Brooks, *The Secret Flotillas*, London: HMSO, 1999.
Rickman, Alexander, *Swedish Iron Ore*. London: Faber & Faber, 1939.
Rieul, Roland, *Soldier into Spy*. London: William Kimber, 1986.
Robertson, K. G. (ed.), *British and American Approaches to Intelligence*. London: Macmillan, 1987.
Sampson, Anthony, *The Changing Anatomy of Britain*. London: Hodder & Stoughton, 1982.
Schecter, Jerrold, *The Spy Who Saved the World*. New York: Charles Scribner, 2002.

Scott, Lord Justice, *Report of the Inquiry into the Export of Defence Equipment and Dual-Use Goods to Iraq and Related Prosecutions*. London: HMSO, 1996.
Seton-Watson, Hugh, *Neither War nor Peace*. London: Metheun, 1960.
Seaman, Mark, *GARBO: The Spy Who Saved D-Day*. London: PRO, 2000.
Sheffy, Yigal, 'British Intelligence and the Middle East, 1900–1918: How Much Do We Know?' *Intelligence and National Security*. Vol. 17, No. 1.
Smith, Michael, *Foley*. London: Hodder & Stoughton, 1999.
——— *New Cloak, Old Dagger*. London: Cassell, 1996.
Spicer, Tim. *An Unorthodox Soldier: The Sandline Affair*. Edinburgh: Mainstream, 2000.
Stafford, David, *Camp X*. Toronto: Lester & Orpen Dennys, 1986.
——— *Churchill and Secret Service*. London: John Murray, 1997.
——— *Spies Beneath Berlin*. London: John Murray, 2002.
Stephenson, William, *British Security Coordination*. London: St Ermin's Press, 1998.
Stewart, Brian, 'Winning in Malaya: An Intelligence Success Story'. *Intelligence and National Security*. Vol. 14, No. 4.
Strong, Sir Kenneth, *Intelligence at the Top*. London: Cassell, 1968.
——— *Men of Intelligence*. London: Cassell, 1970.
Stuart, Sir Campbell, *The Secrets of Crewe House*. London: Hodder & Stoughton, 1920.
Suvorov, Victor, *Inside the Aquarium*. London: Macmillan, 1986.
——— *Inside the Soviet Army*. London: Macmillan, 1982.
——— *Inside Soviet Military Intelligence*. London: Hamish Hamilton, 1984.
Teague-Jones, Reginald, *The Spy Who Disappeared*. London: Victor Gollancz, 1990.
Thatcher, Margaret, *The Downing Street Years*. London: HarperCollins, 1993.
Thomaselli, P. , 'C's Moscow Station – The Anglo-Russian Trade Mission as a Cover for SIS in the early 1920s'. *Intelligence and National Security*. Vol, 17, No. 3.
Thurloe, Richard, *The Secret State*. Oxford: Basil Blackwell, 1994.
Tokaev, Grigori, *Betrayal of an Ideal*. London: The Harvill Press, 1954
——— *Comrade X*. London: The Harvill Press, 1956.
——— *Soviet Imperialism*. London: Gerald Duckworth, 1954.
——— *Stalin Means War*. London: George Weidenfeld, 1951.
Tomlinson, Richard, *The Big Breach*. Edinburgh: Mainstream, 2001.
Trevor-Roper, Hugh, *The Philby Affair*. London: William Kimber, 1968.
Urban, Mark, *UK Eyes Alpha*. London: Faber & Faber, 1996.
Verrier, Anthony, *Through the Looking-Glass*. London: Jonathan Cape, 1983.
Verschoyle, Derek, *The Balcony*. London: 1949.
Wark, Wesley, *The Ultimate Enemy*. London: I. B. Tauris, 1985.
Waugh, Alec, *A Spy in the Family*. London: W. H. Allen, 1970.
Weldon, L. B., *Hard Lying*. London: Herbert Jenkins, 1925.
West, Rebecca, *The New Meaning of Treason*. New York: Viking, 1964.
Whinney, Patrick, *Corsican Command*. London: Patrick Stephens, 1989.
Whitelaw, William, *The Whitelaw Memoirs*. London: The Aurum Press, 1989.

Whitwell, John [pseud. Leslie Nicholson], *British Agent*. London: William Kimber, 1966.
Williams, Valentine, *The World of Action*. London: Hamish Hamilton, 1938.
——— *The Man with the Clubfoot*. London: Herbert Jenkins, 1931.
Winterbotham, F. W., *Secret and Personal*. London: William Kimber, 1969.
——— *The Ultra Secret*. London: Weidenfeld & Nicolson, 1974.
——— *The Ultra Spy*. London: Macmillan, 1989.
Wise, David, and Thomas Ross, *The Espionage Establishment*. London: Jonathan Cape, 1968.
Woodhall, Edwin, *Detective and Secret Service Days*. London: Mellifont Press, 1932.
——— *Spies of the Great War*. London: Mellifont Press, 1933.
Woodhouse, C. M., *Apple of Discord*. London: Hutchinson, 1948.
——— *Something Ventured*. London: Granada, 1982.
Wright, Peter, *The Encyclopedia of Espionage*. London: Heinemann, 1990.
——— *SpyCatcher*. New York: Heinemann, 1985.
Wynne, Greville, *The Man from Moscow*. London: Hutchinson, 1967
——— *The Man from Odessa*. London: Robert Hale, 1981.
Young, George K., *Subversion and the British Riposte*. Glasgow: Ossian, 1984.
——— *Who Is my Liege?* London: Gentry Books,1972.
Younger, Kenneth, *Changing Perspectives in British Foreign Policy*. Oxford: Oxford University Press, 1964.

Index